Active Social Capital

Active Social Capital

*Tracing the Roots of Development
and Democracy*

Anirudh Krishna

COLUMBIA   UNIVERSITY   PRESS   NEW   YORK

COLUMBIA UNIVERSITY PRESS
Publishers Since 1893
New York   Chichester, West Sussex
Copyright © 2002 Columbia University Press
All rights reserved

Library of Congress Cataloging-in-Publication Data

Krishna, Anirudh
    Active social capital : tracing the roots of development and democracy /
    Anirudh Krishna.
        p. cm.
    Includes bibliographical references and index.
    ISBN 0–231–12570–4 (cl. : alk. paper) — ISBN 0–231–12571–2 (pa. :
    alk. paper)
    1. Social capital (Sociology). 2. Economic development — Social aspects.
    I. Title.

HM708 .K75 2002
306.3 — dc21

2002019244

Columbia University Press books
are printed on permanent and durable acid-free paper
Printed in the United States of America

c   10   9   8   7   6   5   4   3   2   1
p   10   9   8   7   6   5   4   3   2   1

To Ma and Papa

Contents

Preface

Does social capital provide a viable means for advancing economic development, promoting ethnic peace, and strengthening democratic governance? This question has particular importance for our times. The world is richer than ever before, but more than a fifth of its people are poor and miserable. The Cold War is over, but civil wars and ethnic strife continue to mar the prospects for peace. Democracy is in place in most countries, but large numbers of citizens cannot avail themselves of its benefits. Something more needs to be done for making development, peace and democracy more fruitful for the ordinary citizen, and building social capital is thought to constitute a promising line of action.

Social capital represents a propensity for mutually beneficial collective action, and it derives from the quality of relationships among people within a particular group or community. Communities with high social capital will achieve superior outcomes in multiple domains, it is claimed; and communities with low social capital can be assisted to build up stocks of this resource, so their performance will also improve over time. Economic development, community peace, and democratic participation can all be promoted in this manner, simply by investing in the stock of social capital. Novel, wide-ranging and full of promise, this claim deserves to be investigated carefully.

This book investigates what social capital is, how it operates in practice, and what results it can be expected to produce. Theoretical premises related to social capital are tested with the help of evidence collected over two years in 69 village communities, located in two Indian states, Rajasthan and Madhya Pradesh. Nearly 2,500 village residents were interviewed for this purpose, and I spoke separately with village leaders, government officials, party politicians, and market operators. Appendix A describes the methodology used for these investigations. Additional data were gathered from official statistics and with the help of focus groups assembled in each of these villages. Different hypotheses related to social capital were generated from a review of the academic literature on this subject, and a locally relevant scale was developed to measure and compare social capital and to test the competing hypotheses.

Social capital is not directly observable; people carry it inside their heads. What one can observe and measure are some manifestations or behavioral consequences given rise by social capital. Different cultures permit and promote different expressions of social capital, so its observable aspects will vary contextually. Developing an independent and locally appropriate index of social capital is thus the necessary first step toward verifying the claims associated with this concept. A locally appropriate scale is developed in chapter 4 for measuring social capital.

How much does social capital matter for economic development, community peace, and democratic participation? In the second part of the book, I assess the usefulness of social capital separately in relation to each of these goals. Alternative explanations are also considered in each case. What else — instead of or in addition to social capital — might influence results in each of these three domains? Competing hypotheses are operationalized and tested using the Indian data.

This field-based investigation is important for assessing the worth of the social capital argument relative to its competitors. It is useful also for understanding the changing bases of social and political organization in rural communities.

Some quite significant changes in leadership have occurred as state and market operations have penetrated deeper into rural areas and as education and mass communications have become more widespread. Leadership based on caste and landed wealth is becoming less salient in these villages, and at the grassroots a new group of political entrepreneurs has arisen who are playing catalyst roles in making social capital more productive for the ordinary villager. By building bridges between communities and their external environment, these new political entrepreneurs help to expand the range of possibilities that villagers can exploit to their common advantage.

Collective action in support of shared goals is more likely where social capital is high. However, *effective* collective action and *superior* goal performance are achieved only where — in addition to high social capital — capable agents are also available. The new non-caste-based political entrepreneurs activate the stock of social capital for achieving benefits related to economic development and participation in democracy. Another set of agents, the traditional and hereditary heads of village groups, make social capital productive for the purpose of community peace. In the absence of such capable agents, social capital remains a latent resource, an unrealized potential for mutually beneficial collective action.

Agency helps to make social capital active. Investing in the stock of social capital is unlikely to be very productive unless steps are taken at the same time to enhance agency capacity. This is the principal message of this book.

Published and official sources do not usually provide high-quality data for the village level in India, and emergent trends need to be investigated at first-hand. I was amply assisted in this task by the Chitra Management team — K. P. Singh, Mahesh Kapila, R. S. Pathak, Mahendra Porwal, Pankaj Mishra, Veerpal Singh, Vinay Singh Bhati, G. N. Mathur, and a group of 16 field investigators — with whose help I investigated trends in 69 villages and interviewed more than 2,500 persons, a far larger number than I might have managed on my own.

Officials of the state government of Rajasthan helped me with archival sources and official statistics, and many of them, including Anil Chaplot, Arvind Mayaram, M. L. Mehta, and C. S. Rajan, also served as commentators and critics. R. N. Meena, Secretary for Rural Development, and C. P. Joshi, Minister for Rural Development and Education, heard me patiently on more than one occasion and responded critically to my views. A special debt of gratitude is owed in this regard to Inderjit Khanna, Chief Secretary (highest-ranking civil servant) of the state of Rajasthan, who chaired a special discussion session in Jaipur in June 2000, where I presented my findings before senior officials of the state government.

Cornell University, my old home, helped me start this enterprise and carry it through various stages. Travel to India was supported by the Mario Einaudi Center for International Studies at Cornell University, and the Cornell International Institute for Food, Agriculture and Development (CIIFAD) provided supplementary support and office space. My new home,

Duke University, has proved equally supportive for completing the final stages of this work.

Earlier versions of the argument and draft chapters were presented at sessions organized by the Environment Institutions Group at Duke University, the South Asia Program at Cornell University, the Graduate School of International Studies at the University of Denver, the Institute of Development Studies, Jaipur, Jawaharlal Nehru University, the Kennedy School of Government, and the World Bank. Walter Mebane provided guidance with the quantitative analysis, and Joe Foudy and David Rueda read through innumerable first drafts, never failing to come up with useful advice and constructive criticism. Bo Rothstein, Niraja Jayal, Bob Keohane, Francis Lethem, Nan Lin, Bishnu Mahapatra, Shail Mayaram, Ellen Mickiewicz, N.C. Saxena, Dietlind Stolle, Narayan Upadhyaya, Eric Uslaner, and Steve Wilkinson have also helped refine the argument.

Arun Agrawal, Valerie Bunce, Milton Esman, Ron Herring, Bruce Jentleson, Philip Oldenburg, Elinor Ostrom, and Peter and Mary Katzenstein read through most or all of the manuscript, and I gratefully acknowledge their advice and encouragement. I owe a special intellectual debt to Norman Uphoff, advisor, co-author of other projects, friend, and possibly the most painstaking (and pains-giving) critic that anyone can have.

Earlier versions of the arguments presented here, particularly in chapters 5 and 7, have been published, respectively, in *World Development* (29, no. 6: 925–43) and *Comparative Political Studies* (35, no. 4: 437–60), and I am grateful to the editors of these journals for permission to use this material. I am also grateful to Peter Dimock, Anne Routon, and Leslie Bialler of Columbia University Press for very competently guiding the production of this book and to two anonymous reviewers for improving the arguments.

I have worked on this piece of research for the past four years, and my children, Aditi and Abhay, have progressed from early to mid teenage during this time. It was nice watching them grow, for they kept me alert and prevented any lapse of concentration, even at home. Vidya alternatively supported them and kept them at bay. Without these distractions provided by a close and loving family, I would surely have despaired at times.

Active Social Capital

1   Introduction: Can Social Capital Help Support Development and Democracy?

Advancing Civil Society Solutions for Development and Democracy

Five decades and more of state-led development in many less developed countries have failed to make any considerable dent on poverty. Half the population of India and up to three-quarters in some other countries — more than a billion persons in all — continue to live in miserable conditions, earning and spending less than a dollar a day.[1] A third of all children born in these countries will not live beyond the age of forty, it is expected, before malnutrition and disease take their toll (UNDP 1999).

As the state is beginning to retreat after having failed to fulfill its promises, and as markets are only just beginning to penetrate the rural areas (and then hardly always to the advantage of the poor), many analysts are calling for civil society solutions for dealing with the enduring problems of poverty and powerlessness. Concerted action made possible by civic associations enables citizens to engage state and market agencies more effectively, it is contended; service delivery is improved, accountability and transparency are enhanced, and the pool of resources is enlarged when organized groups of citizens engage constructively with the state. Development is promoted in this manner, and governance is made transparent and more efficacious.[2]

As globalization threatens to erode the authority of the state from above, governmental leaders are simultaneously being urged to share resources and decisionmaking authority with community associations and local organizations below the level of the nation state (Barber 1995; Rosenau 1992). "Co-production" — where organized groups of citizens produce public services in cooperation with government agencies — needs to be formally recognized, carefully analyzed, and actively promoted, especially in developing countries (Ostrom 1996; Tendler 1997). A larger vision of human development is served when citizens' associations participate widely in diverse tasks of provisioning and self-governance (Sen 1999).

Faith in such solutions is premised on the assumption, however, that organized action by citizens is not a problem, and that citizens in all parts of the world can act collectively in a coordinated and effective manner. For civil society solutions to be effective and viable over a wide range, either the factors that enable coordinated action by citizens must be abundantly available, or these factors should be easy to reproduce at relatively little cost. One or both of these assumptions must be upheld if civil society solutions are to be valid and effective in all parts of the world. The growing literature on social capital provides some support for taking an optimistic view, but it needs to become more precise and predictive, particularly within developing country contexts.

Social Capital and Collective Action

Social capital is defined by Putnam (1995: 67) as "features of social organization such as networks, norms and social trust that facilitate coordination and cooperation for mutual benefit." Relatively stable patterns of social interaction exist within some communities that are useful, social capital theory suggests, for sustaining mutually beneficial collective action.

Social capital is an asset, a functioning propensity for mutually beneficial collective action, with which communities are endowed to diverse extents. Communities possessed of large amounts of social capital are able to engage in mutually beneficial cooperation over a wide front. Communities that have low levels of social capital are less capable of organizing themselves effectively (Fukuyama 1995; Putnam et al. 1993; Putnam 1995, 1996).

Is it possible, however, to build social capital relatively rapidly even among communities that are less well endowed with this asset? Regarded originally as being a relatively immutable endowment, inherited from a distant past (Putnam et al. 1993), social capital can be created and built up, more recent analyses suggest, even within a relatively short period of time (Hall 1997; Schneider et al. 1997).

Citizens' capacities for mutually beneficial collective action can be enhanced through purposive action. The state can retreat gracefully in this manner. And its remaining agencies can engage fruitfully in co-producing services alongside community groups, made more effective by public investments in social capital.

A new bottom-up dynamic of development is proposed by social capital theory (reviewed in greater detail in chapter 2) to replace those failed efforts that were intended to deliver economic and social benefits from the top down. Instead of considering macro-economic policy or design of state institutions as the principal concerns of public policy, attention needs to be directed equally, this theory claims, toward grassroots-level capacities for public action. How many civic organizations exist in any given setting and how effectively these organizations perform will have a close bearing not only upon rates of economic growth, but also on levels of communal harmony and patterns of political participation. Governments and development agencies are being urged, therefore, to "invest" resources in building stocks of social capital (e.g., by Grootaert and Narayan 1999).

Social Capital and Developing Countries

Is social capital available in equal abundance in developing countries? Can it be built up reasonably easily? Research conducted mostly in Europe and America has regarded levels of social capital to be high among communities where a larger number of people register for membership in a greater number of civic associations. By this measure of social capital, most developing countries appear to be extremely poorly stocked with this asset.

Large numbers of citizens are members of civic associations in the industrialized countries of the West. According to the World Values Survey for 1991, 85 percent of citizens in Sweden, 84 percent in the Netherlands, 71 percent in the United States, and 67 percent in what was then West Germany reported membership in at least one association. These proportions are much lower in the developing countries. Thirty-six percent of citizens in Mexico, 24 percent in Argentina, 13 percent in India, and even fewer in other developing countries are members of one or more associations. Even this low extent of associational activity is concentrated for the most part in towns, leaving the huge mass of rural residents unaffiliated with any formal organization.

"Very few Indians belong to associations," asserts Chhibber (1999: 57–59), "Less than two percent were members of caste and religious or neighborhood and peasant associations. . . . the associations that have existed for a long time in India [include] particularly trade unions and student groups [which function almost exclusively in urban areas]. . . . Rural organizations are few and far between."

Data that I collected in 69 central Indian villages in the states of Rajasthan and Madhya Pradesh showed only one in fifteen rural residents to be a member of any formal association. In 80 percent of these cases, the association concerned has been formed by public law or at the initiative of some state agency. It is neither voluntarily nor horizontally organized, two requirements that any organization must meet before it can add to the index of social capital proposed by Putnam et al. (1993).

What we have before us then is a thesis of social capital — derived mainly from Western evidence — and some indications that this thesis does not apply equally well for the developing world. Because involvement in civic associations is substantially higher in countries that have gone farther down the paths to industrialization, social capital will accumulate slowly as countries undergo economic growth and social development. Attitudes and networks facilitating civic engagement derive from economic development, it has been suggested (Almond and Verba 1965; Lipset 1960, 1994), so social capital will become visible only after levels of per capita income have risen above a certain level. Growth precedes social capital formation, this argument suggests. This historical continuity cannot be reversed easily, and social capital cannot be invoked at will to support faster development and higher rates of economic growth.

I will review social capital theory and its criticisms in greater depth in chapter 2, and I will argue in chapters 3 and 4 that this particular view results largely from confusing the concept of social capital with some of its manifestations. Density of membership in *formal* associations has been used as a proxy measurement for scaling and comparing levels of social capital in the West. A considerable misunderstanding results, however, if this proxy measure is equated with the concept itself.

It is not simply the fact of membership in any number of associations that induces a propensity for mutually beneficial collective action. What matters more for social capital are attitudes and behaviors of different kinds that might be exhibited even without the support of any formal organization. A person might trust her neighbors implicitly and she might engage with them in collective efforts to clean and improve their neighborhood — without the help of any formally registered association of neighbors.

Aggregating memberships in formal organizations thus provides an imprecise measure of social capital. Using this measure of social capital leads to overestimating this asset in certain cases (as when formal organizations such as the Ku Klux Klan are also counted) and underestimating its level in other cases (by not considering neighborhood groups and other informal organizations that facilitate collective action among citizens).[3] Underestimation can be quite severe in certain contexts.

In developing countries, particularly in the rural areas, it is informal rather than formal associations that have most value for citizens.[4] Most collective action in the 69 villages that I observed occurs within mutual support networks that come together and disperse as the need arises. The only enduring evidence for the presence and efficacy of these networks exists in the cognitive maps that people in these villages carry around in their heads. Neighbors come forward to help neighbors at times of need, and it is known that such help will be offered and accepted. Villager helps villager in raising crops, in training children, in combating disease, in any number of tasks that are associated with life in these agrarian settings. Few formally registered associations exist, however, to assist villagers with such efforts.

More than 80 percent of rural residents, 1,522 of 1,898 persons interviewed in Rajasthan for this study, participate regularly in labor-sharing groups, sharing work either on their own fields or for some external employer: 63 percent stated that they had got together with others in the village one or more times in the past year to do something about a community problem; 64 percent said that working in these and other informal networks was associated with feelings of trust for other villagers; 54 percent of villagers expected that if some natural calamity were to occur, their entire village would come together and cope jointly with this situation; and 92 percent of villagers felt sure that if someone's house burned down in the village, the rest of the villagers would immediately come forward to help the affected family.

Features of social organization that promote cooperation, including norms, networks and social trust, are hardly nonexistent in these communities, as these data indicate. Formal organizations are, indeed, not much in evidence, but a scale of social capital which measures the density of such organizations to the neglect of all these other indicators will grossly underestimate social capital in these contexts.[5] The instruments that social scientists use, therefore, to observe and measure social capital will need to be calibrated anew for rural developing country contexts. A locally relevant scale of social capital is developed and presented in chapter 4.

Tradition or Modernity?

Yet another doubt raised about social capital in the Third World concerns not the level of this asset but the uses to which it might possibly be put. Will high levels of social capital suffice to shake rural residents out of the inertia that is often attributed to them, especially by urban observers? "Centuries of unequal struggle against his environment have taught him to endure," says Nehru (1946: 357), depicting a typical Indian farmer, "and even in poverty and submission he has a certain calm dignity, a feeling of submission to an all-powerful fate." Will solidarity among rural residents not be used principally in defense of tradition, as some analysts of rural communities have observed (Anderson 1994; Magagna 1991; Scott 1976), rather than in quest of modernity?

Once again, however, depicting rural residents as passive or tradition-bound is a view taken more often by academics and policymakers, and not so much by the villagers themselves. Asked to name the five principal needs of their community, more than 90 percent of respondents in villages (1,714 of 1,898) mentioned items such as roads, schools, agricultural technology, drinking water, and environmental protection, which are associated with their aspirations for a better life. For only 115 (six percent) of respondents did temple construction, religious training, or any such "traditional" item figure anywhere among the top five priorities.

Activities associated with economic development form the principal demand for the majority of villagers, and those associated with traditions are secondary for most. The vast majority of villagers (1,653 of 1,898, or 87 percent) were strongly agreed that productive development works should invariably be taken up in the village even if these have the effect of undermining the traditional way of doing things.[6] Tradition and custom, far from being important concerns to uphold, are readily given up by most villagers in favor of economic development; 84 percent of respondents agreed that there could be no effective development in the village if villagers persisted with their old ways and traditions. Among villagers between 18 and 45 years of age, the corresponding figure is as high as 91 percent.

New cleavages are becoming apparent in the village as tradition gets eroded in the face of modernizing impulses. Only 331 respondents (17 percent) felt that caste or religion formed the most important cleavage in the community, dividing people "considerably" or "a lot." Almost three times as many villagers (974 or 51 percent) regarded differences between the younger and older generations as being considerably more divisive. Caste is the least important among four different cleavages considered here; age (or intergenerational difference) is the most important, followed by education and wealth in that order.

New social organizations have come up (described in chapter 3) that cut across caste and religious lines and that mobilize villagers to act collectively for economic development. Because they are relatively new and not formally registered, perhaps, the rise of these new organizations has gone mostly unheralded in the literature.[7] Such organizations are present in all 69 villages that I visited, however, and they are valuable for diverse development tasks, even though the effectiveness of such organizations varies considerably from village to village.

The rise of these new attitudes, desires, cleavages, and organizations can to a large extent be attributed to the slow diffusion of an ideology of modernization, embodied in and propagated by the post-colonial state. In India as in other newly independent developing countries, "the new state represented the only legitimate form of exercise of power because it was a necessary condition for the development of the nation. . . . A developmental ideology was a constituent part of the self-definition of the post-colonial state" (Chatterjee 1997: 277). What might originally have been an aspiration primarily of the urban middle classes is by now fairly commonly shared even among the illiterate rural majority, as evidence from these north Indian villages shows.

Most rural residents want economic development, even if it means sacrificing the old ways of life, and most desire not to remain isolated within their villages but to engage more productively with agencies of state and market.[8] The question remains, however: Even if villagers are keen to press ahead in quest of the benefits of modernity, does social capital assist them in any way to attain these ends?

Social Capital and Performance

This book investigates whether and how much social capital contributes toward achieving *economic development, community peace,* and *democratic participation* — three separate outcomes that correspond, respectively, to major goals within the economic, social, and political domains. The social capital thesis and its critiques are examined in terms of three competing hypotheses, presented in chapter 2. Other competing and complementary accounts are also examined, including those that invoke caste (Srinivas 1987; Rudolph and Rudolph 1987), relative need (Wade 1994), or party strength (Huntington 1968; Kohli 1987) as principal ways to explain villagers' predilection and capacity for collective action.

Which among these factors helps us to understand the differences that exist among villages in terms of the three outcomes to be explained? Is social capital relevant either separately or in combination with any of these other factors? Are there any limits to what can be achieved with high social capital?[9] Do any of the alternative explanations modify the social capital hypothesis or moderate its effects?

Competing hypotheses are examined empirically for each of the three dependent variables — economic development, community peace, and democratic participation — with the help of a database compiled for 69 villages, 60 of them located in five districts of the state of Rajasthan, India, and nine located in the adjoining state of Madhya Pradesh. Together, Rajasthan and Madhya Pradesh have a population of 116 million persons,[10] a not insignificant chunk of humanity in which to test the social capital hypotheses.

I selected these areas because I have previously worked in Rajasthan for 13 years as an official of the Indian government. I served mostly in rural areas during this time, and I learned to understand and also to speak, albeit haltingly and with mistakes, dialects (of Hindi) local to these areas. I was careful, however, to avoid villages that I had known intimately before and where people might have recognized me as a government official. Social distance between state agents and citizens is considerably large in rural India, and it is likely that villagers might not have spoken so openly or critically had they taken me for anything other than a visiting researcher.

I lived for nearly a year in a representative set of 16 villages, and I spent another year collecting survey data for the full sample of 69 villages and interviewing key respondents in urban centers. Appendix A provides details about the methodology followed for these field investigations.

Social capital does serve villagers well for achieving results in multiple domains, these data indicate. Social capital is significantly associated with each of the three outcomes of interest. But social capital by itself does not explain the major part of the variation in any of these outcomes. Villages high in social capital do not always perform well with respect to economic development, community peace, or democratic participation; and villages that have relatively lower levels of social capital often perform better.

In addition to high levels of social capital, the analysis shows, there also needs to be an appropriate *mediating agency*, which activates the stock of social capital and makes it more productive. High levels of social capital do not automatically translate into better outcomes within any of the three domains — unless there are agents present in the village who are capable and effective.[11]

Agency and Social Capital

Possessing a high level of social capital enables members of any community to act collectively for achieving diverse common goals. Agency is required, however, to help them select goals that are feasible and likely to be achieved, given the constraints and opportunities available within their institutional environment. Agents who have regular contact with state officials and market operators and who are familiar with their procedures and practices can help villagers organize themselves in ways that are more likely to succeed. Collective action can occur even in the absence of informed and effective agents, but it is not likely to be as productive or as sustainable. This proposition is developed further in chapter 2, and it is supported by evidence presented in chapters 5, 6 and 7.

Parties have traditionally performed such agency roles,[12] especially in the West, and so have local-level government officials.[13] But agency in Rajasthan and Madhya Pradesh is provided neither by political parties nor by local government officials. Party organization is moribund below the state level in Rajasthan as it is in most of India (Kohli 1990). Party organizers and members of state legislatures whom I interviewed in six district capitals (five in Rajasthan and one in Madhya Pradesh) all held the view that votes are gathered at the time of elections through forging temporary alliances with pre-existing social organizations. No permanent party organization exists in most villages or even at the subdistrict and district levels.[14] Parties serve very poorly in these contexts as vehicles for expressing grassroots-level demands to the official hierarchy.

Public bureaucracies are also organized from the top down, and it is quite widely held that local governments serve merely to implement programs that are funded and sent down by the centralized state (Bagchi 1991; Jain 1993; Mayaram 1998). No more than 108 of 1,898 respondents in Rajasthan and a similar proportion in Madhya Pradesh (less than six percent) had attended even one of four public meetings called by the *panchayat* (village government) during the past year. Most villagers felt that *panchayats* existed primarily for the purpose of executing programs handed down from above, and hardly 11 percent of villagers thought these bodies useful for channeling villagers' demands to some higher authority.

Mediating agency has a different set of structural antecedents in central India, and different agencies exist to serve the three community objectives that are examined here. These trends are explored in greater detail in the following chapters, but some bare facts can be presented here.

Modernization Theory and the Rise of Appropriate Agency

Agents who help villagers set appropriate goals for collective action and who mediate on their behalf with state and market agencies can be identified in rural India and their emergence understood by considering directions of change suggested by modernization theory. A fairly significant gulf exists that separates the written-down world of state and market from the oral tradition practiced by most villagers in India as in many other developing countries. It is not just that villagers are illiterate and poorly informed. The rules and operating procedures of government agencies are also extremely complex, more complex by far than those observed by similar agencies in the West (Etienne 1988; Robinson 1998; Vithal 1997).

Specialized knowledge is required to gain access to government agencies and to their stock of development benefits. Such knowledge is not easily available to all villagers, but only to some few who have the capacity and who have invested time and effort in acquiring the necessary information and contacts.

Gradually increasing literacy within an economy that is itself growing only very slowly has resulted in making available a small pool of educated but unemployed youth in most villages (chapter 3). Agents who mediate with state agencies on behalf of villagers are usually drawn from this reservoir. Demand for such agency is provided both by villagers who wish to connect with the developmental state and also by state officials who are eager to have villagers organize collectively for implementing agency objectives. Interactions with market agencies are also better handled by agents who can read newspapers, compare prices, and who are able to use this information to obtain the best deals for their fellow villagers.

The factors that are responsible for the rise of mediating agency — among them the spread of literacy, mass media and voting, and the growth of state agencies intent on promoting change from above — have been identified earlier by modernization theory. The spread of schools and mass media and the introduction of voting and the cash economy will be accompanied, it is believed by modernization theorists, with the rise of a "participant culture" (Lerner 1958). Persons exposed to these influences will be more willing and more able to play meaningful parts in modernizing their societies. Being more empathetic to strangers and outsiders, they will be able to fashion productive links with agents and institutions outside their immediate communities (Inkeles 1981; Inkeles and Smith 1974). New roles of innovator and coordinator will arise in convoy with the spread of literacy, modern communications, and urbanization (Apter 1965; Rogers 1969). Markets and state agencies will be engaged collectively by rural communities led by men and women who play the new role of innovator.[15]

Such directions of change are clearly visible in Rajasthan and Madhya Pradesh villages. Younger and relatively better educated leaders have arisen, mostly within the last twenty years, who have made careers out of understanding the procedures and practices of state agencies, and who mediate with these agencies on behalf of fellow villagers. Collective economic gains are much higher in villagers where social capital is high and where such agents are available and effective (chapter 5).

Understanding variations in the second outcome of interest, community peace, requires identifying a second type of mediating agency. The analysis in chapter 6 demonstrates that communal harmony is highest in villages where the traditional council of caste elders is effective. Because the police in the main cannot or will not attend to complaints that do not involve murder, armed robbery, or some other more serious crime, and because dealing with the police is still replete with real or imagined tales of torture and corruption, most villagers continue to take their disputes before the traditional Village Council, where, as has been the case for generations, more than 85 percent of all conflicts are resolved. Incentives arising from the institutional environment (disincentives in the present case) are responsible once again for explaining which agencies arise to tackle community tasks in any particular social domain. Social capital is also important; everything else being the same, villages with higher social capital also have higher levels of communal peace. Everything else is seldom the same, however; in particular, the effectiveness of the informal Village Councils varies considerably from village to village.[16] Villages that are located closer to market and administrative centers tend, in general, to have somewhat weaker Village Councils, suggesting that factors associated with modernization theory might once again serve to complement social capital theory in providing a more complete explanation for this case.

Directions of change indicated by modernization theory can be helpful, therefore, for understanding how new agency roles arise that help villagers' make their stock of social capital more productive. Top-down influences and bottom-up capacities complement each other in providing a more complete explanation.

To explain democratic participation (in chapter 7), I draw also upon these two interwoven strands of theorizing. Lacking their own organizations at the grassroots, political parties in India have usually tapped into some pre-existing form of social organization (Brass 1997; Jalal 1995; Kothari 1988; Migdal 1988). Although they have previously relied almost exclusively on caste associations and patron-client links in the villages, parties in Rajasthan and Madhya Pradesh are turning increasingly toward new and emergent forms of leadership in villages.

Rather than aligning themselves with any particular party, most of which have broadly similar programs anyway (chapters 3 and 7), young development-oriented leaders in villages usually drive hard bargains by playing off one political party against another. What they seek most often in return for votes are greater economic benefits for their village. The new village leaders use political and bureaucratic exchanges to promote economic development for the village. Villagers accord status and respect to these new leaders only so long as the leaders can maintain a steady flow of economic benefits.

The developmental ideology of the post-colonial state has thus percolated down and given rise to new political alignments. The programs of government agencies have generated modernizing influences, giving rise to new forms of leadership, which are responsible, in turn, for influencing the alignments and programs that political parties embrace.

The particular agency forms observed here might be specific to this context. However, a similar dynamic might be emerging as well in other parts of the developing world. Some form of agency is usually necessary for converting a stock of social capital into a flow of benefits. Collective action can occur when social capital is high, but effective collective action requires agents who recognize and who can help others take advantage of the opportunities that exist in their environment. Parties have usually performed this agency role in the West. Where parties and state bureaucracies are constructed largely from the top down, however, mediating agency will emerge as an independent presence at the grassroots. Its form and its objectives will be influenced to a large extent by the nature of modernizing influences that are generated by state and market forces. But its capabilities will be reinforced by those relatively stable patterns of social organization that persist at the grassroots.

2 How Might Social Capital Matter?

Three Alternative Hypotheses

Concern with social capital has exploded into public prominence in the 1990s, but a series of works has challenged the validity and utility of this concept. Described by Putnam (1995: 67) as "features of social organization such as networks, norms and social trust that facilitate coordination and cooperation for mutual benefit," social capital has attracted almost as much criticism as acclaim.

Its harshest critics have charged that social capital has no independent conceptual basis. It is a result rather than a cause of institutional performance, they charge, thus any effects it might have cannot be verified independently.

Others, less hostile, contend that the thesis is valuable but seriously incomplete. Social capital does have some conceptual validity, they agree, but its explanatory value is partial. Rather than being the principal cause explaining results in the economy and the polity, social capital is but one of many independent variables.

Proponents of social capital continue, however, to support their thesis strongly. Social capital, they maintain, is necessary for democracy and development and sufficient on its own account for attaining each of these ends. The reader of the social capital literature is left facing contrasting and contrary views.

Testing social capital against competing explanations is a task that has not so far been systematically undertaken, at least for developing countries. Analysts looking at social capital in the developing world have demonstrated that social capital can make a difference to economic growth rates and household welfare, but no one so far has looked at competing explanations.[1] Might social capital be what its critics have claimed — a mere resultant or residue of state structures? Does social capital matter only in some contexts and not in others?

This book is intended to fill some of these analytical and empirical gaps. I will recast the three contending positions in terms of alternative hypotheses. These are, first, the social capital thesis (claiming substantial cause on behalf of social capital); the structuralist or institutionalist position (asserting causal priority for structures, and claiming social capital to be a residual effect of structures); and the intermediate position, implying contingent causal value.

Necessary and Sufficient Cause: The Social Capital Thesis

The broadest argument made on behalf of social capital can be briefly summarized as follows. Persons bound together in dense social networks, infused with norms of reciprocity and trust, are better able and more inclined to act collectively for mutual benefit and social purposes. Compared to persons not so well endowed with norms and networks, those possessed of these features "can more efficiently restrain opportunism and resolve problems of collective action" (Putnam et al. 1993: 173).

The existence of such norms and networks enables these groups — and society as a whole — to deal smoothly and effectively with multiple social and economic issues.[2] In addition to cooperating with each other for mutual economic betterment, citizens bound together by norms and networks are also able to obtain better governance.

> Citizens in civic communities . . . demand more effective public service, and they are prepared to act collectively to achieve their shared goals. Their counterparts in less civic regions more commonly assume the role of alienated and cynical supplicants. . . . On the supply side, the performance of representative government is considerably facilitated by the social infrastructure of civic communities and by the democratic values of both officials and citizens (Putnam et al. 1993: 182).

The level of social capital is thus a critical variable affecting overall societal achievement. Development, democracy, as well as community peace — all three social domains examined in this study — benefit, it is concluded, in situations of high social capital.

These conclusions are supported by comparisons of the performance of regional governments in Italy. Newly formed, all at the same time, by a common set of legislative reforms instituted in 1970, and similarly endowed with the same administrative powers and roughly equal financial resources, the governments of different Italian regions nevertheless displayed strikingly different levels of performance. Ranked on any of 12 important indicators, regional governments in the northern part of the country have markedly superior achievement levels compared with those in the south (Putnam et al. 1993, chapter 3).

None of the variables usually implicated in political and economic analysis — levels of economic and technological development, education, urbanization, stratification, and conflict — is at all significant for explaining differences in institutional performance. What matters — alone and to the exclusion of all other factors — is social capital, or the level of civic engagement observable in the different regions.

If the social capital thesis has it right, then the form of the structural reforms had little, if anything, to do with comparative results. Given *any* set of formal institutions, regions in the north of Italy would still have outperformed those in the south. Higher levels of civic engagement would serve to ensure that citizens in the north of the country demand better governance and supply better leaders and administrators compared to those in the south — regardless of the specific structural forms selected for the country's and the regions' governments.

Social capital is thus both necessary and sufficient for explaining societal outcomes. It is necessary because low institutional performance corresponds invariably with low social capital, and high institutional performance with high social capital. It is sufficient because no other factor apart from social capital has much value for explanation. Neither economic variables nor state structures matter much for explaining the observed differences among the Italian regions.

Present as well as future performance will be better, it is claimed, in societies that have high levels of social capital. "Societies well supplied with social capital will be able to adopt new organizational forms more readily than those with less, as technology and markets change. . . . Such a

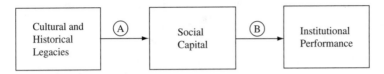

FIGURE 2.1 The Social Capital Thesis

society will be better able to innovate organizationally, since a high degree of sociability will permit a wide variety of social relationships to emerge" (Fukuyama 1995: 27, 30).

The social capital thesis can be represented graphically as shown in figure 2.1. Link A suggests that since social capital is not a product, for instance, of institutional conditions that can be changed in the present day, it can be measured independently of variables proposed by the competing hypotheses. Link B completes the analysis by indicating the causal primacy of social capital. Development and democracy are both underwritten by the same common factor: "Social capital . . . bolsters the performance of the polity and the economy. . . . Strong society, strong economy; strong society, strong state" (Putnam et al. 1993: 176).

The first hypothesis for this study can be worded, therefore, as follows:

Hypothesis 1. *Differences among social units in performance related to multiple domains of human endeavor can be accounted for substantially with reference to social capital alone.*

Presented in such strong terms, the social capital thesis has, not unexpectedly, attracted considerable criticism from diverse quarters. One reason behind the storm of criticism that has greeted social capital relates to the reversal that this thesis makes of the usual causal arrows.

No Causal Value: Social Capital as Effect or Residue

Academics of different persuasions have debated development and governance most often in terms of alternative formulations for macro-structural change — state vs. market-led growth, centralized vs. decentralized government, liberal vs. guided democracy, etc. What happens at the bottom of society, these accounts suggest, depends critically on the nature of structures erected at its top.

The social capital thesis reverses this causal arrow: what matters instead of structures reaching downward from the apex of society is the nature of social relations existing at its base. "Democratic institutions," it is claimed on behalf of the social capital thesis, "cannot be built from the top down. . . . They must be built up in the everyday traditions of trust and civic virtue among its citizens" (Laitin 1995: 172).

Structuralists have responded to the social capital thesis, quite predictably, by challenging its representation of causal arrows. Structures, they argue, remain causally prior to social relations. "Political structure and political context" are critically important, they affirm, and "can go a long way toward shaping both the kinds of organizations represented in society and their impact on the behavior and attitudes of citizens" (Edwards and Foley 1998b: 128). "Social capital may be caused by how government institutions operate and not by voluntary associations" (Rothstein 2001: 207).

> Governments [are] a source of social capital. . . . A large body of social democratic theory claims an important role for the state in reducing the narrow and often risky dependencies of people on each other. The new economic institutionalism stresses the importance of the state in establishing and enforcing the property rights that make trust possible. Recent work by political economists and economic historians emphasizes the role of government institutions in establishing peaceful equilibria among otherwise combative groups (Levi 1996: 50–51).

Social democratic theory, new economic institutionalism, and other venerable traditions are cited in support of restoring causality from the top down. Tarrow reviews the historical evidence presented by Putnam to present a radically different conclusion that reverses cause and effect in the Italian case.

> Every regime that governed southern Italy from the Norman establishment of a centralized monarchy in the twelfth century to the unified government which took over there in 1861 was foreign and governed with a logic of colonial exploitation. . . . [Through 200 years and more] the Italian state has continued to intervene in the South with 'extraordinary' initiatives and institutions, interacting with the local elite in

ways that are far different from its interactions with north-central Italy
... *civic capacity [has been variously] shaped by patterns of state building and state strategy* (Tarrow 1996: 394–95; emphasis added).

Claiming that "civic capacity [is] a *byproduct* of politics, state building, and
social structure," structuralists dismiss the social capital thesis (Tarrow 1996:
396). Instead of social capital explaining institutional performance, thus,
institutions are invoked to explain social capital.

How are these two opposite conclusions derived from the same body of
evidence? The structural rejoinder against social capital picks up on what is
perhaps the weakest point of the social capital thesis: the issue of origins.
How is social capital brought into being, and why do levels of social capital
vary from one society to another? Putnam's attempts to depict social capital
in path-dependent terms — as a carry-forward of historically inherited patterns of civic association — has been challenged by knowledgeable observers
of Italian history.[3]

Contradictory positions taken by Putnam have not helped to make any
convincing case about origins. While he supports a case for historical deter-
minism in Italy, Putnam takes an entirely different tack when approaching
the American evidence. Within the historically short space of a few decades,
he claims, social capital has deteriorated severely in the United States. "For
the first two-thirds of the twentieth century a powerful tide bore Americans
into ever deeper engagement in the life of their communities, but a few
decades ago — silently and without warning — that tide reversed and we were
overtaken by a treacherous rip current" (Putnam 2000: 27). Generational
change accompanied by increased television viewing accounts principally
for this deterioration of social capital in America, according to Putnam
(2000, 1996). But declining social capital in America "directly contradicts
the logic of *Making Democracy Work.* In Putnam's Italian model, the kind
of overnight deterioration of civic virtue that he proposes regarding America
would be inconceivable — once civic virtue is in place it is incredibly durable
over centuries" (Lehmann 1996: 25). In the absence of any persuasive argument about origins, structuralists have strengthened their claim against
the social capital thesis.

Examining United States data for the period 1972–1994, Brehm and
Rahn (1997: 1018) conclude that social capital is "as much a consequence
of confidence in institutions as the reverse." Institutions stand prior to social
relations, they suggest — a view expressed most stridently by the new eco-

nomic institutionalists. "Institutions are the rules of the game," one of the foremost exponent of this school maintains, "the humanly devised constraints that shape human interaction. . . . they structure incentives in human exchange, whether political, social, or economic" (North 1990: 3–4).

Knack and Keefer (1997: 1252, 1284) conclude their 29-country analysis echoing this new institutionalist view. "Trust and norms of civic cooperation," they declare, "are stronger in countries with formal institutions that effectively protect property and contract rights. Formal institutional rules that constrain the government from acting arbitrarily are associated with the development of cooperative norms and trust." Kenworthy's study of the 18 richest market economies concludes similarly: "the principal economically beneficial forms of cooperation tend to be products of institutional incentives" (1997: 645).

Political scientists provide additional evidence to support the priority and primacy of structures. Schneider et al. argue that levels of social capital can be altered through induced structural change. "Design of public institutions," they contend, "affects the level of social capital" (1997: 82). Hall concludes that levels of social capital in Britain have risen or fallen depending on actions taken by that country's government. "The character of both educational policy and social policy in Britain seems to have had profound consequences for social capital" (1997: 28).[4]

There is a fundamental difference in the view of trust and cooperation implied in the social capital thesis and the view that emerges in these structuralist accounts. While the first view considers social capital as exogenous, an independent and explanatory variable for the analysis, the competing view casts it as endogenous and dependent. This difference in opinion has profound consequences for policy. "Considering trust endogenous encourages us to ask which arrangements provide incentives for trust. Considering trust exogenous, however, means that we take levels of trust as given and not subject to change in the short-to-medium term" (Jackman and Miller 1998: 51).

Which is the correct view? For now we must keep an open mind on this issue and treat the structuralist view as offering one more competing hypothesis:

Hypothesis 2. *Differences in institutional performance can be accounted for by variables associated with formal institutions and to the incentives deriving from these institutions. Social capital has no impact on comparative societal performance that is independent of such institutions and their effects.*

Graphically, this hypothesis can be represented as shown in figure 2.2.

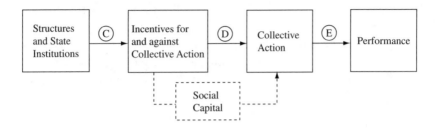

FIGURE 2.2 The Institutionalist Perspective

Incentives for collective action arise from structures and state institutions (Link C). Collective action occurs when the incentives are right, and it falters when these incentives are weak (Link D). Societies will perform well where institutions give rise to incentives that promote effective collective action; else, performance results will be disappointing (Link E).

Where states have permitted citizens to associate freely and where they have supported free enterprise and free association by instituting appropriate rules and legal systems, in those countries and at those times, economic growth has been the fastest, it is contended (De Soto 2000; North and Thomas 1973; North 1981; Olson 1982). Social capital does not matter in this reckoning. At best, social capital is a "byproduct" of institutional incentives, thus unimportant to the causal account. The broken lines in figure 2.2 suggest such a subordinate role for social capital.

Another structural reversal of the social capital thesis is suggested by Wade's (1994) study of collective action among villages in south India. He found that villages located at the tail end of irrigation canals were more likely than those located nearer the head-works to form collective organizations for water supply and distribution. Head-end villagers, who are well supplied with abundant water, have less need to act collectively. But water supply is more unreliable and less adequate in tail-end villages, and the risks of crop loss and water conflict are greater. Tail-end villagers are more in need of community organizations that can mitigate the common risk by sharing scarce supplies equitably and preventing wastage and misuse.

Whether villagers do or do not act collectively depends, therefore, on relative need. Villagers more in need of collective action act together; where the need is less, collective action is less evident. "The basic argument is simply that the benefits of common irrigators are higher in tail-end villages, the costs are no higher, and therefore the net incentive to organize common irrigators is higher than in villages with better water supply locations" (Wade 1994: 164).

Wade supports his relative-need-based explanation of collective action, by looking at arrangements made by villagers for protecting common pastures. Corporate organization at village level for pasture management is more evident, he finds, where the density of grazing livestock is greatest. "The greater the density, the greater the risk of crop loss and conflict" (p. 184). Villagers who have larger numbers of cattle to feed on relatively smaller and less productive patches of grazing land are also more disposed to act collectively for protecting these lands. Once again, as in the case of irrigation, differences in relative need account for differences in collective action.

"We need give no more than a little weight," Wade argues, "to sociological variables such as power structure . . . *or general norms of solidarity and cooperation*" (p. 187; emphasis added). If social capital has any value whatsoever, it is an effect of relative need in Wade's view, a byproduct, once again, and not an independent cause of collective action.

Wade's formulation of relative need can be represented as a corollary to Hypothesis 2. In either case, social capital does not explain differences in institutional performance. Social capital is a byproduct — of state structures in one case, and of relative need in the other. The hypothesis and its corollary are examined in the following chapters. Next, a third strand of literature is considered that provides another hypothesis to be evaluated here.

Partial Causal Value: Social Capital as Incomplete Explanation

The third position on social capital asserts the need for intermediary links between social capital and institutional performance. What enables the effect of social capital, it is asked, to flow from grassroots-level associations and localized social networks into decisionmaking at higher levels? How exactly does social capital existing among members of community organizations affect the performance of regional and national institutions?

The issue of intermediary links marks the point of departure for presenting the third perspective.

The co-occurrence of civic associations and effective government in the same region does not demonstrate that the people in the associations are the ones making the government work. To address that question, one must systematically introduce *a mediating level of analysis* that can demonstrate the actual avenues of influence among civicly engaged people, civic associations, and institutional performance (Foley and Edwards 1996: ff. 8; emphasis added).

Intermediary links are unimportant, recall, for the social capital thesis. "Strong society, strong economy," it is alleged, "strong society, strong state." The cause is sufficient to account for the effect, and mediating links are unnecessary.

The exact mechanisms that link leisurely interaction to good government are somewhat under-specified . . . but the elements of a logical chain are available. The members of secondary associations, who are used to cooperating, know the basic rules of (self) government and are thus particularly sensitized to poor governmental performance. As they interact on a regular basis and trust one another, they can easily mount collective protest against governmental inefficiency and abuse. Should the anticipation of negative sanctions from such trained constituents not suffice to keep the rulers on the right track, they would be easily replaced with more diligent ones, conceivably drawn from those with a long training in self-government (Piattoni 1998: 1).

But such automatic transmission of community-level social capital into state- and national-level performance might be problematic in practice. Quite severe problems of aggregation and transmission might arise to prevent the conversion of social capital into institutional performance.

For instance, it is not clear how members of any social network agree on the ends toward which their social capital should be used. Do all members of any voluntary organization always want the same things from the state and from the economy for which they will be willing to work cooperatively with one another? Is there anything about social capital that guarantees harmony of individual interests?

The point is made for the case of heterogeneous groups:

Co-operation among unequals is problematic because there will always be incentives for the poor, who will naturally be dissatisfied with the existing distribution of assets, to defect from co-operative arrangements that perpetuate the status quo. Moreover, to maintain their political and economic privileges, the rich will maneuver to undermine any co-operative arrangements that the poor may undertake to better their lot (Boix and Posner 1998: 688).

The point is made as well for homogeneous groups by Berman (1997a, 1997b) who considers the example of interwar Germany. Civil society organizations, which were "organized primarily along group [and class] lines rather than across them," not only failed "to contribute to republican virtue, but in fact subverted it." This "fragmented but highly organized civil society . . . proved to be the ideal setting for the rapid rise to power of a skilled totalitarian movement." "Without the opportunity to exploit Weimar's rich associational network . . . the Nazis would not have been able to capture important sectors of the German electorate so quickly and efficiently" (Berman 1997a: 414–422).

Dense social networks are not enough, therefore, to achieve more effective and more accountable government. "Associationism," Berman concludes, is "a *politically neutral multiplier* — neither inherently good nor inherently bad." Dense networks of "civil society can often serve to weaken rather than strengthen democracy" (Berman 1997b: 564).

Whether associationism weakens or strengthens institutional performance depends, in her view, on the nature of the mediating links. In the Western contexts studied by Berman, party organizations are expected to provide such linkages. Where parties are weak, it is argued, the capacity of civic associations "to make effective demands and sanction government action may remain limited . . . certain issues do not even reach the public's attention. . . . Even with a free press, information about policy and policy consequences is costly and confusing" (Levi 1996: 49). By providing members with relevant information about state activities, and by acting as an organized conduit to governmental decisionmaking, political parties have traditionally performed this task of "multiplier" or agency.

For Italy also, it is claimed, parties play much of the role for which Putnam gives credit to social capital. According to some observers, associational activity in the Italian regions has been coordinated mostly by political parties.[5] Association density and party strength rise and fall together among different Italian regions, so it becomes possible for the analyst to consider only one of these factors while ignoring the other. Analyses undertaken in other parts of the world will have to take account separately of party structures and social capital, for these variables are unlikely to coincide as well in every other place.

Mediating agency will need to be considered separately in its own right along with levels of social capital. Issues of interest formation, interest aggregation, and interest representation may remain unresolved even where social capital is abundant. Without the agency function performed by political parties or some other form of mediating agency, social capital, however plentiful, may remain disconnected from state institutions' performance. So long as it pays no heed to the role played by mediating agency, thus, the social capital thesis remains seriously incomplete.

Consider, for example, Bates's and Popkin's discussions of Scott's Southeast Asian peasants.[6] United within a moral economy framework — sharing common interests (sustaining the subsistence economy equilibrium) and a deeply rooted set of internalized norms — peasants in many villages did not act collectively even in the face of flagrant norm violation by landlords.

Until interests were formulated and aggregated appropriately with the help of skilled political activists, the potential for collective action remained latent and unexplored. Scott's norms-based account tells us, he says, of "the creation of social dynamite rather than its detonation" (1976: 4). He has little to account for why peasants revolted when they did. How norms came to be converted into collective action is suggested, not by Scott, but by Popkin. "The difference between the two reactions [collective action and its absence] was . . . *organization*, particularly communication and coordination" (Popkin 1979: 248, 252).

Internalized norms along with membership in labor groups and mutual aid organizations did not prove sufficient in the Southeast Asian case to equip peasants with the wherewithal required for grievance representation and collective revolt. For the latter purpose, some specific agents were required who were sponsored in this case by the communist party and also by church-based organizations. Even when norms are strongly internalized, thus, agents will often be necessary who make it possible for individuals to cooperate for some specific objective, particularly one that is new and different from the past.[7]

Social capital may predispose individuals to cooperate, and pre-existing social networks will facilitate cooperation generally, but in specific spheres of actions, especially where the external environment needs to be engaged, specific agencies such as political parties or organized interest groups will be additionally required. Tasks must be assigned and task performance coordinated, objectives must be set and reviewed in the light of changing circumstances, and relations built and maintained with key decisionmakers of the state and the market. For each of these purposes, specialized knowledge and specific areas of competence will often be required, and agents specially equipped for dealing with particular areas will help with these tasks.

Lowi (1985) informs us that for decisionmaking at the national level, each issue area has its own specific constituency and operating rules. Actors who are competent in engagements with any one of these constituencies and rule structures are often unable to act effectively in other areas. If agency is required at all for social capital, it is very likely that different agents will be selected to act in different areas. But is agency required at all? This question is approached with the help of the third hypothesis.

Hypothesis 3. *Social capital is brought to bear upon institutional performance through the mediation of agencies or conduits, each of which is concerned specifically with issues related to some particular social domains and not others. The effectiveness of the mediating agency is as important as the level of the asset (social capital) for understanding variations in institutional performance.*

Graphically, this hypothesis can be represented in figure 2.3. Social capital is by itself a "politically neutral multiplier" (Link F). Its effects on institutional performance depend on the nature and strengths of the mediating agency (Link G). Agencies mediate the effects of social capital and translate

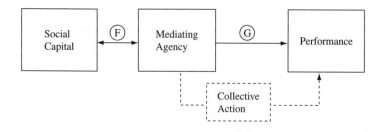

FIGURE 2.3 The Mediating Agency Perspective

it into collective action that is directed toward particular ends. The ends that are served as also the means that are employed depend critically on the nature of the mediating agency.

In defense of their thesis, proponents of social capital might argue, for instance, that even if it is true that social capital is mediated by issue-specific mediating agencies, any such mediation will itself work better in situations where social capital is high. High social capital gives rise to multiple organizational endeavors, so strong mediating agencies will arise of their own accord whenever social capital is high. The mediating agency argument is, thus, of no practical value. High levels of social capital will always be found to be associated with superior societal performance in multiple realms of human endeavor. A detailed examination of these contrasting positions must be deferred until the evidence is presented in full. I must mention, however, that this argument — that strong agencies arise whenever social capital is high — does not find support in the India data examined later in the book.[8]

To recapitulate, we are considering three alternative and competing hypotheses. These hypotheses make the claims shown in table 2.1.

TABLE 2.1 Three Alternative Hypotheses

Hypothesis	Does Social Capital Matter?
1 Differences among social units in performance in multiple domains of human endeavor can be accounted for substantially (if not solely) with reference to social capital.	Social capital matters a lot.
2 Differences in institutional performance can be accounted for by variables associated with formal institutions, both state and market, and to the incentives deriving from these institutions. Social capital is a resultant or residue of these structural effects.	If social capital matters at all, it does so as a result of structures and incentives that derive from these structures.
3 The effects of social capital are translated into performance by mediating agencies, which vary by issue area. The effectiveness of the mediating agency is as important as the level of social capital for understanding variations in institutional performance.	Social capital matters contextually and in part — neither as much as Hypothesis 1 holds nor as little as Hypothesis 2 suggests.

A Brief Look at the Evidence

The evidence examined in this book provides support to a modified version of the third hypothesis. "Civil society requires political agency," suggests Walzer (1995: 14), and different types of agency are required, it is seen here, to deal with different societal objectives, namely, economic development, community peace, and political participation. For each of these dependent variables, social capital is an important independent variable, but the effects of social capital are considerably magnified when mediating agency is brought within the analysis.[9]

The structuralist view, corresponding to Hypothesis 2 above, finds little support in the evidence examined here. Similar institutional structures will provide a similar set of incentives for action and should result in similar institutional performance scores, this hypothesis suggests. So villages located within the same institutional setting and sharing a common set of legal, administrative, and also market-related structures should exhibit no marked differences in performance results. If some differences do exist among these villages, then other structural variables should suffice to account for the same.

These expectations are not, however, substantiated by the data. Conspicuous differences are apparent in performance levels among institutionally similar villages compared on any of the three dependent variables. These differences in village characteristics and performance scores can be accounted for by none of the variables that structuralist theories would have us consider.

Population size, the strength of the dominant caste, social polarization, ethnic differences, party structures, economic associations, nearness to or distance from market, higher education, asset distribution, relative need — not one of these variables achieves any significance in regression analysis. Nor are the corresponding theories supported to any greater extent by the interviews and other case materials collected in a representative set of 16 among these 69 villages.

The social capital view, corresponding to Hypothesis 1, is not fully supported either. If the social capital thesis is substantially correct, it can be argued, villages with high social capital scores should perform highly in respect of all three social indicators, and villages with low social capital scores should perform poorly on all three scales. High scores on any one scale of performance should go together with high scores for the other two scales, and low scores should similarly be found to cluster together.

These expectations are not well supported by the data. There is no significant correlation among village scores on the three different scales. Some
villages that have done well on the economic development scale, for example, have performed very poorly on the other two scales. While social
capital is statistically significant in explaining variations with respect to each
of the three scales of performance, it does not suffice by itself to explain the
major part of the variation in any of these scales.

In addition to social capital, the evidence indicates, performance in any
specific issue area is related also to the capacity of a particular set of agents
who are relevant for that domain. Social capital is an asset that remains
latent until agents activate this stock and use it to produce a flow of benefits.

Different sets of local agents are found in Rajasthan and Madhya Pradesh
villages to be associated with collective action related to different social objectives. Traditional village leaders — elders representing all caste and ethnic
groups of that village — provide agency and activate the stock of social capital
for the community peace objective. Mentioned in the historical literature as
being effective even during Mughal times, i.e., as much as 500 years ago,
these leaders continue to organize residents for collective peace and communal justice in most villages of this region.[10] Levels of community peace are
high, the analysis in chapter 6 shows, where these traditional leaders are effective and where social capital is high. These two variables — social capital
and traditional leaders' effectiveness — are not highly correlated with one another, indicating that agency exerts an influence separately from social capital.
Factors that contribute to high social capital levels are different from those
that influence the capacity and effectiveness of community leaders (chapter 4).

As economic development has been elevated ahead of law and order in
the modernizing state's list of priorities, new forms of leadership and agency
have developed in the countryside.[11] Better educated and much better informed than the traditional leaders about the world outside the village, these
new leaders are more at home in the labyrinths of bureaucratic procedure.

This new set of younger leaders is neither usually high-caste nor from the
richest households of the village. But they are the agents whose services
villagers find useful for wresting state funding for development projects and
for petitioning state agents on behalf of villagers' needs. High social capital
villages do not perform so well for development if agents of this type are
weak or incapable.

Table 2.2 captures some of the main differences between new and old
forms of leadership. The new leaders are relatively younger and somewhat

TABLE 2.2 Old and New Leaders in 60 Villages

		OLD (Related to Community Peace)	NEW (Related to Development)
	n =	197	211
Age		54.5	38.3
Education (years)		3.5	9.6
Caste Rank (0 to 4)		2.9	1.7
Land per capita (ha)		0.84	0.48
Assets (out of 7)		2.8	2.4
FUNCTIONS*			
Dispute Resolution		12.5	2.1
Religious and Social		5.9	1.2
Government (Development)		5.3	22.1
Government (Regulatory)		6.3	16.7
Market Brokerage		1.4	11.6
Party Politics		2.8	4.3
FEATURES (average score)			
Information Sources (out of 7)		3.2	6.1
External Contacts (out of 10)		3.6	7.9

* Note: Scores for each function are measured by the number of times the respondent performed this function in the preceding six months. "Government (development)" and "Government (regulatory)" measure the number of times contact was made with government agencies of these two types on behalf of someone else in the village. "Party politics" mentions the number of times the respondent contacted or was contacted by party officials from outside the village.

lower in caste hierarchies. They own less land and are less well off materially than the old group of caste-based leaders, but they have much higher levels of formal education and greater access to state and market agencies.

Power and influence in the village have been dispersed more broadly with the rise of this new leadership.[12] More and more villagers are looking to these new leaders for support and assistance in dealing with the world outside the village. As they help villagers transact effectively in economic activities outside the village, the new village leaders acquire influence and status both within the village and outside.

The new leaders have with them a means of getting things done from the state — a most potent currency of political exchange in the villages of present-day India. Their rise to power has been assisted, as I will discuss in the following chapters, by the spread of education and mass communications, by a huge increase in the development programs of state agencies, and also by a sharp rise in the intensity of party competition. These factors — identified earlier by modernization theorists — are useful for understanding the changing leadership roles in the Indian countryside.

Briefly, thus, the data show agency as providing an important mediating link between social capital and societal performance. Social capital matters for development, for communal harmony, and for democratic participation, and it matters even more when is activated and made productive through the intervention of capable agents.

3 Structure and Agency
New Political Entrepreneurs and the Rise
of Village-Based Collective Action

Before examining the competing hypotheses about social capital presented in the previous chapter, it is necessary to agree upon an appropriate unit of analysis. Political analysts have mostly considered caste and extended patron-client links as the building blocks of political organization in rural India.[1] Because of events occurring within the last two decades, however, new networks and new forms of leadership — based on non-ascriptive criteria — have arisen in villages. These new leaders provide superior opportunities for collective action by villagers, and they help mobilize social capital for diverse economic and political purposes. The village has gained consequently as a unit of mutually beneficial collective action.[2]

Three sets of factors have operated to support the emergence of new village leaders and the strengthening of new village-based networks of collective action and political mobilization:

1. Rural education that was almost entirely neglected before 1947, and which spread only very slowly in the first three decades after independence, has increased greatly in the last twenty years. Starting from a low base, educational achievement has risen even faster among lower and scheduled castes. Lower caste and other historically excluded groups have gained a new ability to negotiate independently with state bureaucrats and party officials.[3]

2. A fourteen-fold increase in state expenditures over the last fifteen years accompanied by proliferating government activity in rural areas has vastly expanded points of interface and mediation between the village and the state.

The monopoly of access that higher caste and better connected villagers previously had to agencies of the state has been worn down simultaneously as villagers of all caste groups have gained in education and negotiating ability. New leaders have arisen, who are more able to gain benefits and services from the state, and villagers look to these persons for assistance, regardless of caste and economic background.

3. Weak grassroots organization and lack of ideological separation have led political parties in India to rely for support on pre-existing social organizations. Where they relied previously on caste- or patronage-based voting, they are now finding it more useful to forge links at the village level with the rising group of young and educated leaders. Intensified two-party competition, especially since 1977, has provided incentive to each party for reaching out to new leaders with influence among villagers. The old caste-based leadership is no longer the only or even the primary contact that party organizers seek when they enter these north Indian villages looking for votes.

The emergence of these new non-caste-based political entrepreneurs is not an entirely new phenomenon. Bailey (1960) had anticipated that new forms of leadership would come up, based on new relationships that individual villagers would forge outside village boundaries. Such new forms of village leadership had started becoming evident in the late 1970s and early eighties, as reported by Reddy and Haragopal (1985) and Mitra (1991, 1992). These trends have picked up pace considerably in the past twenty years, and I found new non-caste-based leaders to be quite widespread and influential in the 69 villages of Rajasthan and Madhya Pradesh that I studied between 1998 and 2000.[4]

The village has gained, in consequence, as a unit of mutually beneficial collective action. Villages that can mount collective action effectively have gained more than others in terms of outcomes in the economic, social, and political realms. Stocks of social capital possessed by village communities are important for understanding variations in these outcomes and also the capacities of agents who help villagers derive benefits from these stocks.

The Village in North India

The village in India is a relatively stable territorial unit. All 16 case-study villages, where I stayed for periods of two weeks or longer, have a history that traces back 500 years and more. Population has increased in the fifty years following national independence, but village boundaries have remained relatively intact.[5]

Most male villagers live and die in the village to which they are born, without spending any significant part of their lives outside its boundaries. Women live out their lives after they are married (usually by the time they are 18 years of age) in villages to which their husbands belong.[6]

Average population in my sample of 69 villages is 1,089 persons and average village area is 867 hectares, which is not dissimilar from the rest of Rajasthan, or for that matter, from much of the rest of India.[7] About half of the total village area consists of agricultural fields, while the rest is wasteland, scrub forest, and common grazing grounds. The table at Appendix B provides these and other village details.

Each village has a center, where people of all caste groups live, albeit in distinct caste-denominated neighborhoods.[8] The village map at Appendix C depicts the rough map that I drew while staying in Balesariya village of Bhilwara district, Rajasthan. The center of this settlement is bordered on all sides by fields where crops are grown in the rainy season, usually ranging from late June to late September.

More than 90 percent of villagers have agriculture as their principal occupation. Average landholdings are quite small, however — 1.4 hectares per household on average, or 0.25 hectares per capita (given average sample household size of 5.5). Yields vary greatly from year to year on account of scanty or untimely rainfall. Production of major crops has not consistently risen over the past fifty years, as discussed in chapter 5, but population has grown by almost 25 percent every decade. All villagers keep cattle and other farm animals to insure against low and variable crop yields.[9]

Nearly half of all villagers supplement their incomes every year by working as casual and mostly unskilled labor. 861 of 1,898 villagers surveyed in 60 Rajasthan villages — or 45 percent — stated that additional income derived from working as casual labor for at least one month every year were essential for meeting their household expenses. A similar proportion (46 percent) was recorded among 334 villagers interviewed in nine Madhya Pradesh villages. Many more villagers go looking for wage employment on public works in years when the harvest is particularly bad, which is two years out of every five, and the government is the largest provider of casual employment in this area.[10]

Government-sponsored employment-generating works have come to form an essential lifeline for nearly half of all villagers who depend on these works for meeting subsistence needs. Villagers jostle with other villagers to get employment-generating public works approved for their village, and caste plays little part in these negotiations. People of different castes mobilize together for these purposes, and their efforts are made more productive by the new group of non-caste-based village leaders, who have arisen and gained influence in the last twenty years.

Villages in this region are usually multi-caste units, as the map at Appendix C indicates, and different caste groups have been living in the village since antiquity. What has changed, however, quite visibly and rapidly over the last twenty years, is the relationship between caste and influence in the village.[11]

Village and Caste in Historical Perspective

High caste was associated up to fifty years ago with greater wealth and larger political clout, and these privileges were backed by an influential ideology that allotted occupation and status in the village according to the caste to which a person was born (Dumont 1970; various). Higher caste persons, particularly Rajputs and Brahmins, owned the largest and richest land areas within villages in my study area, and they exercised administrative control on behalf of the ruler over all other lands in the village. Relations with the state were mediated exclusively and monopolistically by Rajputs (in most villages) and by Brahmins (in villages such as Sunderchha or Sema, where local control was handed over to groups of Brahmins especially favored by the ruler).[12] Village chiefs belonging to the highest landowning castes administered justice in the village on behalf of the state. "In cases regarding the distribution of justice or the internal economy of the chief's estates, the government officers seldom interfere" (Tod 1971 [1829]: 120).

Duties and rights were allocated according to caste, and the lowest castes were expected to perform forced labor, or *begaar*, whenever it suited the highest castes. "A Chamar or for that matter, a Bhil, could be asked to do *begaar* right at the time of sowing and harvesting. This resulted in shattering the economic life of the poor. In cases where the victims of *begaar* showed some resistance or delay in compliance, the results were very much injurious for the former," consisting of beatings, torture, death or eviction from the village (Chaubisa 1988: 41–42).

All persons took up the occupations allotted to their own caste group.

Chamars flayed dead cattle, turned their skins to leather, and made shoes that the upper castes could wear (lower castes, including Chamars themselves, were denied the right to wear shoes in public). Nais worked as barbers, and their women helped as midwives. Kumhars made earthen pots for storing grain and water; Dholis beat the drum on festive occasions and funerals; Suthars were the carpenters of the village community; and so on. In the relatively autarchic economy of the village, fifty or a hundred years ago, all necessary tasks were divided up among castes within the village — or alternatively, people were divided into castes in order that particular tasks could be performed (Pinhey 1996 [1909]).

Economic exchange among castes usually followed a closed patron-client arrangement based on mutuality and barter. "The relationship of artisan castes, service-rendering castes, and priestly castes with . . . [landowning] castes are known as the *Jajmani* system. The *Jajmans* are patrons of those groups which require their services. . . . For these services, payment is generally made in kind."[13]

"The Lohar (blacksmith) would repair a farmer's implements and not ask for money at that time. He would come at the time of harvest and be paid in grain. At childbirth, the Nai's wife would come to our house. Seller and buyer were closely tied up with one another in this system. We could not ask for any other midwife, and she could not serve more clients [than her household had inherited]. To have pots made, we could only go to a certain Kumhaar, who took two bags of grain from us at every harvest."[14]

Each person had a fixed place in this system that he or she knew at birth. The system was regulated and enforced by the upper caste group, Rajput or Brahmin, which was delegated judicial and magisterial authority by the state, and which also owned the largest tracts of land in the village and could thus keep all other groups submissive by threat of eviction. The state relied upon these people not only for gathering the revenue and keeping the peace (of a certain kind), but also to procure other services and to place other demands upon villagers (Lupton 1908). [15]

Even after independence and the advent of democracy, this inglorious tradition — of banking upon the strong to gain the allegiance, or at least the compliance, of the weak — was found useful and continued by political parties. Not just in southern Rajasthan but also in many other parts of rural India, the modus operandi of the Congress Party, imitated less successfully by other parties, consisted of enlisting the largest landlords of the area and using their inherited influence to garner votes among the lower classes.[16] These landlords' influence was bolstered by providing them with exclusive access to agencies of the state, much as rulers of the princely states had done in their days, and by letting development benefits from the state pass as patronage through their hands.

The Congress Party spoke the language of equality and nationhood, but it got its votes in southern Rajasthan through men like Gulab Singh Shaktawat, a Rajput leader and feudal landlord of the old regime, who used his connections with other Rajput bosses to persuade or compel villagers to vote for the Congress Party. Colonel Ram Singh (retired), ex-Sarpanch of Village A,[17] and close crony of Gulab Singh, had the following to say about his relationships with other villagers:

> No villager used to go directly to the police or to the courts. They came here first [to my house]. If anyone had any problem with any government department they came to me. People in the village are still honest and give you respect according to your status and position. Any new official who took his position in the village came first to my house [it is the largest and most visible house in the village]. All government officials cooperated with me after they learned who I am. If I had any problems with any of these officials, I would tell Gulab Singh, and they were transferred out of this area. I would tell the *panchayat* secretary what proposals to send from the village. There was no need for a meeting; what can these villagers tell me? I would tell the *Thanedar* [police station officer-in-charge] what the truth was in any case involving this village. Lately there are a few mischievous youngsters. They have got a little bit of education, and so they think they know everything. . . . Education is another evil visited upon us by the government. What good does it do to educate a Bhil [scheduled tribe] or a Meghwal [scheduled caste] boy when all he is good for is a menial job in some government office?

Political and economic outcomes of up to twenty years ago could be substantially explained in terms of the efforts and influence of individual strongmen. Like the Colonel in Village A, a particular set of individuals, privileged by high caste and economic status, stood as gatekeepers to the state. Parties won or lost votes depending on what these individuals did; and villagers gained economic benefits depending on how effectively their strongman could connect with agencies of the state.

This situation has changed, however, and most notably over the last two decades. The Colonel is still an important figure in his village, but his influence and authority have been challenged successfully by other villagers. Because of the spread of education, the vastly increased involvement of the state in the rural economy, and the heightened intensity of two-party competition — three factors that I will examine in the following paragraphs — new village-based networks have gained influence over the last two decades. Much more than the residual capacity of individual strongmen, villagers' collective capacities have become more important indicators of what they can achieve. Characteristics of village communities, such as level of social capital, become salient consequently as factors influencing results in the economic, political and social realms.

The Rise and Spread of Education

Changes occurring over the past fifty years have affected social relations in the village. Increasing cash-based transactions have had the effect of weakening *Jajmani*, and the previously exclusive relationship between seller and buyer has been sundered on account of the cash economy. People are no longer bound to follow the occupation of their caste. Barbers have become telephone operators, sweepers have become *patwaris*,[18] and skinners and tanners have become tractor repairmen. Not all barbers, sweepers, and tanners have moved up in life, to be sure, but there are no longer strict rules or effective enforcers who can hold them back at all times. Even as caste continues to be a primary source of social identity in these villages, caste, occupation, and income category are no longer always closely aligned.[19]

Land ownership is no longer a monopoly of the upper castes. Even though they own more than three times as much land on average than Scheduled Castes (SCs), as Table 3.1 indicates, upper castes are usually no longer in a position to evict the lower castes at will or to command *begaar* from them. Land reform in Rajasthan as in other parts of India has hardly equalized land ownership among all villagers, nor has it bestowed much land on those who were previously landless. What it has done, however, is to transfer ownership to those, particularly middle and backward castes,[20] who were the actual cultivators of land, even though Rajputs and Brahmins were the recorded owners. Additionally, security of tenure has been significantly enhanced even among smaller farmers and lower caste tenants (Ladejinsky 1972; Saxena and Charan 1973, 1993; Varshney 1995).

More than Rajasthan's and India's incomplete land reform, however, it

TABLE 3.1 Distribution of Land and Educational Achievement by Caste

CASTE GROUP*	Land owned per capita (hectares)	Average Educational Achievement: Years of School Education (by age-group)				
		All ages	Less than 40 years	Less than 35 years	Less than 30 years	18–25 years
Upper (n = 326)	0.45	4.8	5.8	6.1	6.8	7.1
Middle (n = 206)	0.55	3.0	3.4	3.8	3.9	4.2
Backward (n = 702)	0.23	2.8	3.5	4.0	5.4	5.9
ST (n = 410)	0.18	1.8	2.3	2.8	3.2	4.5
SC (n = 254)	0.14	2.4	3.7	4.7	5.3	7.0

* SC refers to Scheduled Castes; ST to Scheduled Tribes; Backward includes those caste groups that have been classified officially as "Other Backward Castes" (OBC); Upper Castes includes Brahmins, Rajputs, Mahajans and Jains; and Middle Castes includes landowning castes such as Jats and Dangis that have not been recognized as OBC

is education that is proving to have a more radical influence, especially among lower-caste and poorer villagers. The distribution of education is becoming almost equal among different caste groups. This trend is not immediately apparent if educational achievement is considered for villagers of all age groups, but it is more readily visible when education figures are broken down by age and caste categories. Tables 3.1 and 3.2 present figures for educational achievement subdivided by caste and age-group for the random sample of 1,898 villagers consulted for this study in Rajasthan.[21]

When educational achievement is considered among villagers of all age groups, Scheduled Castes (SC), Scheduled Tribes (ST), and backward castes are seen to be considerably less well educated than upper castes. A difference of more than two years in average educational achievement separates upper castes from SCs, and this difference is even larger (three years) between upper castes and STs.

TABLE 3.2 Percentage of Villagers with Five or More Years of School Education

	Age Group					
Caste Group	Over 65 years	55–65 years	45–55 years	35–45 years	25–35 years	18–25 years
Upper (n = 326)	32.6	49.5	51.7	58.1	69.9	81.0
Middle (n = 206)	9.3	14.2	21.7	37.8	42.9	50.0
Backward (n = 702)	9.7	27.7	28.7	34.4	55.8	72.0
ST (n = 410)	0.0	7.4	12.1	14.6	23.9	52.6
SC (n = 254)	0.0	11.7	18.3	23.6	40.4	72.4
AVERAGE (all castes)	15.2	22.5	27.6	32.8	48.2	69.6
Decadal Increase: *Improvement Over Previous Cohort (percent)*		7.3	5.1	5.2	15.4	21.4
Gap A: *Between Upper Caste and SC (percent)*	32.6	37.8	33.4	34.5	29.4	8.5
Gap B: *Between Upper and Backward Castes (percent)*	22.9	21.8	23.0	23.7	14.1	9.0

The difference among the castes narrows significantly, however, when we consider villagers who have received their school education within the last two decades. Among villagers aged between 18 and 25 years of age, SCs have nearly the same education on average (seven years) as the upper castes. SCs have overtaken the dominant land-owning category, the middle castes, in educational attainment. Similarly, backward castes and STs have also gone ahead of middle castes, but they are still some distance behind upper castes.[22] These trends become even clearer when we consider the figures presented in table 3.2.

The picture of rural India as a largely illiterate and ignorant mass fragments considerably when educational achievement is broken down by age group. While only 31 percent of all rural Rajasthanis were literate in 1991, i.e., they could barely write their names,[23] almost 50 percent of villagers between 25 and 35 years of age and nearly 70 percent of those aged 18–25 years have five or more years of school education. Though not yet as high as in the industrialized countries, these rates compare favorably with those observed in China or in India's much vaunted state of Kerala just ten years ago (Dreze and Sen 1995; Heller 2000). And the results in terms of political mobilization are beginning to resemble those observed in Kerala.[24]

The fastest gains in educational achievement across caste groups have been recorded in the last two decades, and especially among SCs and backward castes. Villagers who went to school about 40 years ago (i.e., those who are presently 55 to 65 years of age) are more educated than other villagers who went to school ten years before them (those aged 65 years or more). The decadal increase in this case is, however, quite small — only 7.3 percentage points. The largest and most significant decadal increase has been registered within the past twenty years. 21.4 percentage points separate 18 to 25-year-olds from those aged 25–35 years, and 15.4 percentage points separate the latter cohort from other villagers who attended schools ten years previously (i.e., those aged 35–45 years).

All younger villagers have gained rapidly in educational achievement, but scheduled and backward castes have registered a higher rate of increase compared to upper and middle castes. The last two rows of table 3.2 show that the difference in average education between upper and lower castes has reduced considerably over the last 20 years. Not a single SC or ST person above 65 has five or more years of school education, but 72 percent of SCs between 18 and 25 years of age and 53 percent of STs of this age group are educated to this level. Among upper castes aged 65 years or more, 32 percent have five or more years of school education. Among upper castes who went to school forty years later, i.e., those aged from 18 to 25 years, this proportion is as high as 81 percent. The increase in average educational achievement among upper castes has been of the order of 47 percentage points in the past forty years. The corresponding increase among SCs has been much higher — 72 percentage points on average.

Two facts emerge from these statistics that have gone largely unnoticed so far.

1. Educational achievement is more than double among villagers aged 18–25 years compared to other villagers who went to school more than twenty years ago. Average literacy rates conceal the substantial marginal gains that have been made by younger villagers.

2. The gap in educational achievement between upper and lower castes has closed considerably in the last two decades. The gap between upper castes and SCs — in terms of the proportion of people of each caste who attended school for five or more years — was stable at around 33 percent until 20 years ago. This gap has narrowed rapidly in the last twenty years.

Marginal rates of educational achievement are substantially higher than average rates. And younger villagers who are benefiting from this trend — particularly younger villagers of scheduled and backward castes — are beginning to make a considerable impact upon patterns of leadership and influence in these villages.[25]

These trends are continuing into the future. I do not have similarly detailed figures for persons who are less than 18 years of age (villagers were selected for interview based on a sample drawn from the voters list, which has the result of excluding anyone under 18 years of age). But in the 16 villages where I stayed for long periods of time it was clear that more than 90 percent of children of all castes are currently going to school. 33,758 state-run primary schools serve 37,889 villages of Rajasthan (GOR 1997), and more are being set up, including non-formal and privately run schools. Nearly all villages have one or more primary school within their boundary, and there is none from which a school is more than five kilometers distant.[26]

Higher education levels acquired by younger and lower caste villagers, especially over the last two decades, have provided them with a greater ability to deal directly with the complex procedures of state agencies, free of their patrons and caste leaders.[27] As the government machinery has been vastly extended in the rural areas — also over the last twenty years, as I will review in the next section — contacts between villagers and government officials have expanded substantially. Villagers as well as government officials look for reliable and competent persons to mediate these transactions. And the pool of newly educated but unemployed villagers provides a source of potential mediators.[28] The supply of young and educated villagers has grown rapidly in the last twenty years, and demand for their services has also grown at the same time.

This group of educated young men help villagers take advantage of the opportunities for collective action that have arisen as state programs have expanded vastly over the past two decades. They enable villagers to draw upon their stock of social capital, and they provide the agency that is necessary to maximize the flow of benefits from this asset.

Expanding State Programs

Regulations relating to the industrial sector are the subject of frequent academic and policy discussions in India. There is a vast "array of public controls over the private industrial sector, controls which have only begun to be streamlined in the last decade" (Vanaik 1990:31). Though they are less well covered by the literature, state interventions in the rural sector are no less intrusive and encompassing. Instead of being dismantled or streamlined in the last two decades, moreover, state intervention in the rural sector has been intensified in the name of rural development and poverty reduction (Mishra 1997; Singh 1995).

At nearly every stage of the agricultural cycle, the farmer is confronted with barriers erected by the state. Distribution of fertilizer and certified seed is controlled by the state; state-run cooperatives and nationalized banks provide all institutional credit; crop insurance can be acquired only from nationalized insurance companies; produce can be bought and sold legally only in market yards established by the state and supervised by its inspectors. To sell, donate, bequeath, or subdivide land, the farmer must first get this transaction registered in the *Tahsil* (subdistrict) office, and then he must get the *patwari* to "mutate" the village land record. If he wants to open a shop in his village, he needs to get nine licenses and permits from different government agencies.[29] To get his children admitted to a high school or college, he must often get a certificate of residence from the area magistrate. To cut down trees on his own land, he needs one permit from the Forest Department and another from the *Tahsil*.[30]

Not one of these statutory requirements has been liberalized or streamlined. On the contrary, villagers' transactions with a complex and procedure-ridden state bureaucracy have increased many times since a plethora of welfare and development programs began to be launched starting in the late 1970s. "These projects of social transformation arose out of a deliberative-legislative [i.e., a top-down] rather than a participative-democratic [or bottom-up] process" (Jayal 1999:1), and people have to line up to establish their eligibility for program benefits before government officials whose mandates and program funding come from above.

Rural development schemes were few and far between in the period before 1971 when Indira Gandhi gave her call for *garibi hatao* (abolish poverty). The Janata Party government of 1977–1980 gave this slogan a programmatic basis, and it introduced two new programs which, after being expanded and re-christened many times over, have formed the core of successive governments' thrust toward community infrastructure development, employment generation, and poverty reduction in the rural areas.

Vastly expanded budgetary provisions were allocated to rural development starting in the late 1970s. Funding for rural development schemes has expanded *seven-fold* (in inflation-adjusted terms) in the period between 1980 and 1995 (GOI 1998), and it is being increased further.[31] A vast network of District Rural Development Agencies (DRDAs) was established covering each of India's more than 500 districts to cope with this huge inflow of funds.

The first major program introduced by the Janata Party government, the Food for Work Program, was meant to fund construction of community assets, such as school buildings, approach roads, and health centers. Simultaneously it was intended to provide employment and wages to large numbers in rural areas. Labor-intensive projects were preferred, and the material component of program expenditure was restricted to 25 percent of total program funds. Successively termed the National Rural Employment Program (NREP) and the *Jawahar Rozgaar Yojana* (JRY), these employment-generating schemes have been continuously expanded. In the five-year period 1992–1997, upward of four billion rupees were allocated for various rural employment schemes in Rajasthan, and 104 million person-days of employment were generated, approximately *ten days* of wage employment for every adult who lives in the rural areas.[32]

As these programs have been sustained and expanded continuously for more than twenty years now, they have come to form a part of normal life for the ordinary villager. Nearly half of all villagers — 45 percent in Rajasthan and 46 percent in Madhya Pradesh — depend on such employment for at least one month every year merely in order to make ends meet.

The other major program introduced by the Janata government was *Antyodaya* (literally "rise of the last," and implying development for the poorest). This scheme, the forerunner of the Integrated Rural Development Program (IRDP), aimed to identify the poorest households in each village and to assist them with grants and subsidized loans for purchasing "productive assets," such as cattle, sewing machines, or carpentry kits, with the help of which these households could raise their incomes. Training was provided under a parallel program. In fiscal year 1996–97, just before IRDP was being replaced by a successor scheme, it was targeted to provide benefits to more than 50,000 poor families in the state of Rajasthan. Between 1980 and 1995, it has been estimated, nearly a million rural households in Rajasthan — almost a sixth of all rural households — were provided with some form of IRDP assistance (Bhargava 1997).

The budget for rural development has not only been expanded many times, it has also been fragmented into larger numbers of tiny parcels. As villagers have become more assertive in demanding community development and employment-generating schemes for their village, ruling party politicians have stretched the state budget thin in order to reach out to the largest number of village communities. Forest department officials who used earlier to guard large tracts of state-owned forests are now spending the bulk of their time implementing social forestry schemes on relatively tiny tracts of village forests.[33] Irrigation Department officials spend comparatively little time planning and building large dams or canal projects. Most of their energy goes into garnering resources from the NREP and JRY programs for implementing isolated minor irrigation projects in individual villages.[34]

The span of supervision has increased vastly among government officials charged with implementing these projects. And they have turned increasingly to villagers who can informally supervise site implementation on their behalf.

Caste and status hardly matter while selecting villagers for these tasks, but education matters greatly. The village supervisor must first and foremost be able to comprehend and apply complex procedures on behalf of the government official. One government official recounts his experiences in this regard:

I have been in this [Soil Conservation] Department for 21 years. First there were large works. Four or five engineers used to work on the same site. Now there are many more sites. Small works have been opened in many villages. Three Junior Engineers work under me, and my Unit has work sites in 24 villages, located many kilometers away from each other. It is not easy to get around. I cannot visit any site more than once every month or two months. My Junior Engineers cannot go more than once a week. In between, we have selected local persons to supervise the work. . . . without their help we cannot achieve our targets. . . . We soon find out when we go to any village who are the persons who can work on our behalf. Everyone knows

who has supervised [labor-generating] works in the past. . . . We had
such "mates" earlier also in our large sites, but they worked under our
direct supervision. Now we must rely on these persons much more.
They measure and record the work, they take the attendance of laborers, they handle payment.[35]

The pool of educated and unemployed youth provides a near-ideal set of
intermediaries upon whom government officials can rely in the village. They
are educated, so they can be relied upon to maintain records and accounts.
They are unemployed, so they can work long hours, supervising construction
on public works. They will continue to live within the village, so they cannot
hope to get away easily if they conspire with officials to cheat, exploit, or
under-pay villagers. And they establish their status and leadership in the
village by providing regular employment opportunities to laborers (up to 45
percent of all villagers), so they are keen to keep faith with government
officials who control this work and who appoint the village supervisor.

Logar Lal Dangi, a new leader of Nauwa village, tells of the role that
such leaders play vis-à-vis government officials.

I was eight years old, and my mother and father were dead. There was
very little land in the family, hardly two bighas [one-third of a hec-
tare]. My uncle sent me to school for eight years. Then I had to go to
work. I started by helping the village *sarpanch.* I supervised labor on
[government-sponsored] works implemented by the village *panchayat,*
and I looked after accounts for these construction projects. I could
read and write well, and there were few such persons at that time in
the village who were also willing to stand all day in the sun and work
with laborers. Then a new NGO project was started in the area for
farm forestry. They looked for a person in the village who knew some
official procedures, who could work hard, and who was trusted by
laboring villagers.

Trust is important. Many times labor is not paid for weeks after the
work is done, so they come to work only on the say-so of someone in
the village whom they trust and who can compel these agencies to
make payments on time. The NGO supervisor saw me laboring day
after day in the hot sun. He came to me and he asked me to lead the
new project in the village. . . . After that there have been other projects.
We have a *team* now. . . . Tekaram among the Bhils, Sangram Singh

among Rebaris, and others; we all work together. I convince the villagers that the project is sound and that they will be paid fairly, even
if the payment is a little delayed. On my guarantee, the village shop-
keeper gives *atta* [flour] and other goods to them against future wages.
To government officials and NGO supervisors, I promise a loyal and
hardworking labor force. We protect these officials against complaints
and inquiries — but they must pay the laborers fully and on time.[36]

Not only agencies undertaking construction works, but also other state
and market agencies look out for such intermediaries. Bankers need local
persons who can fill out loan application forms on behalf of other villagers
and who can help them recover the loaned amounts.

Since the early 1980s, we have large targets of loaning in each rural
branch. Only three to four full-time persons are available to a rural
branch to serve from 40 to 60 villages. We are severely overloaded.
Villagers need intermediaries to come to us. . . . In my experience [of
25 years], about 30 percent of applications are presented on behalf of
villagers by *gram sevaks* [local government officials] and about 70 percent by the young fellows who have come up in every village. They
[the young fellows] help us also at the time of recovery. They want us
to advance more loans in their village every year, so they help us in
the recovery process.[37]

As targets of work have expanded in the rural areas, and as officials who
serve in these areas must fulfill higher and higher individual quotas every
year, the demand for village intermediaries has been rising consistently. Construction agencies — critical for almost half of all villagers who depend on
them for supplementary incomes — need to rely on these intermediaries and
also government agencies concerned with many other subjects, including
law and order,[38] and family welfare.[39] Bankers must rely on these persons to
achieve their targets of work, along with insurance agents, lawyers and whole-
sale merchants of grain.[40]

For multiple tasks that involve interacting with state and market agencies,
many more villagers contact the new village leaders compared to any other
type of village notable. 1,172 villagers (53 percent) said they would seek the
assistance of new, young, and educated leaders if they had any business with
the police or the *Tahsil*; 1,431 said that these leaders helped them procure
employment in construction works carried out by different government de-

partments; 1,118 said that these leaders had helped them get a bank loan or a subsidy from some government program; and 1,253 (66 percent) said they consulted such leaders regularly whenever they needed to procure commercial seed or fertilizer. Many fewer villagers — less than 15 percent in any case — reported seeking the assistance of caste leaders or *Jajmans* (patrons) or *panchayat* officials for any of these purposes.

Known commonly among villagers as *naya neta* (new leader) or *naya karyakarta* (new social worker), the new set of younger and more educated village leaders consolidate their positions by building large cross-caste networks in the village. Few new leaders have as yet gone very far toward achieving this goal, and Logar Lal Dangi of Nauwa village is clearly furthest along among the new leaders that I met. But nearly all new leaders are concerned to have a widespread network for it increases the bargaining power they have vis-à-vis state bureaucrats and party politicians.

Government officials need large numbers of laborers in order to implement agency targets, and they are not usually concerned about the castes to which these villagers belong. Party politicians recognize and reward the new leaders, as we shall see in the next section, according to the numbers of voters they can influence. In either case, the new leaders have hardly any incentive to confine their activities to any specific caste or group of castes. It benefits them, instead, to build large cross-cutting coalitions in their village.

Competition among rival new leaders takes different forms among different villages,[41] but it is hardly ever organized on caste lines. In not one among the villages that I observed closely did new leaders ever try to build caste-based constituencies. Their raison d'être, their basis for survival as leaders, lies in being able to wean villagers away from the influence of the old caste-based leaders. By looking to caste as a possible source of influence for themselves, they know they would merely be playing into the hands of the old leadership.[42]

The cross-cutting village networks that new leaders attempt to mobilize are useful for achieving multiple individual and collective benefits. Roads are constructed or repaired, drinking water and electricity are supplied, dispensaries and nursing staff are allocated, schools constructed or upgraded, and teachers deployed or replaced depending on how well villagers can mobilize to get these facilities for their village. Employment generation schemes are awarded by the state to a village, and so are the benefits of other development and anti-poverty programs.[43]

Villagers who can mobilize effectively are able to gain a larger share of these benefits for their village community. Others must remain content with the dregs. Social capital becomes important for this reckoning, and also the capacity of agents who enable villagers to derive larger benefits from this stock.

Some new leaders use their superior education and information and their better access to the machinery of the state for extracting rents from their fellow villagers. However, this is hardly the norm for all new leaders. Usually, there is more than one new leader in a village, and monopolistic rents are competed down where they arise. Villagers are free to select which among these new leaders they will use for any particular service, and they are wont to prefer persons who abide by local norms of decent behavior, including rendering neighborly assistance at times of need without profiteering from others' misfortunes. Since new leaders are unlikely to have equal influence outside their native village — where they are not known and may not be trusted — their activities are most often confined within the village of their birth.[44] Local knowledge and social sanction are often effective to deter aspiring leaders from crossing the bounds of decent behavior.

Many new leaders, and especially those who command some sizeable political influence among villagers, are moved in addition by a social and political purpose. They acquire status and respect in their village by working seemingly selflessly on behalf of their neighbors — and status and respect are important motivations for people who hail mostly from quite humble origins. The hope of acquiring high political position in future also acts as an incentive. Babulal Bor, a *naya neta* of Kundai village, Udaipur district, recalled:

> I have been working for the villagers for about 10 years now. It is hard work. People come in the middle of the night, and I cannot refuse. I take them to the hospital on my motorcycle. I am available to them night and day. I have no time for my family. . . . But it has become my life now. If a day goes by when no one comes to my door, I cannot sit peacefully. I feel unwanted. . . . We get by all right. I have a small salary from the work that I do for the Cooperative Department. I will never be rich . . . but someday I might be MLA [Member of the State Legislative Assembly]. I came close to getting a ticket [party nomination] the last time [elections were held].[45]

Villagers who think they have paid a lot of money to new leaders feel no obligation to pay in votes. Leaders who wish to impress officials and politicians and who can assemble a large support group do so by trading favors and not by extracting rents from villagers in need. By helping their fellow villagers — regardless of caste or other considerations — they acquire a fund of obligations, which can be translated at election time into votes. Party organizers are aware of this newfound influence, and they try hard to attract these new leaders within their fold and away from the competing party.

Intensified Party Competition

Lacking any organizational bases of their own, especially at the grassroots level, party politicians are keen to strike deals with local leaders who can help to collect large numbers of villagers for electoral purposes. Where caste- and patronage-based leaders had served these purposes before (Weiner 1989, Manor 1990), party politicians are increasingly tapping into the multi-caste village networks that have come up and gained strength within the last two decades.

Knowledgeable observers of village politics date this trend to 1977, a year that in many ways marks a watershed in the politics of Rajasthan and the country.

> Politics was a one-sided game [before 1977]. People would put their stamp on [cast their vote for] whoever got the Congress Party nomination. In 1977, the Janata Party won . . . since then, *jagriti* [awareness of issues] has come to the village. Before 1977, people voted on *vishwas* [faith alone]. After that, work and performance have become the primary considerations. . . . Before 1977, when we [Congress Party workers] went into any village we thought it enough to speak to the *Mukhiyas, Patels* and *Lambardars* [village headmen, caste leaders, and feudal strongmen], and these persons would tell all other villagers to vote in a certain way. Now every villager has to be contacted individually. People get upset if we contact only the old leaders. They say, "Why did he only meet *Ba-saab* [a term of respect for an old man] and not me? Have I not got a vote to give?"

> People's attitudes have changed since 1977. Individuals have realized that their votes *can* make a difference to the results. We [parties] have made them feel this way. . . . People's concern for development has also increased enormously; *vishwas* has no worth any more. Even the smallest village wants electricity, a road, a school, a health center — these basic minimum requirements are wanted by all villagers. Leaders

are judged by what they can achieve. . . . The MLA [Member of the (state) Legislative Assembly] and MP cannot look after every village personally, so they all rely upon local workers. We can no longer rely on the *Mukhiyas* and *Patels* as we did in the past. We look for persons in the village who understand how government offices work and who can get villagers' works done in these offices. . . . Youth have come up in large numbers in politics since 1977. Old leaders who were not able to get villagers' work done are now in the corner [they have been sidelined]. Because no party has any fixed organization in the village, we all have to rely upon these young village workers.[46]

Table 3.3 gives parties' strength in the Rajasthan State Assembly. For 20 years starting in 1952, the Congress Party regularly captured half or more of all seats in the Rajasthan State Assembly, thereby succeeding in forming the government of this state. The fortunes of all the other parties fluctuated in

TABLE 3.3 Party Strength in Rajasthan State Assembly (Number of Members)

	1952	1957	1962	1967	1972	1977	1980	1985	1990	1993	1998
Congress*	82	119	89	103	146	41	133	113	50	76	153
BJP**	8	7	15	19	8	—	32	38	84	95	33
Janata Party	—	—	—	13	—	150	8	10	—	—	—
Janata Dal/ Lok Dal	—	—	—	—	—	—	7	27	54	6	3
Ram Rajya Praishad	24	17	3	—	—	—	—	—	—	—	—
Swatantra Party	—	—	37	35	11	—	—	—	—	—	—
Communist Party	1	—	5	—	4	2	2	1	1	1	1
PSP/ Pragitishil	1	26	7	1	—	—	—	—	—	—	—
Independents	34	—	20	4	11	6	12	9	9	21	7
Other Parties	10	7	—	9	4	5	6	2	2	1	3
TOTAL SEATS	160	176	176	184	184	200	200	200	200	200	200

* From 1952 to 1972 the Congress Party was known simply as 'Congress.' In 1971, the party split and the dominant faction was renamed the 'Indian Congress.' Between 1980 and 1990, the dominant faction was known as the Congress (I). From 1992 on, its name has been the Indian National Congress.

** The BJP (Bhartiya Janata Party) was remade in 1980 from constituents of the earlier Jan Sangh that merged in 1977 with the Janata Party. Electoral results before 1977 reported against the BJP relate in fact to the Jan Sangh.

this period, but none of these parties was ever able — either singly or in combination with all other non-Congress parties — to form a government.

The election in 1977 brought about the first change in the administration of the state. The Janata Party came into power, displacing the Congress, and a new dynamic of alternation was set in place. People felt that a viable alternative did exist in terms of who ruled at the state capital, and parties intensified their efforts to gain the reins of power. Knowing that they needed to reach out to all possible networks since competition was now so intense, party politicians engaged in new forms of political exchange with emergent types of village networks.[47] Particularly since ideological and programmatic differences are relatively minor among the major parties,[48] each party tries to get its votes by striking a better deal with influential people in villages.

"We look for persons of influence in each village where we go," claimed Mangilal Joshi, President of the BJP for Udaipur district. "Those persons are gaining most influence in villages who are able to get villagers' day-to-day work done in government offices. Persons who take a sick villager to the district hospital and who can get doctors to attend properly are remembered by the patient's family for long afterward. Those who can do *jugaad* [liaise effectively] with the police, with the Tahsil [land records office], with banks — these are the persons who matter in the village today. They can get the most number of votes, especially if they are personally honest and not out to make money from these activities."[49]

Sheshmal Pagariya, President of the Congress Party, the other major party in this district, reflects a similar view. "The criterion for voting was earlier *jati* (caste), now it is *vikaas* (development). Development work done in a village has the most effect on voting. People ask us: 'What have you done for us? How many new works can you open? How much labor will be employed?' We cannot watch over development in every village, so we support and rely upon the local worker. We catch hold of these worker-type persons in every village, and we know that the other party will also do the same, so we try to get to them first at election time."[50]

The view of politics expressed by these party leaders is reflected in the judgments expressed by individual villagers. 352 villagers (15.7 percent) felt that candidates to the state Legislative Assembly or Parliament would do well to contact caste leaders for mobilizing votes in their village. A much larger number (1,018, or 54 percent) felt that candidates could gain the most votes by contacting the *naya netas* (the new development-based village leaders).

The majority of villagers want economic development benefits over any other kind. As we saw in chapter 1, more than 90 percent of villagers consider roads, schools, health clinics, and employment generating works to be the principal needs of their communities. And most are willing to give up traditional practices if these come in the way of achieving these ends.

Caste continues to be a primary form of social identity in these Rajasthan and Madhya Pradesh villages. People in these villages live in caste-denominated neighborhoods, and the clothes that they wear reveal the caste identity of the wearer. In terms of economic and political mobilization, however, caste has been overtaken in most of these villages by other forms of local alliances. Caste and political organization are not closely aligned in these villages.[51] Whether these trends might extend as well to other parts of India and what impacts they might have on the future of Indian democracy are discussed below in chapters 7 and 8.

In these Rajasthan and Madhya Pradesh villages, however, cross-caste political actions intended to obtain benefits for the entire village, and led by the new political entrepreneurs, are more productive and more popular among villagers, by and large. Villages where residents are more united and where the *naya netas* are more effective are able to get larger development benefits in return for political support.

The expansion of education in these villages has resulted in enhancing the supply of potential leaders. Rapidly increasing state expenditures have generated a demand for new kinds of leadership. And increasing two-party competition has helped consolidate the position of emerging new leaders.

Far from resisting the newly powerful mode of political exchange in which villagers barter their votes for collective development benefits, leaders of major political parties are actively embracing it. Starting from fiscal year 1993–94, Members of Parliament have been allotted discretionary amounts that they can use to finance community asset creation and employment-generating activities in villages within their constituencies.[52]

Amounts allocated to MPs for these discretionary village grants have risen steadily. In fiscal year 1998–99, a sum of Rs. 10 million was allocated for this purpose to every MP. By 1999–2000, the allocation had been *doubled*, and each MP was provided with Rs. 20 million under the Members of Parliament Local Area Development Scheme. There are approximately a thousand villages in each MP's constituency, so the incumbent can allocate nearly Rs. 100,000 to each one of them during his or her five years' tenure. Not all villages are equally targets of MPs' vote-gaining strategies, however, and villages that can organize better for collective action have gained several times this average amount. Nauwa's residents received more than five times the average amount from Shanti Lal Chaplot after they had united to help elevate him from Member of the State Assembly to member of the national parliament.

Not to be left behind, Members of the state Legislative Assembly (MLAs) have also voted similar budgetary subventions for themselves. These amounts have also been raised every year, reflecting the rising competition to attract votes on a full-village basis. In fiscal year 1998–99, each MLA in Rajasthan had recourse to Rs.500,000 which he or she could use to fund development works in villages. For 1999–2000, each MLA has been allocated Rs.2.5 million under a newly expanded MLA's Local Area Development Scheme, an increase of *five times* over the previous fiscal year.[53]

Political parties have responded in these ways to the emergence of a new basis for leadership in villages. In the process, the new leadership has been fortified. Collective action organized with the village as unit has acquired a strong basis over the past twenty years, and variations in social capital at the village level become important to investigate for explaining economic, political and social outcomes. Social capital is not so potent, and its results do not flow so copiously, when leaders, the agents, and the connectors, are less effective. But agents' capacity to strike deals is greater when there is village-wide backing for their efforts. Social capital matters in this reckoning and so do agent's intelligence, shrewdness, and perseverance. This account is illustrated in the chapters that follow.

4 Measuring Social Capital

Before testing the three hypotheses about social capital that were presented in chapter 2, a final set of tasks remains. Variables corresponding to each of these hypotheses must be defined, and measures must be developed to scale these variables in north Indian villages. While variables representing the structuralist hypothesis (Hypothesis 2) are relatively easy to define and measure, special attention must be paid to social capital and agency strength that correspond, respectively, to Hypotheses 1 and 3.

I will briefly review empirical measures of social capital that are available in the literature. I will then develop a measure to compare social capital rankings among villages in the database, and I will provide measures for other structural and agency variables.

Measures of Social Capital

Putnam (1995: 67) defines social capital as "features of social organization such as networks, norms and social trust that facilitate coordination and cooperation for mutual benefit." He ranks social capital in Italian regions according to a measure of density of membership in formal organizations.

Two facts must be noted about this measure. First, it is a proxy measure of social capital: it is not directly concerned with norms or with trust but it looks, instead, at certain manifestations that accompany social capital in this setting. It is not obvious that social capital will be manifest in other cultures in a similar fashion. In particular, formal organizations are notoriously thinly spread within rural areas in the Third World, as we observed in chapter 1.

Even though the concept of social capital travels well outside an Italian setting, its empirical referents will vary as different cultures manifest social capital differently. Institutions do not have "an ontological status apart from the human activity that produces them" (Berger and Luckmann 1966:57). Varying forms of human activity develop to deal with different needs and compulsions of life in different ecological and cultural settings. Networks, roles, rules, procedures, precedents, norms, values, attitudes, and beliefs are different among people who have different patterns of life. Measures of social capital that are relevant for one set of cultures might be quite irrelevant for others.

Different measures of social capital have consequently been developed as analysts have scaled social capital in different cultural settings. Table 4.1 provides details on 13 empirical studies where social capital has been measured as an independent variable.[1]

The connotation of social capital, i.e., its sense and meaning, and even more so its denotation or empirical referents, have changed considerably with usage.[2] In their seminal work on the Italian regions, Putnam et al. present a measure of social capital — the Civic Community Index — that they construct entirely out of factors related to networks. Norms are not separately considered for this measure of social capital, since it is believed that "an effective norm of generalized reciprocity is likely to be associated with dense networks of social exchange" (1993: 172).[3] Norms form part of the definition of social capital, but they have no part within Putnam's measure of this concept. "Social norms are . . . a product of the institutional conditions," other analysts claim in support of this step, "specific institutions give rise to a particular collection of social norms" (Rothstein 1998: 139). So norms can be dropped and only networks retained while measuring social capital.

However, there is no unanimity about what sorts of networks should be observed and measured. The concept of appropriate networks has changed considerably as the concept of social capital became operational in different settings. Vertically or hierarchically organized relationships were thought to inhibit social capital formation in northern Italy.[4] Only organizations that are not hierarchical, where relationships among members are organized horizontally, were aggregated within this density measure.

A different type of network was identified, however, when the concept was scaled in the United States. Horizontal networks are not all equally well

TABLE 4.1 Alternative Measures of Social Capital

Study and Location	Definition of Social Capital	Measurement Concept	Data Sources	Dependent Variable	Conclusions	Implication
(A) Individual or Household Level						
1. Schneider et al. (1997) *United States*		**Networks-based.** Membership of PTA, engagement in volunteer activities, conversations with other parents.	Individual interviews (n = 1,270)	Social Capital	Giving parents a choice of school for their children is associated with increasing their social capital.	Government policies influence the level of social capital. *Structure influences social capital,* and not vice versa as Putnam et al. (1993) suggest.
2. Narayan and Pritchett (1997) *Tanzania*	Quantity and quality of associational life and the related social norms	**Networks-based.** Multiplicative Index (number of memberships; but also heterogeneity and satisfaction level.)	Household survey (n = 1,370)	Household income	Strong association exists between social capital and household income.	More *heterogeneous groups* are associated with higher social capital.

TABLE 4.1 Alternative Measures of Social Capital (*continued*)

Study and Location	Definition of Social Capital	Measurement Concept	Data Sources	Dependent Variable	Conclusions	Implication
3. Brehm and Rahn (1997) *United States*	Webs of cooperative relations between citizens that facilitate resolution of collective action problems	**Norms-based.** Interpersonal Trust (Combine responses to three questions using factor analysis)	General Social Survey (1972–1994)	Confidence in political institutions	Higher interpersonal trust leads to greater civic engagement and more confidence in political institutions	More trust leads to higher civic engagement. *Norms influence networks* — an opposite conclusion to that presented by Putnam et al. (1993).
4. Grootaert (1998) *Indonesia*	Institutions, relationships, attitudes and values that govern interaction among people and contribute to economic and social development.	**Networks-based.** Multiplicative Index (number of memberships; as well as heterogeneity and range of activities.)	Household survey (n = 1,200), community leaders, official sources.	Per capita household expenditure.	Household social capital influences household welfare.	More *heterogeneous groups* are associated with higher social capital.

TABLE 4.1 Alternative Measures of Social Capital (*continued*)

Study and Location	Definition of Social Capital	Measurement Concept	Data Sources	Dependent Variable	Conclusions	Implication
5. Rose (1999) *Russia*	Stock of formal or informal social networks that individuals use to produce or allocate goods and services.	**Modified Networks-based.** No single measure. Assessed as membership in specific networks that help with sector-specific needs.	Individual survey (n = 1,904)	Various (related to specific sectors).	Different social networks enhance individuals' efficacy with respect to particular sectors.	*Specific networks* assist solidarity and trust within particular social domains.
		(B) Neighborhood or Community Level				
6. Portney and Berry (1997) *United States*		**Networks-based.** Participation in different social organizations	Individual surveys in five cities (n = 1,100)	Sense of community with others in the neighborhood	Compared to other organization types, participation in neighborhood groups is more strongly associated with a sense of community.	Not all types of networks support community feeling. *Homogeneous* networks are more supportive than heterogeneous ones.

TABLE 4.1 Alternative Measures of Social Capital (*continued*)

Study and Location	Definition of Social Capital	Measurement Concept	Data Sources	Dependent Variable	Conclusions	Implication
7. Sampson et al. (1997) *United States*	"Collective Efficacy": Mutual trust and willingness to intervene for the common good.	**Networks plus Norms.** Combination, via factor analysis, of responses to ten survey questions.	Individual surveys in 343 Chicago neighborhoods (n = 8,782)	Level of violence in the neighborhood	Violence is negatively related to collective efficacy.	More *homogeneous* neighborhoods have higher levels of collective efficacy.
8. Krishna and Uphoff (1999) *India*	Cognitive aspects of social relations that predispose individuals toward mutually beneficial collective action, and structural aspects that facilitate such action.	**Networks plus Norms.** Six survey questions combined using factor analysis.	Household surveys (n = 2,400), focus groups, official sources.	Village development performance	Social capital is positively related with development performance	*Informal groups* are salient for social capital in this context more than formal ones.
			(C) Regional Level			
9. Putnam et al. (1993) *Italy*	Features of social organization, such as networks, norms, and social trust that facilitate coordination and cooperation for mutual benefit	**Networks-based.** Four measures combined using factor analysis (association density, newspaper readership, referenda turnout, and preference voting).	Individual surveys, interviews of councillors and leaders, case studies, official sources.	Performance of regional governments on multiple indicators.	Social capital is strongly and consistently associated with regional governments' performance in multiple social domains.	*Horizontal groups* are associated with higher social capital in comparison with those that are more hierarchical in their organization.

TABLE 4.1 Alternative Measures of Social Capital (*continued*)

Study and Location	Definition of Social Capital	Measurement Concept	Data Sources	Dependent Variable	Conclusions	Implication
10. Morris (1998) *India*		**Networks-based.** Four separate measures, including, women in associations, newspaper readership, and electoral turnout.	Official data, published sources.	Poverty	States of India that are well endowed with social capital have been more successful in reducing poverty.	*State-created* and government-managed groups are included within this measure of social capital.
(D) National Level						
11. Hall (1997) *Britain*	Networks of sociability, both formal and informal, and norms of social trust associated with such networks.	**Networks and Norms Separately.** Separate indicators for associational membership, voluntary and charitable work, informal sociability, and generalized trust.	Diverse	Social capital and political engagement are alternatively specified as the DV	High levels of social capital associate with high levels of political engagement	*State policies influence social capital formation.*

TABLE 4.1 Alternative Measures of Social Capital (*continued*)

Study and Location	Definition of Social Capital	Measurement Concept	Data Sources	Dependent Variable	Conclusions	Implication
12. Knack and Keefer (1997) *Cross-National*	Trust within groups.	**Norms-based.** Trust (single question)	World Values Surveys	Rate of economic growth	Trust is positively related to growth, but density of associations is not related to either growth or trust.	*Social trust and network density are not related to each other. Creating more horizontal networks may actually damage social capital.*
13. Stolle and Rochon (1998) *Germany, Sweden and United States*	Norms and networks that link citizens to one another and that enable them to pursue their common objectives more efficiently.	**Networks and Norms Separately.** 12 indicators grouped into four separate sets: political efficacy, generalized trust, trust in government, and optimism.	Surveys among members of 102 associations in these three countries	Social Capital is the DV	Greater membership diversity in an association is associated with higher level of social capital.	*Different types of networks facilitate building social capital in different cultural contexts.*

regarded for measuring social capital in this new context. Compared to secondary associations, whose members have frequent face-to-face contact, tertiary and mailing-list organizations are considered less likely to manifest trust and mutual cooperation among Americans (Putnam 1995, 1996).

Neither all horizontal associations (valid in Italy) nor even the subset that have face-to-face relationships (valid in the U.S.) are found legitimate for assessing social capital in Germany and Sweden (Stolle and Rochon 1998). Instead, associations that are more diverse, "whose members bridge major social categories are . . . more effective [for] . . . fostering generalized trust and community reciprocity" in these contexts. "Homogeneous associations are less likely to inculcate high levels of generalized trust and reciprocity among their members," and only heterogeneous networks manifest social capital in these countries (Stolle and Rochon:1998: 47, 62). Not too far away yet from its Italian home, the measure of social capital has already been challenged and amended.

Heterogeneity and density are retained for measuring social capital in Tanzania (Narayan and Pritchett 1997) and in Indonesia (Grootaert 1998) but another criteria is added: span of activity. Not all heterogeneous networks are equally valued here; networks that encompass a wider range of activities represent greater social capital. In each of these studies, a household-level index of social capital — computed by multiplying together numbers of associational memberships with internal heterogeneity of associations and span of activities — is found to be positively and consistently related with household economic welfare.

Though it is thought good for social capital in Sweden, Germany, Tanzania and Indonesia, heterogeneity is regarded as the very antithesis of this concept when applied by other observers to the United States. Studying neighborhoods in five American cities, Portney and Berry (1997) find that heterogeneous localities have less effective neighborhood associations. Sampson et al. (1997) find more effective neighborhood associations to be less highly stratified in terms of income, length of residence, and other criteria. Diversity and heterogeneity are counterproductive in these contexts. Homogeneous associations reflect higher social capital, or so these authors believe.

Homogeneity is well regarded in some contexts, while heterogeneity is thought to represent more social capital in others. The context provides the referents that are used to measure social capital. "Groups with high diversity levels in homogenous cultures [such as Sweden's or Germany's] are much more trust producing. . . . These relations look different in countries with more diverse populations. . . . In the United States [with a more heteroge- neous culture], homogeneous groups generate more generalized trust, and not the ones that accommodate people from diverse backgrounds" (Stolle 1998: 28–29). Horizontal networks reflect social capital in some contexts, but they are valueless in others. In the 29 countries they studied, Knack and Keefer found that "horizontal networks . . . [to be] unrelated to trust and civic norms" (1997:1284).[5]

Numerous other disagreements have surfaced regarding what types of networks should be considered and in which particular contexts.

- *Formal versus Informal Groups:* Should one include only formally organized groups in the measure, as Putnam does, or should in- formal groups also be considered, especially since "the socializa- tion role of creating 'habits of the heart' is more likely to be played . . . by informal groups" (Newton 1997:582)?
- *Small versus Large Groups:* Should only small face-to-face groups be considered (Olson 1965; Putnam 1995), or should one look also at large multiregional and multinational organizations? As group size increases, it is contended, it becomes more likely that some subset of members will combine and produce benefits for all, hence social capital is likely to be manifest more often (Minkoff 1997; Oliver 1984; Oliver and Marwell 1988).
- *Strong versus Weak Ties:* Are strong associational ties better, or do weak ones facilitate collective action more effectively (Granovetter 1973)?

No final answers are available to any of these questions. The problem lies, I believe, in conflating norms with network types and in considering only networks for the purpose of measuring social capital. Norms that are not associated with identifiable network types get disregarded in these cal- culations; while networks that are not linked with any particularly cooper- ative norms get lumped within the proxy measure.

Group solidarity is difficult to verify with reference to norms alone, ac- cording to Hechter (1987).[6] Equally, the shape of any network — horizontal or vertical, heterogeneous or homogeneous, formal or informal — does not by itself indicate much about the nature of human relationships within that network.[7] Comparing two similarly structured choir groups in one city, Eastis

(1998) finds that "mere membership in one or another category of voluntary association [is] too crude a measure to capture empirically the complex experience of membership. Members of both choir groups could report very extensive participation yet still come away from the experience with a rather different mix of human, cultural, or social capital. Such variation owes much to the characteristics of the groups and the structure of relations between their members — not to participation per se nor to the types of groups per se."[8]

"Trust," conclude Jackman and Miller (1998: 62) after reviewing a range of empirical evidence, "is clearly not isomorphic with group membership." What sorts of norms are associated with which type of network cannot be assumed a priori; it must be investigated independently for each separate context.[9]

If norms matter in addition to networks, as is strongly implied in the accounts reviewed above; if norms, in turn, are dependent on context; and if context varies by culture and country; then can any measure of social capital be found that is universally valid across all countries and cultural contexts? Perhaps not, I should submit. Instead of devising global measures of social capital that span entire countries and continents, one may learn more from comparisons among social units that are culturally alike and where social capital is similarly manifest. Such a comparison is presented in this book for villages that share a common cultural space in rural north India.

Developing a Locally Relevant Measure

The village is the appropriate unit to investigate and measure social capital in rural India, as we saw in chapter 3. Indicators need to be found among features of village life of factors that promote cooperation for mutual benefit.

Density of formal organizations is a particularly inappropriate indicator. Formal organizations in large areas of Asia and Africa are mostly state-controlled enterprises, created to achieve state and regime objectives.[10] Nearly every formal organization established in Rajasthan and Madhya Pradesh villages is linked to a state agency and is executor of its program. Joint Forest Committees are looked after by the Forest Ministry. The Women's Development Ministry is responsible for Mahila Mandals (women's groups). Sports and Education Ministry officials set up new Yuva Mandals (youth groups) every year. Governments and donor agencies prescribe targets. Local officials are given these targets to implement. Villagers are press-ganged to join in newly formed organizations. There are benefits to be availed. People sign up to get the benefits; the target is nominally achieved; then everyone goes home.[11]

Villagers in Rajasthan have set up hardly any formal organizations voluntarily. On average, there is just one formal organization in every two villages, while 50 percent of villages have no formal organizations at all operating in their midst (Krishna and Uphoff 1999). Informal networks exist in large numbers, however, and many villagers participate in these networks regularly. Because the process of registration is costly and time-consuming, however, villagers have little incentive to have their informal networks registered as formal associations.

Measures that rely upon density of formal organizations reflect the state's organizing zeal in these contexts. To scale social capital, however, one will need to look among informal networks. The structural dimension of social capital — relating to networks, roles, rules, precedents — must be considered and also the cognitive dimension — relating to norms, values, attitudes, and beliefs. While cognitive elements *predispose* people toward mutually beneficial collective action; structural elements of social capital *facilitate* such action (Uphoff 2000; Krishna 2000).

Both structural and the cognitive dimensions matter, and they must be combined to represent the aggregate potential for mutually beneficial collective action that exists within any community. To understand the separate importance of these structural and cognitive elements, consider the following example. Someone's house or barn burns down at night and people of the neighborhood come together the next day to help the afflicted family rebuild the structure. This kind of collective action is possible to find not just in villages in north India but also among diverse social groups in all parts of the world. What is interesting to examine, however, are the factors that lead people to behave in this way.

Two constructions are possible. In one scenario, there is a well-recognized group of community leaders within the neighborhood who, when they learn of the unfortunate event, direct villagers to collect at the site, bringing along whatever tools and implements and building material they might possess. In the other scenario there is a community in which nobody has the role of organizer. Motivated, instead, by norms of what is appropriate behavior — i.e., it is only right and proper that one should help out any one of their community who is faced with a similar situation — people collect spontaneously and assist with the rebuilding.[12]

In both instances, the same cooperative outcome resulted. In the first case, it was the structural dimensions of social capital — roles, rules, networks — that facilitated cooperation and coordinated action. In the second case, collective action was based on norms and beliefs, i.e., it has a cognitive and not a structural basis.

Considering only networks within the measure of social capital results in neglecting mutually beneficial collective action that has such a cognitive basis. Considering only norms similarly underestimates social capital by ignoring its structural dimensions. Both norms and networks must be assessed, and the measure of social capital must represent the aggregate potential for mutually beneficial collective action.

A locally relevant scale relying upon both structural and cognitive indicators was devised by Krishna and Uphoff (1999) for a previous investigation conducted in Rajasthan. Six survey questions considering cognitive and structural aspects of social capital were included within a questionnaire administered to 2,400 persons. Responses to these six questions were very highly correlated with one another, and factor analysis supported the proposition that these were manifestations of a single underlying factor. These six constituent items were aggregated within an index of social capital.[13]

To assess social capital in this agrarian context, quite different from northern Italy, we started by considering the types of activities with which people of this area are commonly engaged. Not all activities observed in this area are valid for investigating dimensions of cooperation and coordination, both structural and cognitive. Social capital exists "in the *relations* among persons" (Coleman 1988: S100–101), and only those activities are valid for comparing social capital that inhabitants of this area regard as appropriate to carry out collectively rather than individually.

The extent of social capital in any community must be verified in relation to activities that are usually carried out collectively for mutual benefit. What these activities are, however, varies from one context to another. Crop diseases are usually dealt with collectively in Rajasthan, but not crop harvesting. House building is an individual's enterprise in Rajasthan and a collective one in Somaliland (Farah 1992). Investigators comparing social capital among Somali communities should look among networks that build houses. In Rajasthan, we looked at social behavior dealing with crop disease. We looked also at other tasks and at norms concerning other activities that are typically collectively undertaken here.

Even though residents of all villages share similar conceptions about what are properly individual and appropriately collective activities, we found that past practice and future expectations vary considerably from village to village. Some villagers have acted collectively more often in the past. In the future too, residents in these villages expect that their fellows and they will cooperate a great deal. Other villagers have poorer records and lower expectations.

Revisions were made to the scale and to its component questions based on reviewers' comments, and a modified version was used for the present investigation. Once again, structural and cognitive features were separately considered for the revised six-item index. Alternative responses were provided to each survey question after discussing each of these questions with two focus groups of villagers constituted for this purpose. The revised questionnaire was pre-tested in four villages, and then applied after a final set of modifications in 69 villages studied for this book.

Individual responses for each of the six questionnaire items reported below were aggregated for all individuals surveyed in each village. The resulting village averages have been used for constructing a village-level Index of Social Capital.

Structural Features

1. *Membership in Labor-Sharing Groups.* Are you a member of a labor group in the village, i.e., do you work often with the same group, sharing the work that is done either on your own fields, on some public work, or for some private employer? Responses were coded as 0 for "no" and 1 for "yes."

These responses were aggregated for all individuals interviewed in each surveyed village, thereby measuring the proportion of villagers who do participate in such networks. Among all informal networks considered here — including irrigator associations, youth and sports clubs, women's groups, *bhajan mandalis* (choir societies), and religious associations — labor groups were the most important, attracting the largest range of participants. 1,522 of the total number of 1,898 respondents interviewed in Rajasthan (more than 80 percent) gave a "yes" response to this question, though this proportion varied from a high of 98.5 percent (in village Sadariya) to a low of 73 percent (village Sinhara).

2. *Dealing with Crop Disease.* If a crop disease were to affect the entire standing crop of this village, then who do you think would come forward

to deal with this situation? Responses ranged from "Every one would deal with the problem individually," scored 1, to "The entire village would act together," scored 5. The full range of responses is as follows:

- Every person would deal with the problem individually [1]
- Neighbors among themselves [2]
- Villagers by locality [3]
- Village leaders acting together [4]
- The entire village [5]

Individuals' responses were averaged for each surveyed village. The highest average response score came from village Balesariya (3.07), while the lowest was from village Sema (1.11). This item and the next relate to the cognitive maps that people have concerning the breadth of mutual support networks in their village.

3. *Dealing with Natural Disasters*: At times of severe calamity or distress, villagers often come together to assist each other. Suppose there was some calamity in this village requiring immediate help from government, e.g., a flood or fire, who in this village do you think would approach government for help? The range of responses was as follows:

- No one [1]
- Government employees posted in this village [2]
- Some political leaders of the village [3]
- A committee of villagers [4]
- The entire village collectively [5]

Averaged villager responses varied from a high of 4.64 (village Chawandiya) to a low of 2.58 (village Sodawas).

Cognitive Features

4. *Trust*: Suppose a friend of yours in this village faced the following alternatives: which one would he or she prefer?

- To own and farm 10 bighas of land entirely by themselves[14] (scored 1)

- To own and farm 25 bighas of land jointly with one other person (scored 2)

This item scales the factor of trust in terms of an empirical referent that is valid for these agrarian communities. The second alternative would give each person access to more land (12.5 bighas, instead of just 10 bighas represented by the first option), but they would have to work and share produce interdependently. The question was framed so that the respondent was not making an assessment of his or her own level of trust, but rather of how trusting other people in the village were in general. Average villager responses ranged from a high of 1.76 (village Chautra), showing a high level of mutual trust, to a low of 1.05, showing a virtual absence of inter-personal trust (village Chachiyawas).

5. *Public Spiritedness*: Is it possible to conceive of a village leader who puts aside his own welfare and that of his family to concern himself mainly with the welfare of village society? Responses ranged from "Such a thing is not possible," scored 1, to "It is sometimes possible," scored 2, to "Such a thing happens quite frequently in this village," scored 3. Averaged individual responses ranged from a high of 2.26 (village Balesariya, once again) to a low of 1.23 (village Kunda).

6. *Solidarity*: Some children of the village tend to stray from the correct path, for example, they are disrespectful to elders, they disobey their parents, are mischievous, etc. Who in this village feels it right to correct other people's children? Four alternatives were posed: "No one," scored 1; "Only close relatives" scored 2; "Relatives and neighbors," scored 3; and "Anyone from the village," scored 4. Averaged individual responses ranged from a high of 3.45 (village Khemaroo) to a low of 1.70 (with village Sema once again occupying the lowest spot).

These six items load highly on a single common factor.[15] The factor pattern is reported in table 4.2.

This common factor is highly correlated with each of these six individual items,[16] and these items are also closely correlated among themselves, as could be expected given the high factor loadings.[17] The single common

TABLE 4.2. Social Capital: Factor Pattern

Variables	Factor 1
Membership in labor-sharing groups	0.64131
Dealing with crop disease	0.68887
Dealing with natural disasters	0.74042
Trust (sharing land)	0.74162
Public Spiritedness	0.84012
Solidarity	0.84192

factor accounts for about 61 percent of the combined variance of the six individual items.

Village scores on the six separate items were aggregated to form the Social Capital Index.[18] This Social Capital Index is highly correlated with each of its six constituent items, as reported earlier. It is correlated also with other indicators of local norms and informal networks. All of these correlation coefficients are significant at the 0.01 level or better.[19]

- If some epidemic were to occur among cattle or humans in this village, what do you think the people of this village would do? (Will they act unitedly?) (correlation = 0.592)
- Suppose some person from this village had to go away for a while, along with their family. In whose charge would this person leave their fields? (Can only close relatives be trusted, or a larger group of villagers?) (correlation = 0.712)
- People here look out mainly for the welfare of their own families, and they are not much concerned with society's welfare. How strongly do you agree or disagree with this statement? (Strongly agree scored as 1, strongly disagree as 4; indicating the extent of reciprocity practiced in this village) (correlation = 0.645)
- Who is responsible for maintaining the cattle drinking ponds of this village? (Is no one responsible and the ponds are in disrepair, or do villagers collectively maintain these assets?) (correlation = 0.662)

Mean score for villages on the Social Capital Index is 38.8 points (out of a possible 100 points) and standard deviation is 23.6.[20] Eight villages have scores of 75 points or more, including three of the sixteen case-study villages: Balesariya, with 88 points, leads this list, and Sunderchha (82 points) and Nauwa (74 points) are next. Twelve villages have scores of 25 points or lower, including four of the sixteen case-study villages: Kundai (21 points), Sare (20 points), Ghodach (18 points), and Sema (13 points).

Balesariya's high stock of social capital manifests itself in many different ways. People trust each other a great deal here. No walls separate houses of this village, and doors are left open all day. Large numbers get together every Tuesday in Balesariya to sing *bhajans* (devotional songs). Every household takes its turn to fill the communal trough for animals to drink. Morning and evening, turns are taken by rotation. Water from an irrigation tank is also distributed by rotation. Households all pay a fee to receive water, and this money is used to finance repairs and watchmen's salaries.

Trust and collective goodwill are nowhere nearly as manifest in Kundai, Sare, and Ghodach, where social capital scores are low. People in Ghodach are suspicious of each other, and they are constantly scheming to put each other down. People in Kundai speak guardedly. They are afraid that something they might say will be misunderstood by a neighbor. There is an irrigation tank in Ghodach, but all households takes water any time they can and there is no organization. People in Sare, Kundai, and Ghodach celebrate festivals only among family and close relatives. In Balesariya and Nauwa, the whole village turns out for major community events. At times of emergency, villagers borrow money from other villagers in these high social capital villages, and they return these amounts as quickly as they can — without being charged any interest on the loan. In low social capital villages, such as Ghodach, Sare and Kundai, on the other hand, people can only turn to the *mahajan* (professional moneylender) at such times.

High social capital manifests itself in multiple acts of cooperation and mutual goodwill, and low social capital is associated with less cooperation and lower expectations. The question for analysis, however, is whether and to what extent their propensity for mutually beneficial collective action is valuable to villagers for achieving the objectives of economic development, communal harmony, and political participation. Is social capital helpful for achieving these objectives? Does it matter only in conjunction with appropriate agency? Or is social capital unimportant and merely a residue of structure? Agency and structural variables corresponding to the two competing hypotheses are presented in the next two sections.

Agency Variables

Six agency variables will be considered for analysis. These types of agency are common among villages in this region, and they are also regarded by some body of literature as being effective for one or more of the three objectives. Figure 4.1 lists these agencies and also the corresponding sources in the literature. The effectiveness, utility, and range of functions of each type of agency differ from village to village, and I look to these variations for developing scales that compare agency strength.

Apart from one type of agency, the Village Council, the effectiveness of none of the other agency types is related to the level of social capital in a village. Correlation coefficients between the Social Capital Index and measures of the effectiveness of the six different agency types are quite insignificant, as we shall see later in this chapter. Let us first, however, develop some scales for measuring the effectiveness of each different agency type.

For comparing agents' capacities among villages, I do not look just at whether any of these agency types exist within any given village, but I also assess how *effectively* each type performs in that village. Each scale presented below is used for comparing a particular type of agency across villages. Since they rely upon different items, however, scores on one scale cannot be compared with scores on another. Political party strength cannot be compared with, say, the strength of caste associations in any given village; their units of measurement are quite dissimilar. But the same agency can be compared across multiple villages. Villages can be compared to see which of them has stronger caste associations. Similarly, villages can also be in respect of the other five modes of agency — political parties, *panchayats* (local governments), new leaders, traditional Village Councils, and patron-client links. Are variations in the strength of any of these agency forms related significantly with economic development or with any of the other two dependent variables?

Strength of Political Parties: Party registration lists are not available for villages, probably because no party in Rajasthan or Madhya Pradesh has enrolled members for more than 20 years. "Strength of political parties" is measured by considering responses to three separate survey questions adapted from Rosenstone and Hansen (1993):

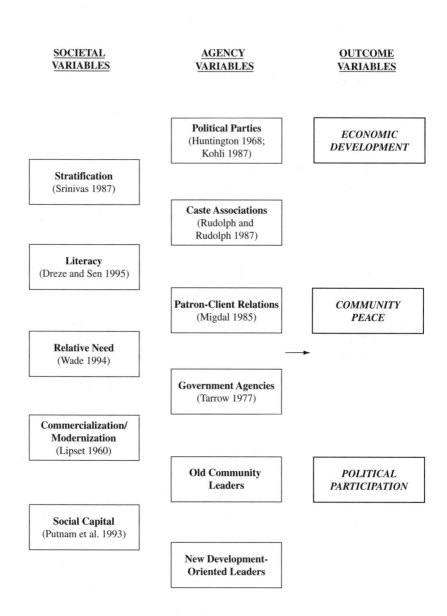

SOCIETAL VARIABLES	AGENCY VARIABLES	OUTCOME VARIABLES
	Political Parties (Huntington 1968; Kohli 1987)	*ECONOMIC DEVELOPMENT*
Stratification (Srinivas 1987)		
	Caste Associations (Rudolph and Rudolph 1987)	
Literacy (Dreze and Sen 1995)		
	Patron-Client Relations (Migdal 1985)	*COMMUNITY PEACE*
Relative Need (Wade 1994)		
	Government Agencies (Tarrow 1977)	
Commercialization/ Modernization (Lipset 1960)		
	Old Community Leaders	*POLITICAL PARTICIPATION*
Social Capital (Putnam et al. 1993)		
	New Development-Oriented Leaders	

FIGURE 4.1 What Combination of Societal and Agency Variables Has Relevance for the Three Outcomes Variables?

- Some people are members of a particular political party, whereas others belong to no party. Are you a member of any party or do you consider yourself close to no particular party? (Close to no political party was scored 1, while close to some political party was scored 2.)
- In the previous few elections have you always voted for the same party or have you voted for different parties at different times? (Voted for different parities in different elections was scored 1, while voted for the same party in each election was scored 2.)
- Within the political party that you presently prefer, how would you rank yourself—as a leader, as an important member whose opinions matter, as a member who has some importance but not too much, or as a person who does not express their opinion at all to party leaders? (These options were scored, respectively, from 4 to 1.)

The variable STR_PARTY was constructed by adding together average response scores for all respondents in a village. Notice that this variable does not relate to the strength of any particular political party. It is intended, instead, to take stock of allegiance, loyalty, and influence in respect of political parties in general. Low scores were received on this variable by villages where most respondents considered themselves neither close or loyal to any political party or influential within its ranks. Villages in which respondents reported more closeness, loyalty, and influence within political parties received higher scores on this variable.

Strength of Caste Associations was scaled by referring to three other survey questions:

- How often do you get together with other members of your caste in your village to do something abut your common welfare? ("Never was scored as 1, "rarely" as 2, and "often" as 3.)
- How would you rate the persons who lead these associations in your village: Are they very knowledgeable and effective, reasonably effective, or not effective? (These options were scored 3, 2 and 1 respectively.)
- Do you feel the effectiveness of caste associations has increased in your village? Has it weakened? Or has it stayed more or less the same over time? ("Weakened" was scored as 1, "stayed the same" as 2, and "increased" as 3.)

- Which of the following activities do you usually undertake together with your caste fellows or where your caste leaders provide you with support? (Response scores were calculated by adding the total number of Yes responses.)

  - Contact with the police or tahsil   Yes/No
  - Contact with government departments providing   Yes/No
    subsidies and loans, such as Panchayat Samiti or DRDA
  - Contact with government departments providing   Yes/No
    casual employment (such as PWD, irrigation, forest,
    or watershed development)
  - Contact with banks or insurance agencies   Yes/No
  - Contact with seed or fertilizer suppliers   Yes/No
  - Contact with other market agencies   Yes/No
  - Looking after the affairs of religious buildings, such   Yes/No
    as temples or mosques
  - Organizing religious ceremonies   Yes/No
  - Resolving disputes among individual villagers   Yes/No
  - Dealing with disputes between husband and wife   Yes/No
  - Punishing people who have broken a moral code   Yes/No

Scores were summed over these four items for each individual respondent, and these aggregate scores were averaged over a village to provide its score for the variable, STR_CASTE. Places where caste associations were relatively more salient — where villagers met more often with their caste fellows, where leadership was more effective among caste associations, where effectiveness had not declined over the years, and where the range of activities was larger — were given higher scores on this scale. Where salience, effectiveness, continuity and scope were low, conversely, low scores were received on this variable.

Strength of Government Agency: The only local government agency elected directly by villagers and accountable to them on a day-to-day basis is the village *panchayat.* Other elected agencies are not local,[21] and no other local agencies are elected.[22] I consider the *panchayat* as the appropriate general-purpose government agency for this analysis. I will also consider other special-purpose government agencies where I deal with economic development and community peace, respectively.

Strength of village *panchayats* (STR_PANCH) is scaled by considering average village responses summed over three survey items:

- How often in the last one year have you attended public meetings called by the village *panchayat*? (Response scores varied from 1 for "never," to 2 for "just one or two meetings," to 3 for "attended most or all meetings.")
- Are you or is anyone close to you active in the village *panchayat*? (Response scores varied from 1 for "I have no contact with the *panchayat*," to 2 for "someone I know well but not related to me is or was an official," to 3 for "another member of my household is or was a *panchayat* official," to 4 for "I am myself an official (or former official) of the *panchayat*.")
- How effective do you consider the *panchayat* in this village compared to other villages? (Response scores ranged from 3 for more effective, to 2 for equally effective, to 1 for less effective.)

Participation, range of influence, and effectiveness form the three criteria for comparing *panchayat* strength across villages. Do villages with stronger *panchayats*, measured in these terms, show significantly better performance in terms of economic development, communal harmony, or political participation? That is the main question which is being examined here. Next, I consider the new development-oriented leaders that were found in the previous chapter to have acquired significant influence within the past two decades.

Strength of New Development-Oriented Village Leaders: Three survey questions were asked relating to their existence, utility, and contact by villagers.

- Some people have told me about new village leaders, who assist them in various works outside the village. Are there any such persons in your village? ("Yes" was scored as 2, and "No" as 1.)
- Some people think that these "new leaders" provide a useful service to other villagers, while others think that they simply take advantage of fellow villagers for their own personal benefit. We would like to know what you think in this regard. (Response scores were 1 for "These leaders simply take advantage of other villagers," and 2 for "They provide a useful service to fellow villagers.")
- How many times in the last 12 months have you yourself contacted any such new leader on a matter of concern to you? (Response scores considered for analysis ranged from 1 for "never," to 2 for "once or twice," to 3 for "many times.")

In addition, a fourth question was asked for assessing scope of activity:

- With which of the following activities do these new leaders assist other villagers? (Response scores were calculated by adding the total number of Yes responses.)

    - Contact with the police or tahsil   Yes/No
    - Contact with government departments providing   Yes/No
      subsidies and loans, such as Panchayat Samiti or DRDA
    - Contact with government departments providing   Yes/No
      casual employment (such as PWD, irrigation, forest,
      or watershed development)
    - Contact with banks or insurance agencies   Yes/No
    - Contact with seed or fertilizer suppliers   Yes/No
    - Contact with other market agencies   Yes/No
    - Looking after the affairs of religious buildings, such   Yes/No
      as temples or mosques
    - Organizing religious ceremonies   Yes/No
    - Resolving disputes among individual villagers   Yes/No
    - Dealing with disputes between husband and wife   Yes/No
    - Punishing people who have broken a moral code   Yes/No

The variable STR_NEW was constructed by summing across responses averaged for each village.

Strength of Traditional Village Council: This type of agency is described in more detail in chapter 6, and only a brief description is provided at this point. The traditional Village Council is an informal body,[23] different from the *panchayat*, and it is not recognized by the administration or the courts. Respected elders from all caste groups in the village chair this body. Some of these elders are also leaders of their respective caste associations. When they sit on the Council, however, they play a different (and more collaborative) role, and they deal with a different range of issues that concern the entire village and not just a particular caste.

Among all the different types of agency considered here, the Village Council is the only one whose effectiveness is at all related to the level of social capital in the village. The Village Council is entirely an internal feature of village communities. All representatives belong to the village, its sphere of decision making is confined to matters within the village, and decisions are taken in accordance with local precedent and locally-established rules. Neither political parties nor *panchayats* or the new development-oriented leaders are similarly circumscribed by features internal to the village. Even so, the capacity of the Village Council, in terms of effectiveness and range of functions, is only partially associated with the level of social capital, as we shall see presently.

The Village Council has existed since antiquity and, as I discuss in chapter 6, it is particularly useful for maintaining harmonious relations and resolving conflicts among villagers. To test this hypothesis, Village Council strength is compared among villages.

Council functions are less well known in some villages, meetings of the Council are held less frequently, fewer villagers attend these meetings, and a much smaller range of issues is discussed. Strength of Village Councils is assessed in terms related to familiarity, frequency, range of activities, and attendance at meetings.

Four survey items were considered for scaling the variable, STR_VC:

- In some villages, respected elders of all castes sit together in a village council. Does your village have any such council of village elders? ("No" was scored as 1, and "Yes" as 2.)
- In the last 12 months, how many times has this village council met? (Response scores ranged from 1 for "never," to 2 for "rarely, just one or two times," to 3 for "often, three times or more," to 4 for "regularly, six times or more," to 5 for "frequently, every month or more often.")
- How often have you attended the meetings of this council? (Response scores range from 1 for "never" to 4 for "attended all meetings.")
- With which of the following activities do the Village Councils leaders assist other villagers? (Response scores were calculated by adding the total number of Yes responses.)[24]

  - Contact with the police or tahsil   Yes/No
  - Contact with government departments providing   Yes/No
    subsidies and loans, such as Panchayat Samiti or DRDA
  - Contact with government departments providing   Yes/No
    casual employment (such as PWD, irrigation, forest,
    or watershed development)
  - Contact with banks or insurance agencies   Yes/No

- Contact with seed or fertilizer suppliers   Yes/No
- Contact with other market agencies   Yes/No
- Looking after the affairs of religious buildings, such   Yes/No
  as temples or mosques
- Organizing religious ceremonies   Yes/No
- Resolving disputes among individual villagers   Yes/No
- Dealing with disputes between husband and wife   Yes/No
- Punishing people who have broken a moral code   Yes/No

Once again, individual responses were summed over these four questions that are related, respectively, to existence, regularity, familiarity and scope, and village scores were derived as an average of these individual scores.

Strength of Patron-Client Links: Three sets of survey items were considered for this purpose, which relate, respectively, to utility, frequency of interaction, and range of functions.

- Do you have any patron (*jajmaan*) in this village to whom you have turned for help in times of need, or are you yourself a patron who has traditionally provided assistance to others?
- If you do have a patron-client relationship with any person or persons, then how often do you meet with these people — rarely, seldom, frequently or very often?
- How many of the following functions are performed by patrons in this village? (Response scores were calculated by adding the total number of Yes responses.)

- Providing credit in times of need   Yes/No
- Providing employment in times of need   Yes/No
- Providing protection against enemies   Yes/No
- Arranging for votes   Yes/No
- Arranging medical care   Yes/No
- Resolving disputes among villagers   Yes/No
- Contacting government agencies on behalf of   Yes/No
  villagers

The variable STR_PCR was constructed by summing together responses averaged over each village.

Social Capital and Agency Variables

How do the different agency variables relate to the measure of social capital? Correlation coefficients were calculated between the Social Capital Index and each of these measures of agency strength. Table 4.3 reports these results. Apart from the Village Council, which is significantly though not highly correlated with the Social Capital Index, none of the other agency variables has a correlation coefficient that is either statistically or substantially significant. The absolute size of each of these coefficients is quite small and — more important — just one of these correlation coefficients is significant at the 0.05 level.

Social capital is neither an effect nor a cause of the strength of different types of agency, these data indicate, and (with the partial exception of Str_VC) the two sets of variables can be considered as separate and unrelated independent variables for the purpose of analyzing the three outcomes of interest.[25] Two reasons suggest why social capital and agency strength are not highly correlated with each other. First, while social capital reflects the nature of relations within a community, i.e., it is a collectively possessed resource, agency strength relates most often to the capacities of particular individuals. While the level of social capital depends principally upon factors that are internal to the village, factors operating from outside have a critical influence upon agency capacity.[26]

TABLE 4.3 Correlation Between Social Capital and Agency Strength

Agency Variable	Correlation Coefficent with Social Capital Index	Significance Level
Str_PCR	-0.24	0.12
Str_PARTY	0.06	0.63
Str_PANCH	-0.06	0.65
Str_NEW	0.19	0.13
Str_VC	0.45	0.05
Str_CASTE	-0.05	0.68

Social capital and agency strength are both high in some of the 69 villages where I measured these variables. In most villages, however, there is no correlation between social capital and the strength of any particular agency type. As a result, many villages are unable to convert their stocks of social capital into flows of benefits, as we shall see in the next three chapters. Local-level resources, however plentiful, need to be marshaled strategically and directed toward incentives available within the broader institutional environment of state and market. When the intermediate links are weak, as they are when agency is not capable, social capital does not translate into equally good results.

Statistical results parallel observations in the sixteen case-study villages. Social capital is high in Balesariya, but there are no new leaders (Str_NEW is zero). Social capital is low in Ghodach, but political parties are strong (Str_PARTY is high). No clear pattern emerges between village scores on these variables. Table 4.4 provides this picture with respect to two types of agency.

TABLE 4.4 Social Capital and Agency Strength in 16 Villages
(H = High, M = Medium, L = Low)

Village	Social Capital	Str_New	Str_VC
Sangawas	H	H	L
Nauwa	H	H	H
Sunderchha	H	L	M
Balesaria	H	L	H
Gothra	M	M	M
Dantisar	M	L	H
Khempur	M	H	H
Sema	M	H	H
Devali	M	L	L
Losing	M	M	M
Palri	L	L	L
Ghodach	L	H	M
Kundai	L	H	M
Kundali	L	L	M
Sare	L	M	L
Hajiwas	L	L	L

Measuring Structural Variables

Agency variables are helpful for testing Hypothesis 3; the Social Capital Index helps test Hypothesis 1; but variables are still required for testing the structuralist hypothesis (Hypothesis 2). Recall that this hypothesis regards societal outcomes as well as social capital as products of structural conditions. Differences in economic development, communal peace, and political participation should be associated, if this hypothesis is true, with the structural differences that exist among these villages. The following structural variables are considered for testing this hypothesis:

Stratification is measured in two different ways:

The variable N_CASTES is a measure of the number of different caste groups that reside in any village. This variable provides one measure of the extent of homogeneity within the population of a village, and it is helpful for testing the claim that greater caste differences result in weaker (or stronger) collective action.[27]

The variable CASTE_DOM measures the proportion of village households that belong to the most numerous caste group, corresponding to the hypothesis of Srinivas (1987) that villages where the dominant group is larger will act collectively more often and more effectively than others. Both of these variables have been generated from information obtained during the field survey.

In addition, stratification is also measured in terms of the percentage of village population belonging to Scheduled Castes (SC) and Scheduled Tribes (ST), respectively, and also in terms of the Gini coefficient of land ownership. While figures for SC and ST have been taken from District Census Handbooks, relating to census year 1991, the latest year for which these data are available for the village level at the time of writing, the Gini coefficient of land ownership is calculated for the random sample of individuals interviewed in each village.

Commercialization and other indicators of relative modernization are expected by Lipset (1960) and others to be associated with greater civic involvement and higher levels of mutually beneficial collective action. For the purpose of this analysis, these variables are scaled in two different ways.

Commercial influences are likely to be less within villages that are located farther from markets. The variable, DISTMKT, measures the distance in kilometers to the market town that villagers visit most frequently.[28]

Relative modernization is measured in terms of the surrogate variable, density of infrastructure facilities. The variable INFRASTR combines scores for level of facility related to transportation, communications, electrification, and water supply.[29]

The hypothesis by Wade (1994) proposing *Relative Need* as a cause of collective action is relevant for economic development but not so much for the other two outcomes. Variables scaling this attribute are presented in chapter 5, which deals exclusively with economic development.

Though it is neither a structural nor an agency variable, literacy is also considered within the analysis, especially for testing the hypothesis by Dreze and Sen (1995) that communities with higher educational achievement will also have faster economic development.

Literacy figures are available from the District Census Handbooks. Since these figures are more than eight years old, however, and since change in literacy rates has been quite marked in this period — far more marked than changes in, say, infrastructure or stratification — I have opted to rely, instead, on the sample information. LITERACY is calculated as the sample percentage of persons having five or more years of formal education.

We are now equipped with a full set of independent variables that we can use to test the three competing hypotheses. Chapter 5 tests these hypotheses with respect to economic development, chapter 6 does so with respect to community harmony, while chapter 7 examines them in the context of political participation. Figure 4.1 presents in graphic form the alternative hypotheses that are being tested and the outcomes that we are trying to understand.

5 Understanding Economic Development: Why Do Some Villages Develop Faster than Others?

In chapter 2, we looked at the social capital hypothesis (high social capital leads to superior results in multiple societal domains); at the structuralist hypothesis, which rejects social capital theory (structures matter, social capital is merely a byproduct, a residue of structures); and we looked at the agency hypothesis, which qualifies social capital theory (social capital matters and agency helps convert its stock into a flow of benefits). Chapter 3 discussed how structure and agency look in the context of north Indian villages. The village, it is seen here, is the appropriate unit for evaluating hypotheses related to social capital in rural India. Chapter 4 presented locally-grounded measures of social capital and of other structural and agency variables. Social capital varies considerably among villages in this region, we saw there; agency strength is unrelated to social capital; and agency strengths also vary significantly from village to village.

The present chapter tests the three competing hypotheses in relation to economic development. Four sets of activities — related to livelihood stability, poverty reduction, employment generation, and essential services (education, health, and drinking water) — are examined that correspond with villagers' needs and their aspirations for a better life. Measures are developed to scale development performance in villages in terms of these four different activities. It is found on analysis that villages which perform well in relation to any one of these four different development activities also perform well in respect to each of the three activities. A single root propensity seems to be at work that makes villages perform similarly well or similarly badly in

respect of multiple development objectives. What factors might account for
this feature of villages which makes some villages high performers, by and
large, and other villages low performers?

Causes for high and low development performance are examined first by
using the case study data that I gathered over an extended stay in a group of
16 villages. Mills's Methods of Agreement and Difference (discussed below)
are utilized to distinguish which among the three competing hypotheses can
help explain the difference between high and low village performance. Factors identified by Millsian analysis are illuminated by detailed case accounts
from a subset of villages. Finally, data for the larger group of 69 villages are
examined with the help of regression analysis. Both the case-study examination and the statistical tests support a similar conclusion: Social capital
matters for development performance, but capable agency is required for
making social capital more productive.

Development in North Indian Villages

Development means different things to different people. To some, development is adequately captured by the measure of per capita income.
Economic development is positive in this conception when people's incomes rise on average — even when the rich gain and the poor lose, and
income inequality worsens. Concerns of equity are central for other measures, such as the United Nations' Physical Quality of Life Index, which
regards progress in development as the provision of basic minimum facilities
to all. Yet other views evaluate development performance in terms related
to the pace of industrialization, export growth, environmental status, etc.

What development means to villagers in Rajasthan and Madhya Pradesh
must be understood in context of *their* concerns and their aspirations for a
better life. What is life like in these villages, and what do villagers need and
want for improving their levels of well being?

Agriculture is the principal occupation of 92 percent of villagers.[1] Even
though nearly all households depend upon the land, however, it provides
neither a bountiful nor an assured existence. Crop yields fluctuate widely
from year to year, depending upon the state of rainfall, and there is severe
drought at least twice every decade, when crops fail and drinking water is
hard to find (Bokil 2000).

People no longer starve to death at these times.[2] But cattle die in large numbers, people's savings get depleted, and the land and its people emerge exhausted from these encounters. Table 5.1 reports yields of major crops in the five Rajasthan districts.[3] Best- and worst-year yields are reported here for Five-Year Plan periods of the Indian government,[4] highlighting the huge fluctuations that occur from year to year.

Average productivity has risen only marginally if at all over the past forty years, a comparison of best-year yields shows. But trend figures are hardly meaningful when seen against the huge swings that occur from year to year.

Maize yields in Udaipur district rose to a high of 1,528 kilograms per hectare in the year 1967–68 but they fell to 458 kilograms in 1968–69, less

TABLE 5.1 Annual Average Crop Yield
(kilograms per hectare)

	DUNGARPUR (Maize)		UDAIPUR and RAJSAMAND (Maize)		BHILWARA (Maize)	
	Worst Year	Best Year	Worst Year	Best Year	Worst Year	Best Year
1956–1961	529	1,058	699	1,253	603	1,116
1961–1966	770	1,348	959	1,394	869	1,156
1966–1974	208	1,380	458	1,528	528	1,429
1974–1980	180	1,312	691	1,328	632	1,248
1980–1985	789	1,098	800	1,492	557	1,544
1985–1990	246	1,232	211	1,441	306	1,444

	AJMER (Jowar)		BHILWARA (Jowar)		AJMER (Bajra)	
	Worst Year	Best Year	Worst Year	Best Year	Worst Year	Best Year
1956–1961	76	180	46	285	177	598
1961–1966	74	257	76	177	380	435
1966–1974	14	344	40	237	279	666
1974–1980	38	100	151	387	190	635
1980–1985	13	312	199	610	162	563
1985–1990	2	206	58	532	130	513

Source: GOR 1991

than a third of what they were a year ago. Twenty years later less than half of even this amount was harvested in a drought year. In 1987–88, yields were a mere 211 kilograms per hectare.

No major improvements have been recorded in terms of stabilizing or enhancing crop yields in all these years. And this is a problem not just in Rajasthan and in Madhya Pradesh but also in more than half of the other Indian states,[5] in other parts of South Asia, and in a broad swathe of countries cutting across northern and central Africa.[6] Sustaining people's livelihoods has become a prime concern of development agencies as large numbers in the Third World continue to fall victim to drought and as crop yields continue to fall as low and lower than they were fifty years ago.[7]

A stable livelihood is, not surprisingly, a principal development requirement of people in these regions. Activities that enable them to raise crop yields sustainably and to improve the availability of fodder and drinking water at all times are highly regarded by villagers. More than 90 percent of them ranked soil and water conservation and pasture development activities as one of three foremost village needs, besides safe drinking water and education and health facilities.

Many villagers wish they could escape from agriculture with its high risks and low rewards. But very few, hardly ten percent, have been able over the last fifty years to make this leap. Employment in organized manufacturing and urban services — which accounts for less than ten percent of the Indian labor force — has increased at a snail's pace. During the period 1986–96, for example, employment in these sectors grew from 25.1 million to 27.9 million persons, representing a compound annual growth rate of less than one percent.[8] Population grew at more than double this rate, and numbers of unemployed in the urban labor force grew even faster. In 1996, 5.9 million unemployed persons were registered with employment exchanges in India, but only 233,000 of them, less than four percent, were provided jobs in this year.[9]

Male villagers stay within the village of their birth, and women stay in the village of their marriage. They must make do with the resources that are available, even though productivity is constant or falling, and each generation must share this fixed resource with a larger number of people.[10] "Rural areas," in which nearly three-fourths of the country's population live, are consequently "characterised by poverty, low levels of productivity, and lack of adequate basic minimum services."[11]

On average, 44.5 percent of households are poor in the 69 villages of Rajasthan and Madhya Pradesh that were surveyed for this study.[12] This figure is as high as 87 percent in Dooka village of Dungarpur district. In 29 of the 69 villages that I studied, the majority of households are poor, i.e., they have incomes too low to acquire minimum nutritional requirements. Poverty reduction is thus another development priority for villagers, along with livelihood stabilization.

Creation of employment is their third major concern. Large numbers of villagers depend on wage employment for supplementing the meager amounts that they make from agriculture and animal husbandry. 45 percent of villagers interviewed in Rajasthan and Madhya Pradesh mentioned that wage employment for at least one month every year was necessary for them to cope with essential household expenditures.

A fourth criterion of development performance mentioned by villagers relates to the quality of health, education, and water supply services. Infant mortality in rural India is upward of 150 per 1,000 live births, and millions of villagers are stricken every year with tuberculosis, polio, malaria, and dysentery — diseases that have nearly disappeared from the industrialized world.[13] The quality of health services they receive is a major concern of most villagers and also the quality of education and water supply.

Health services in rural areas are provided almost exclusively by the Health Department of the state government; school education is provided by its Education Department; and water supply by its Public Health Engineering Department.[14] To obtain better service quality, villagers undertake collective action to protest against poor service delivery or they combine their voluntary efforts to improve service quality locally, at the village level.

For employment provision, also, villagers usually need to interact with several different government agencies. The private sector provides hardly any employment opportunities, and most laboring villagers have come to rely upon programs of the state that expanded enormously, especially during the 1980s and 1990s, as we saw in chapter 3.[15] The other two development objectives — livelihood stability and poverty reduction — are also achieved largely in the context of some state-run program, as we shall see in the next section. Villagers who can deal better with the state are more likely to achieve higher development benefits.

To what extent does social capital matter for village development performance? In order to examine this question, an Index of Development Performance is constructed in the next section, which utilizes village scores related to each of the four principal development concerns expressed by these Indian villagers, namely:

- livelihood stabilization,
- poverty reduction,
- employment generation, and
- service quality. .

The three competing hypotheses related to social capital are examined in the sections that follow.

Measuring Development Performance

Livelihood Stabilization

Almost half the land in every village is not privately owned. Ownership of these tracts vests with a government department (usually the Land Revenue or the Forest Department) or with the village *panchayat*, but there are usually weak or no barriers to entry, and villagers access these lands freely to graze their cattle and to collect firewood. A large proportion of villagers' biomass and energy requirements, up to two-thirds for poorer villagers, is provided by such village common lands (Jodha 1990).

With village population increasing by 25 percent every decade, and with the cattle population growing even faster, most common lands have been severely overgrazed to the point where many tracts stand devoid of any foliage (Brara 1992). Conserving and developing these common lands is critical for the livelihoods of most villagers, and so is conserving soil and moisture on privately owned lands where crops are grown. A government program of integrated watershed development was launched in 1991 that assists villagers in achieving these aims.

Prior to the launch of this government program, few villages had done much to develop common lands or to conserve soil and moisture on private lands. Neither was technology well known that could enable villagers to improve the productivity of these resources reliably and cheaply; nor were most villagers in a position to work free of cost for the entire number of days that are needed to implement these schemes. External support in the form of appropriate technology and supplementary resources was required, and the state government provided these means starting in 1991.[16]

The residents of each participating village elected a five-member Users Committee with responsibility for planning and implementing all program activities on common lands, including soil and water conservation, plantation (of trees, shrubs and fodder grasses), protection, and management. To participate in the program, villagers also had to commit themselves, individually and collectively, to providing voluntary labor amounting to a ten-percent share of program costs. Ninety percent of these costs were provided for in the form of government subsidies.[17]

Rules were devised locally by each Committee to apportion costs and harvesting rights and to allocate tasks and wage employment opportunities equitably among villagers. In some but not all villages, these committees took over a larger set of program activities, involving themselves additionally with drainage line treatments (constructing small dams) and with crop production activities.

Nearly five hundred villages in Rajasthan joined with the program in its first phase (1991–1994), and more than a thousand villages joined later. For the purpose of this study, 60 Rajasthan villages were selected that have participated in this program continuously since 1991. Records of work done and yield improvements were available with the Watershed Development Department. Fodder production has increased ten-fold in some villages, crop yields have trebled and they fluctuate much less from year to year, and the water level in village wells has risen substantially. In other villages, however, these changes are far less impressive (CTAE 1999). Village performance was ranked High, Middle, or Low on the basis of the available record, and 20 villages were selected at random from each of these three categories.

An index of performance was constructed that relies upon the following indicators:

1. *Quantum of work*: measured in terms of the percentage of village common land that was developed under the program. Villages that were able to assemble larger voluntary contributions (of money *and* labor) developed a larger area of common land. In addition to measuring total program expenditures, thus, this variable also scales the extent of voluntary effort by villagers.

2. *Protection and Survival*: measured in terms of seven-year survival rates for trees and shrubs planted during program implementation. Approximately 100,000 trees were planted on average in each village, and survival rates vary from a low of 12 percent (in Kunda village) to a high of 64 percent (Sangawas village). Higher survival is representative of the greater care that villagers took, collectively, of trees and shrubs planted within village boundaries.

3. *Productivity*: seen in terms of the quantity of fodder and fuelwood harvested from common lands in the previous year, measured as headloads

harvested per capita. 18 headloads of fodder grass and dry sticks were collected by every resident of Sunderchha, for example, and 14 headloads by every resident of Nauwa, but residents of Ghodach harvested only three headloads each, and residents of Balesariya, Palri and some other villages harvested nothing at all.

4. *Diversification:* considered in terms of the number of activities, other than common land development, that were undertaken by the Users Committee of each village. It measures the range of activities for which villagers achieved cooperative solutions and common implementation mechanisms.

Information for coding the first item, related to quantum of work, was obtained from the records of the Watershed Development Department. Information for coding the other three items, related to protection and survival, productivity, and diversification was collected through site inspections and focus group interviews.

It is found on analysis that a village's score on any of these four variables is closely correlated with its score on each of the other three measures. A single common factor is found that is closely associated with all of these four measures of performance in livelihood stabilization activities.[18] Because these four variables are so closely correlated with each other, they are combined to provide a single Index of Common Land Development (CLD), with a range from zero to four points.[19] Mean village score on this Index is 1.68 (out of four points), and standard deviation is 0.81.

Among the 16 case-study villages, Nauwa (3.1 points) and Sangawas (3.2 points) have the highest scores. Gothra, Khempur and Sema also have higher than average scores. Balesariya, Sare, and Palri are the lowest scoring villages, getting 1.1, 0.9 and 0.7 points, respectively.

Livelihood stability, seen here in relation to performance in watershed development, is only one of four development goals that villagers consider to be of primary importance. Poverty reduction, employment generation, and basic services are also important, and we must devise appropriate measures to compare village performance for these three other activities.

Poverty Reduction

The second main development objective of villagers — or at least of the 45 percent of them who earn less than subsistence amounts — is measured here in terms of progress in poverty reduction. No direct measures are available of the numbers of people who escape poverty each year. I rely, instead, upon numbers assisted under the official programs — Integrated Rural Development Program (IRDP) and two others[20] — that provide assets and training to poor villagers. With their asset base increased in this manner, it is expected that the poor should be able to earn larger amounts.

However, not all persons assisted under these programs have achieved substantial or sustainable income increases, and assistance has in many cases failed to bring about any significant improvement. Incorrect identification of beneficiaries, insufficient extension and follow-up, inappropriate selection of activities, and misappropriation of funds by officials are mentioned as reasons for these failures.[21] Such failed grants amount, according to different analysts, to between 15 and 60 percent of the total.[22]

Be that as it may, and regardless of whether it is success or a failure overall, IRDP represents quite often the only chance that the poor have for overcoming the limitations of their situation. Their credit-worthiness is low, and they have hardly anything to mortgage to banks and other lenders. Employment in factories and services accounts for a tiny number of villagers, as we have seen earlier, and drastic redistribution of land is unlikely to occur any time soon.[23] The sum of Rs.16,000 ($400) that is provided in grants and cheap loans — and that beneficiaries use to procure cows, buffaloes, machines, and stock-in-trade — cannot usually be acquired by them in any other manner. IRDP has failed in many cases, no doubt; until something better comes their way, however, it represents often the only chance the poor have for enhancing their asset base.

The variable POVASSIST measures for each village the number of grants per hundred villagers obtained over the last five years. Among villages that have the highest scores on this variable are Sema (5.8), Sangawas (5.7) and Nauwa (4.9). Case-study villages that have among the lowest scores are Hajiwas (0.47), Sare (0.65), and Palri (0.95). Mean score for all 60 villages is 2.75, and standard deviation is 1.17.

Employment Provision

Continuing poverty is abated to some extent through the wages provided by public construction projects. 45 percent of all villagers — i.e., 1,262 of 2,232 persons interviewed in Rajasthan and Madhya Pradesh villages — asserted that wages earned in this manner are necessary for their families to subsist from year to year.

Employment creation programs have grown rapidly in the rural areas over the past twenty years, as we saw in chapter 3, as political parties have tried, especially since the mid-1970s, to build constituencies among the rural poor (Kohli 1990). Previously quiescent but now increasingly aware and alert, the rural poor force parties to compete for their votes by providing larger and larger employment programs. A target of 450 million man-days of wage employment was set for one such program alone (Jawahar Rozgaar Yojana or JRY) for fiscal year 1998–99 (GOI 1998). Distributed in the rural areas, this assistance provided support to 15 million Indian households.

The idea is to spread employment out thinly so that all villagers have at least some chance of making the necessary income supplements, so JRY projects are mostly of small size and short duration. Between 1994 and 1998, more than 20,000 village projects were taken up in Rajasthan, each of which provided wage income to between 50 and 60 households for an average period of five weeks in a year (GOR 1999).[24]

The variable EMPPROV measures man-days of employment generated over the previous three years per capita of village population.[25] Mean village score is 2.39, implying that over the three years past, employment opportunities were provided by the state to every man, woman and child villager for an average of nearly two-and-a-half days.[26]

High EMPPROV scores are achieved by three case-study villages: Sangawas (6.45), Nauwa (6.24), and Sema (5.9). Among the lowest achievers are Sare (0.51) and Hajiwas (1.09).

Quality of Basic Services

Finally, I consider three indicators corresponding to the United Nations' Physical Quality of Life Index (PQLI) that bear upon the quality of health, education, and water supply services. No objective measure of quality is available, however, so villagers' subjective assessments are considered for this measurement.

A focus group of villagers was consulted to rank the quality of health, education, and water supply services in their village compared to neighboring villages. Villagers assigned a score of 5 points if they felt the quality of a particular service was "much better" in their village compared to other villages, scores of 4, 3, and 2 if they felt it was "better," "the same," and "worse," respectively, or a score of 1 if they felt it was "much worse." A score of zero was assigned if the particular service was entirely unavailable in their village.

The variable QUALSERV combines the scores for all three services, health, education, and water supply. The highest range of scores, 11–13 points out of a possible 15 points, is achieved by two of the 16 case-study villages, Sema, and Nauwa; and the lowest range of scores, 5–8 points, is achieved by three case study villages, Kundai, Palri and Sare.

Analysis

It is striking to find that the same case-study villages — Nauwa, Sangawas, Khempur, and Sema — are consistently among the top ten performers for each of the four scales of development performance. Conversely, Sare, Hajiwas, Balesariya, and Kundai occupy the bottom third in each of the four sets of rankings.

How do these four aspects of development in this region — livelihood stability, poverty assistance, employment provision, and quality of basic services — relate to each other within the larger group of 60 villages? This question is addressed below by examining the correlation among CLD, POVASSIST, EMPPROV, and QUALSERV.

Correlations among the four development variables are high and statistically significant. Further, these variables load commonly on a single factor, which accounts for 76 percent of their combined variance, indicating that

TABLE 5.2 Four Development Indicators: Pearson Correlation Coefficients
(n = 60; significance levels are in brackets)

	CLD	POVASSIST	EMPPROV	QUALSERV
CLD	1.00 (0.0)	0.632 (0.0001)	0.678 (0.0001)	0.662 (0.0001)
POVASSIST		1.00 (0.0)	0.524 (0.0001)	0.484 (0.0001)
EMPPROV			1.00 (0.0001)	0.457 (0.0001)
QUALSERV				1.0 (0.0)

some underlying propensity exists, which is associated with high performance in each of these enterprises.

Villages that do well in any of these four development programs tend, by and large, to have high performance scores on each of the other three development programs. And villages that perform poorly do so, in general, commonly across all four programs. Villages perform well in multiple activities or they perform poorly in most, these figures indicate. Very few villages do relatively well in some activities and relatively poorly in others.

It is not the nature of activities that matters so much for success in development, the analysis reveals. There is some feature of villages that enables a particular set to succeed no matter what development activity is taken up.

Instead of focusing their energies exclusively on developing newer and better programs and implementing these from the top down, as they have done for so many years, planners of development ought to consider as well the capacities that emerge from the bottom-up and that enable villagers to succeed in multiple development enterprises. What these capacities are and where they come from are examined next.

For the purpose of analysis, the four separate development indicators are combined, since they are so closely associated, into a single *Index of Development Performance*, which is constructed by aggregating the scores received on each of the four separate scales.[27] Mean village score on this index is 48 points, standard deviation is 20.6, and skewness = 0.37.

The Index of Development Performance (DEVINDEX) is closely correlated with each of its four constituent variables, and is also significantly correlated with other measures of development. For instance, it is correlated with the variable FP_CAP, which measures the number of family planning practitioners in the village per unit of population.[28] The correlation coefficient between these two variables is 0.44, which is significant at the 0.01 level.

TABLE 5.3 Development Performance: Factor Pattern

Variables	Factor 1
CLD (Livelihood Stabilization)	0.820
POVASSIST (Poverty Assistance	0.691
EMPPROV (Employment Provision)	0.843
QUALSERV (Quality of Basic Services)	0.712

Comparing the Three Hypotheses: Case Analysis

I will start looking for causes of high development performance by using Mills's Methods of Agreement and Difference to examine data for the 16 case-study villages. Next, I will look at a couple of cases in depth. Finally, I will use regression analysis to corroborate these results within all 60 Rajasthan villages included in the study sample.

Mills's method of examination starts by dividing observed cases into positive cases, where the phenomenon of interest is visible and strong, and negative cases, where the phenomenon of interest is absent or only weakly manifest. The phenomenon of interest in our case is high development performance. So villages are divided into those where development performance is conspicuously high (positive cases) and others where development performance is conspicuously low (negative cases).

Fourteen of 60 villages score 65 points or higher on this index, including five case study villages, and our set of positive cases is made up of these five villages:

High-Performing Villages (Positive Cases)

- Nauwa
- Sangawas
- Gothra
- Khempur
- Sema

On the other hand, fifteen villages have conspicuously low development performance, scoring 35 points or lower on the Index of Development Performance. Six of 16 case-study villages are included within this list of low performers, and our set of negative cases is made up of these six villages:

Low-Performing Villages (Negative Cases)

- Kundai
- Sunderchha

- Ghodach
- Balesariya
- Hajiwas
- Sare

Having distinguished positive and negative cases, we can now go on to the next step of Millsian analysis. Different hypothesized causes for high and low performance are tested in this step to see how well each of them corresponds with the phenomenon in question. To be a "true" cause of this phenomenon, a hypothesized cause must be present whenever the phenomenon is present and absent whenever the phenomenon is absent. To be a valid cause of high development performance, thus, a hypothesized cause, such as social capital, must be present among all positive cases and absent among all negative ones. And no other hypothesized cause should share the same property. Thus, only if social capital is high whenever development performance is high and low whenever development performance is low — and no other factor co-varies in the same way with high and low development performance — can social capital be considered validly to be the cause of high development performance.

More formally, Mills's methods require that:

1. If X is the hypothesized cause and Y the effect, then X should be present whenever Y is present;
2. X should be absent whenever Y is absent; and
3. Factors associated with alternative hypotheses, e.g., Z, should be absent when Y is present.

A property that is shared by all positive cases and by none of the negative cases is a candidate cause, according to this method, especially if theory exists in its support. Positive cases in this instance are the five villages that score very highly on the Index of Development Performance, and negative cases are the six lowest-scoring villages.

Two separate stages are involved in applying Mills's methods. In the first stage, one tries "to establish that several cases having in common the phenomenon one is trying to explain also have in common a set of causal factors . . . what Mills called the 'Method of Agreement,' " i.e., one looks first at the positive cases to assess whether some hypothesized cause is consistently associated with all of these positive cases. In the second stage, one looks at "cases in which the phenomenon to be explained and the causes are both absent, but which are otherwise as similar as possible to the positive cases . . . [what] Mill labeled the 'Method of Difference' " (Skocpol 1979: 36). Thus, in the second stage, one looks only at negative cases. If a hypothesized cause is present in all positive cases (stage one) and absent in all negative cases (stage two), then it can be considered a valid cause of high development performance, especially if no other hypothesized cause is similarly associated with positive and negative cases.

Let us undertake the first stage of this analysis using the Method of Agreement, and let us look first at variables corresponding to the *structuralist* hypothesis. Recall that this hypothesis claims that different villages face different structural conditions, and that differences in development performance arise on account of these structural differences. Now, macro-level structures are not very different among villages in Rajasthan and Madhya Pradesh, which lie within the same country and region, and share similar agro-ecological characteristics and a common cultural inheritance. So micro-level features must be considered that reflect structural differences among villages. Stratification, relative need, and commercialization and modernization are held out by different theories as factors responsible for village-level differences in development performance, and variables corresponding to these hypotheses were developed in chapter 4.

Differences in stratification are measured with the help of two variables, N_CASTES (number of distinct caste groups) and CASTEDOM (extent of domination by a single caste). Differences in the effect of commercialization are measured by DISTMKT (distance to market town), and modernization is measured by INFRASTR (density of physical infrastructure).

Measures of relative need were not provided in chapter 4, however, and these must be described anew in the context of economic development, for need is invariably related to the object at hand. Relative need in the context of economic development is measured in terms of two indicators: DRYLAND and PERCPOOR.

DRYLAND measures the percentage of village land that is not irrigated by any source other than seasonal rainfall. The higher the proportion of dry land in the village, it can be conceived, the greater the need for villagers to seek livelihood stability, poverty assistance, and employment generation. Similarly, the higher the percentage of below-poverty households in a village, i.e., the greater the value of PERCPOOR, the more the need to reach for help to programs of the state.

In stage one of applying Mills's methods, these six structural variables are tested using the Method of Agreement to see if they are uniquely associated with high development performance, represented by the five positive cases. Table 5.4A provides a summary of this analysis.

Not one of the structuralist variables remains at a steady level within the group of positive cases. None of these variables is consistently associated, either at a high level or at a low level, with high development performance. The stratification variables, NCASTES and CASTEDOM take a high value in some of the positive cases but they have low values in others; 16 distinct caste groups live in Nauwa village (NCASTES is comparatively high), but there are only three in Sema (NCASTES is low). The dominant caste (Dangis) are 42 percent of the population of Khempur (CASTEDOM is high), but in Sangawas the dominant caste (Rajputs) make up only 17 percent of its populace (CASTEDOM is relatively low).

The commercialization and modernization variables, DISTMKT and INFRSTR, also fluctuate between high and low values within the subset of positive cases. For instance, Nauwa and Khempur are located more than 20 kilometers away from the nearest market (DISTMKT is high), while from Sangawas the distance to market is comparatively low, a mere two kilometers. Relative need is also not consistently high among high-performing villages (nor is it consistently low). Dryland has a high value in Nauwa but it has among its lowest values of all in the village of Khempur. The poor form 84 percent of the Sema's population (PERCPOOR is comparatively high), but they are much below average, 36 percent, in Sunderchha (PERCPOOR is comparatively low).

None of the structural variables are associated consistently, thus, either positively or negatively, with high development performance. According to the Method of Agreement, these factors can no longer be considered valid causes of the phenomenon to be explained.

Though it is not necessary to do so — a candidate cause rejected by the Method of Agreement need no longer be considered using the Method of Difference — we adopt the latter procedure to see whether any association exists between negative cases and the structural variables. Table 5.4B reports the results of this stage two analysis.

No consistent association exists, these data show, between poor development performance and any of the structural variables. Neither the stratification variables, nor the commercialization and modernization variables, nor even any of the relative need variables are constant in association with low devel-

TABLE 5.4A Mill's Methods Applied to Structural Variables
Positive Cases: High-Performing Villages

| | Stratification | | Commercialization/ Modernization | | | Relative Need | |
	NCASTES	CASTEDOM	DISTMKT	INFRSTR		DRYLAND	PERCPOOR
Nauwa	H	L	H	L		H	H
Sangawas	L	L	L	H		L	H
Gothra	H	L	M	H		M	L
Khempur	L	H	H	L		L	L
Sema	H	H	L	L		H	H

H = High
M = Medium
L = Low

TABLE 5.4B Mill's Methods Applied to Structural Variables
Negative Cases: Low Performing Villages

	Stratification		Commercialization/ Modernization		Relative Need	
	NCASTES	CASTEDOM	DISTMKT	INFRSTR	DRYLAND	PERCPOOR
Kundai	H	H	L	H	L	M
Sunderchha	L	H	L	M	M	L
Ghodach	H	L	H	M	L	H
Balesariya	H	L	H	L	L	L
Hajiwas	M	L	L	H	M	M
Sare	L	H	H	L	H	H

opment performance. According to the logic of the Millsian method, thus, variables corresponding to the structural hypotheses cannot be considered valid causes of high development performance. Other hypotheses and other variables will need to be considered in order to account for this phenomenon.

Two other hypotheses, the social capital hypothesis and the agency hypothesis, were proposed in chapter 2. How do variables corresponding to these other two hypotheses fare when tested with the help of Millsian analysis? The social capital hypothesis would derive support from this analysis if high levels of social capital were associated with all positive cases and low levels of social capital were associated with all negative cases. The agency hypothesis is slightly harder to judge. To recall, we are considering six different agency strength variables associated with political parties (STR_PARTY); caste associations (STR_CASTE); patron-client links (STR_PCR); the government agency, *panchayats* (STR_PANCH); with new development-oriented leaders (STR_NEW); and with old community leaders and their informal village council (STR_VC). The question to be judged in testing the agency hypothesis is whether any of these agency variables is consistently associated with high development performance, either singly or in combination with high social capital.

The Social Capital Hypothesis and the Agency Hypothesis are tested conjointly using Mills's methods. In the first stage of this analysis, the Method of Agreement is employed, and candidate variables are tested against the five highest-performing villages, which constitute the positive cases for this analysis. Table 5.5A presents the summary results of this analysis.[29]

The social capital hypothesis (Hypothesis 1) gets partial support in this analysis. Social capital is medium to high in each of these high-performing villages, and in none of these cases does it take a low value. Among the agency measures, none are clearly and consistently associated with high development performance. Values of these variables are not stable at any given level, high, medium, or low; instead they fluctuate between two or more of these values. Only one of these variables, STR_NEW, has a relatively constrained range of values, and it ranges from medium to high but does not take any low value. So partial support is also derived in the case of this particular agency variable, related to capacity of new village leaders, and described in chapter 3.

However, neither the Social Capital Index nor the variable STR_NEW can as yet be considered valid causes of high development performance. A second stage of examination is required to complete Millsian analysis. Neg-

TABLE 5.5A Mills Methods Applied to Social Capital and Agency Variables
Positive Cases: High-Performing Villages

	SCI	STR_NEW (new leaders)	STR_CASTE (caste associations)	STR_PANCH (government agency)	STR_PARTY (political parties)	STR_VC (old community leaders)
Nauwa	H	H	L	H	L	H
Sangawas	H	H	M	H	M	L
Gothra	M	M	H	H	L	M
Khempur	M	H	H	L	H	M
Sema	M	H	L	L	M	H

ative cases must also be analyzed using the Method of Difference. For a hypothesized cause to be a valid cause of high development performance, its variable should take high values among all positive cases and low values among all negative cases. The structuralist variables, which we examined earlier, passed none of these tests. Social capital and the agency variable, STR_NEW, have both partially passed the first of two tests. Let us see how these variables fare in the second test, the Method of Difference. Table 5.5B reports these results.

Applying the Method of Difference, one finds that considered separately, neither of these two variables, Social Capital Index or STR_NEW, shows any consistent pattern in association with low development performance. Social capital is alternatively high and low among low-performing villages (i.e., it is not always low, as it should be in order to be a valid cause). Similarly, the effectiveness of new leaders, STR_NEW, also ranges from low to high among negative cases. Thus, neither of these variables — Social Capital Index or STR_NEW — can individually be considered to be a valid cause of development performance.

The social capital hypothesis is not supported by Mills's methods. In order for it be a valid cause of development performance, values of social capital should be uniformly high among positive cases and uniformly low among all negative cases. But social capital ranges from medium to high within the list of positive cases, i.e., the Method of Agreement is only partially satisfied

TABLE 5.5B Mills Methods Applied to Social Capital and Agency Variables
*Negative Cases Low-Performing Villages**

	SCI	STR_NEW (new leaders)
Kundai	L	H
Sunderchha	H	L
Ghodach	L	H
Balesariya	H	L
Hajiwas	L	L
Sare	L	M

*Other agency variables were also considered, but as in the case of high-performing villages, none of these variables had any consistent range of values.

by social capital. And the Method of Difference is satisfied not at all; high values of social capital coexist with low values within the list of negative cases. Social capital cannot be accepted, thus, as a valid cause of development performance, nor can the variable STR_NEW be accepted as an individually valid cause of development performance.

The agency hypothesis remains to be fully tested, however, even though none of the agency variables are individually upheld by the Method of Agreement and the Method of Difference. Hypothesis 3 claims, it will be recalled, that social capital is brought to bear upon societal objectives through the mediation of an appropriate agency. The level of social capital matters, it is claimed, and also the strength of the agency concerned. For testing this hypothesis fully, the two variables, Social Capital Index and STR_NEW, must be considered not just individually but also in conjunction with one another.

When the Social Capital Index and STR_NEW are combined, the interaction of these two variables is revealed to have a distinct pattern of association with development performance values. We have seen that Social Capital Index and Str_NEW both ranged from medium to high for all positive cases and they did not take any low value. Among the negative cases, it was seen that either one or the other of these two variables invariably takes a low value. Either social capital is low or agency strength is low among negative cases, and there are no negative cases where at least one of these two variables is not low.

The inference that emerges can be stated as follows: Social Capital must be not low *and* the effectiveness of new leaders must also be not low in order for villages to have relatively higher development performance; if either one of these variables is low, then relatively slow economic development will result. High development performance occurs only when both of these variables are not low. Both social capital *and* agency strength must be medium or high in order that development performance be relatively strong in a village.

Before going on to check these results with the help of regression analysis for the larger group of 60 villages, let us look first look within the case-study materials to see why and how social capital and agency strength matter in conjunction with one another. Examples of two villages will be reviewed in the next section: Balesariya village, where social capital is high but new-development oriented leaders are weak and ineffective; and Ghodach village, which has the reverse situation: social capital is low and new leaders are numerous and strong.

Agency and Social Capital: Why Should Both Matter for Development?

Balesariya (*High Social Capital, Low Agency Capacity*)

Social capital has an almost ambient quality in this village, as we saw in chapter 4. People trust each other considerably, they meet each other often, and they cooperate to deal with numerous community issues and common problems. Why does their highly developed propensity for mutually beneficial collective action not translate into superior results vis-à-vis economic development? A likely cause is to be found in low agency capacity.

Mangilal, *sarpanch* (chief) of Balesariya's *panchayat*, is the only one among the 1,011 residents of this village who has regular contact with any state or market agency. He is not well liked by other villagers, who consider that he succeeded to his position by employing foul means. Though he transacts on their behalf to get projects from the state that assist with livelihood stability, poverty assistance, employment generation, and basic services in their village, the villagers regard him as at best a necessary evil. "Mangilal does what he will. We meet him only if we have to, in connection with some work we have [with the government]. There is no one else in this village to whom we can go for such work."[30]

Though he is the only one that they have, Mangilal is not a very efficient agent of villagers. He cannot easily cheat them — villagers are strongly united, and social sanctions, including ostracism, are imposed swiftly and firmly, with no scope for appeal — and Mangilal serves them to the best of his ability. But Mangilal's abilities are not very great.

"People in the village are not very aware of what is happening in the world outside," says Mangilal, "First there was only a single government department, the *Mahakma Aam* [or general administration department, of the pre-Independence Udaipur state], but now [in the present-day structure of government] any one case has to be walked through ten different offices, so a great deal of time has to be spent [pursuing any case]. . . . Development can only happen when one has some control over government officials and when they listen to one. I find it is no good talking to these officials. . . . First [in earlier times] hardly any [state] funds were given to villages; now there is a lot of money available. But villages take different amounts depending upon their strength."[31]

Strength lies in being able to persuade officials and politicians to allocate schemes and program funds to one's village. Mangilal is particularly weak in this respect. "Mangilal is among those village *sarpanchas* who sit at the back in each meeting [of *sarpanchas* of the local area]. They [the back-bencher *sarpanchas*] know very little about schemes and programs, so they don't dispute whatever officials say. They are thankful for what is given to them. They don't know how to fight for more."[32]

Apart from gaining the entitlements that they cannot be denied — such as some amount of JRY funds that are allocated in proportion to village population — Balesariya's residents have been unable to dig more deeply into sources of funding that are allocated at the discretion of officials and politicians. Where other villages of similar size, such as Nauwa and Sangawas, have got more than half a million rupees each in development funds allotted by MPs and MLAs, Balesariya has received nothing. New leaders in other villages have liaised with bankers and officials to obtain more than five IRDP grants per hundred villagers; but Balesariya in the last three years has received only nineteen grants for its population of more than a thousand people.

Even when development projects, such as the watershed development program, have been implemented in this village, their benefits have not been sustained. Balesariya has among the lowest scores on the Common Land Development index, and it is easy to see why. The quality of work is very poor, and nearly all of the trees and shrubs planted through the watershed development program have died on account of poor management and protection techniques. The users committee in Balesariya is among the least knowledgeable, and they have hardly any contact with officials of the government department. Quality of basic services, health, education, and water supply, is low in this village because, as Mangilal says, "officials don't listen to us."

Despite their ample stocks of social capital, residents of Balesariya have been unable to achieve fast economic development. The approach road to the village is a muddy path, impossible to negotiate during the three monsoon months. Drinking water is still taken from the community well, and there is no piped water supply anywhere in this village. Villagers here make good use of what they have, and they have allocated these resources reasonably effectively and equitably. Without the support of capable new leaders, however, they have been unable to add significantly to their existing resource base. They are good at using what they have; but they lack the capacity to achieve more. Because it has no effective leaders who can help them reach out and attract additional resources from the state (or from the market), Balesariya remains an economic backwater.

Ghodach (*Low Social Capital, High Agency Capacity*)

If the capacity of agents matters such a lot for development, as the case of Balesariya reveals, then why does Ghodach perform so poorly? There are seven new leaders in this village of 2,003 inhabitants, and each of them is capable and effective in his ways.

However, though these leaders are quite skilled at arbitrating villagers' relationships with state and market agencies, they do so more for their own personal benefit and less for villagers' collective advantage.

The meaning of unity in our village is that if some money came here from up there [from some government department] and if you [a local leader] were to use some of this money [for the purpose it was intended] and eat away [pocket] the rest, then I [other villagers] would have no worries on this account. That is why development is at a halt [in our village]. Whatever [misdeeds] I am doing are accepted by you, and whatever wrong you do is accepted by me.[33]

Development is at a halt, according to another Ghodach resident, because "villagers are not able to agree and form a consensus among themselves. That everyone gets together behind some work and behind protecting and maintaining [the assets that are created by] this work — such a thing never happens in this village. Honesty has no value here."[34] Villagers are not united, either for sanctioning individual leaders who cheat and betray them, or even for supporting the interventions these leaders make on their behalf with government officials and party politicians.

Service quality is poor in this village. Two schoolteachers out of four had been missing for over a month during the time I spent in this village, and no one in the village had done anything about it. The local nurse had no stocks of medicine or other supplies left with her. The approach to the village was over two broken bridges, and tarmac cover had disappeared from what remained of the road.

No rules guide the use of common land in Ghodach, and pastures planted under the watershed development program have been destroyed by willful encroachments. "Ghodach*walas* [residents of Ghodach] are not like people of Losing [another village adjoining Ghodach]. In Losing, everyone cooperated, watershed development went on very well, and we won the all-India prize [for best watershed development]. . . . Work went on at the same time in Ghodach, but there was no [local] cooperation. The User Committee was ineffective. It was no fun working here."[35]

Social capital is at a low level in Ghodach village, as these vignettes suggest, and as its low score on the Social Capital Index indicates. Though they have capable new leaders who can help them strike beneficial deals with officials and with politicians, the residents of Ghodach are unable to achieve any coordination among themselves. Villagers here hardly ever get together to cooperate for any purpose. Individuals are suspicious of each other, and they have little faith in initiatives that are taken by anyone else in the village. Ghodach provides an unattractive target, thus, for politicians and for government officials. Politicians prefer dealing with villages that promise a large number of block votes, and they are happier allocating discretionary grants to such villages. Government officials are keen to have large numbers of villagers participating actively in program activities, and they avoid anomic and atomized villages such as Ghodach whenever possible.

Their low stock of social capital prevents villagers in Ghodach from deriving any sturdy flows of development benefits, despite the presence of capable agency. In Balesariya, on the other hand, the stock of social capital is high, but capable agency is absent, so benefits are small. That these two factors — social capital and capability of new leaders — both matter and that they matter in interaction with one another is shown as well by the results of regression analysis performed for the full group of 60 Rajasthan villages.

Comparing the Three Hypotheses: Statistical Analysis

Table 5.6 gives the results of regression analysis. Model 1 tests all of the structural and agency variables in association with the dependent variable, the 100-point Index of Development Performance, DEVINDEX. Not one of the agency variables is individually significant, just as the previous Millsian analysis showed, and not one of the variables corresponding to structural theories and privileging stratification, relative need, and commercialization and modernization, respectively, is significant either. Only literacy matters.[36]

TABLE 5.6 OLS Regressions on Development Performance:
DEVINDEX is the Dependent Variable

	MODEL 1	MODEL 2	MODEL 3
Intercept	22.4 (15.7)	-60.2** (24.7)	-47.2* (22.9)

INDEPENDENT VARIABLES

	MODEL 1	MODEL 2	MODEL 3
(A) *Societal Variables*			
DRYLAND	0.09 (0.19)		
PERCPOOR	0.79 (3.48)	0.61 (3.21)	0.52 (3.24)
DISTMKT	0.21 (0.39)	0.30 (0.36)	0.27 (0.37)
INFRASTR	-0.24 (1.77)		
NCASTES	0.15 (0.97)		
CASTEDOM		-0.001 (0.05)	0.002 (0.04)
Literacy	1.14* (0.44)	0.65* (0.37)	0.52* (0.24)
(B) *Agency Variables*			
Str_PCR	-0.14 (0.68)		
Str_PANCH	1.45 (3.89)		
Str_PARTY	0.97 (5.39)		
Str_CASTE	0.25 (4.41)		
Str_VC	-0.78 (4.82)	-0.89 (4.9)	-0.69 (4.77)
Str_NEW	0.87 (2.68)	1.12 (2.7)	0.61 (2.64)
(C) *Social Capital* (SCI)		1.10* (0.34)	0.35 (0.36)
(D) *Interaction*			
(SCI*Str_NEW)			0.08*** (0.009)
N	60	60	60
R^2	0.12	0.28	0.43
Adj-R^2	0.04	0.21	0.37
F-ratio	1.56	3.39	6.27
F-probability	0.186	0.01	0.0001

Note: Standard errors are reported in parentheses. $*p <= .05$ $**p <= .01$ $***p <= .001$

However, the fit of this regression equation is very imperfect. R^2 is only 0.12 (and adjusted R^2 is almost zero). The F-probability of 0.186 indicates that a regression model consisting of these structural and agency variables is not a good predictor of values of DEVINDEX.

Model 2 drops most of these nonsignificant structural and agency variables and it adds the Social Capital Index (SCI) to the equation. R^2 improves (it now has a value of 0.28), and the Social Capital Index has a significant coefficient, in addition to literacy, which remains significant as before. Model 3 retains all of the variables of Model 2. Additionally, an interaction term is added that is calculated by multiplying together SCI with Str_NEW, the variable that measures the capability of new leadership in each village. Once again, literacy remains significant. The Social Capital Index loses significance, however, and the interaction term is revealed to be highly significant. R^2 improves further to 0.42, and the F-statistics also improve considerably, indicating that Model 3 fits much better with the data at hand.

Social capital and the capacity of new leaders both matter for development performance, and they matter in interaction with each other.[37] It is the multiplication of these two variables in any village that is critically related to its level of development performance, just as we learned previously with the help of Mills's methods and the case analysis.

A village that has the median score of 40 points on the Social Capital Index, for example, and where Str_NEW has the low value of 4 points, scores 25 points lower on development performance when compared to another village where social capital is at the same level but where agency is strong (Str_NEW = 12 points). Similarly, if we compare two villages that have the same score for agency strength (Str_NEW = 10 points, say), the village that has the higher social capital score (80 points) achieves 40 points more on development performance than the other village where SCI is only 30 points.

The higher the value of social capital, the greater the effect made by differences in agency strength; conversely, the greater the agency variable, the more the difference in performance on account of social capital. Social capital and agency interact with one another, and development performance is significantly and substantially influenced by the interaction term.

Differences in agency strength multiply the differences in social capital that exist between these villages. Villages like Nauwa are developing rapidly; others, such as Balesariya and Hajiwas, where new leaders are less effective, i.e., where STR_NEW is low, are falling behind.

New leaders are important for development, recall from chapter 3, because they assist villagers in transacting business with a diversity of state and market agencies. 1,308 (or 69 percent) of 1,898 villagers interviewed in Rajasthan said that they seek the assistance of this type of agency (and no other) when they need to procure employment on government construction works; 1,248 said that these such leaders help them get bank loans or subsidies from poverty reduction programs of the government; and 1,253 (66 percent) said they consulted such leaders regularly whenever they needed to procure seed or fertilizer from the market. Similarly, more than two-thirds of 334 villagers interviewed in the nine Madhya Pradesh villages cited the new leaders as the appropriate agency for multiple development-related tasks, providing both individual and collective benefits.[38]

The new leader understands and fulfills the requirements of villagers as well as government officials, and he becomes the trusted agent of both. Government officials are keen to find effective mediators and facilitators at the village level, who can multiply their efforts and help them implement their programs. Villagers are keen to avail themselves of benefits from expanding state programs, but they are usually unable or unwilling to deal with state agencies directly on their own account. Because of ignorance or unfamiliarity with the Indian bureaucracy's complex procedures, or for other reasons — including lack of time, unwillingness to suffer humiliation, lack of faith that any government business can get transacted without some intervention, etc. — villagers usually prefer to have agents deal on their behalf with the government machinery.

Where these agents are effective, they can help villagers gain larger benefits, individually and collectively, from government departments and market agencies.

> Many different types of schemes and programs are in operation. If they cannot understand these schemes, then of what use are the leaders? Ordinary villagers do not have the means to know about what benefits exist. Leaders perform these functions [for them]. . . . They meet with officials. They [should] know about schemes and programs. They place their village's demands before officials and politicians.[39]

How Can Development Performance Be Improved?

Case study examination as well as regression analysis supports the view, held out by Hypothesis 3, that social capital and agency strength both matter for development performance. Social capital is necessary for high development performance (all high performance villages have medium to high social capital), but it is not a sufficient condition (some low performing villages also have medium or high social capital). Similarly, capacity of new leaders is also necessary for high development performance but it is not sufficient by itself (capacity is high even among some low performing villages). However, both these factors are together sufficient for high development. Development is high in all those villages where social capital is medium or high and where agency strength is also medium to high. Development is not high in villages where even one of these factors is low. A combination consisting of high agency strength and high social capital is both necessary and sufficient for high development performance.

How can development performance be improved? Recall that a single root propensity enables villagers to perform well in multiple development enterprises. Villagers that do well by way of poverty assistance, for instance, also tend to do well in regard to livelihood sustainability, employment provision, and population control. Stimulating the growth of factors associated with this root propensity will be valuable, therefore, for assisting multiple aims of national economic development.

Analysis reveals that social capital, capability of new agents, and literacy are significantly and consistently associated with high development performance. Enhancing the levels of these three factors is likely, therefore, to stimulate faster-paced development.

Literacy is increasing substantially in villages, as we saw in chapter 3. Especially since the last two decades, villagers are increasingly sending their children to school. Development in the future is likely to benefit from the investments in education that are being made by current generations.

What can be said about enhancing social capital and agency strength? I take up this analysis in chapter 8. Social capital may or may not be possible to enhance in the short to medium term, the evidence in this regard is still not conclusive, but agents' capacities can be improved significantly through investments in educational facilities and by supporting measures that enhance public awareness of constitutional rights and government programs. Before taking up analysis relating to the correlates and constituents of social capital and agency strength, however, the effects of these variables are seen in relation to two other societal objectives: community harmony (dealt with in chapter 6) and political participation (chapter 7).

6   Examining Community Harmony: Why Are Some Villages Peaceful and Others Not?

The birth of the independent Indian nation was marred by widespread and open violence among communities divided by religion, and hundreds of thousands of Indians lost their lives and their property in the accompanying bloodbath. Breaches of public peace have occurred several times since, and the preservation of community harmony continues, along with economic development and democratic participation, to be a primary objective of public policy in India (Balagopal 1995; Brass 1974, 1997b; Engineer 1989; Mayaram 1993; Nandy 1990).

Policymakers' plans for community peace have been translated into national laws, and organizations of police and criminal justice have been set up at the national and the state levels to quell violence and to keep the peace. These mechanisms are only partially effective, however, and village-level influences shape community harmony as much or more than systems framed at the national and the state levels.

There are large differences in community harmony indicators among villages located within a small sub-region. The 60 Rajasthan villages studied here share a common framework of criminal jurisprudence, and they are regulated equally by the same police force and the same courts of law.[1] Yet, some villages are peaceful, by and large, and in others there is more conflict, litigation, and unrest.

By exploring these village-level differences and by identifying local-level determinants of peace and community harmony, this chapter makes a contribution to the discourse on community harmony in India. The three hypotheses that were developed in chapter 2 serve as a starting point for this inquiry. Does social capital matter for community harmony (Hypothesis 1)? Do structural features account better for these differences (Hypothesis 2)? Or does agency play the crucial role (Hypothesis 3)?

Social capital does matter for community harmony, the data indicate. Having a high level of social capital enables villagers to mitigate and avoid conflict. In addition, the capacity of a particular type of agency also matters for community harmony: villages that have effective Village Councils are better able to resolve the conflicts that arise.

Conflict is *averted* where social capital is high. Conflicts are *resolved* more efficaciously where Village Councils are capable.[2]

Constituted by the heads of different caste groups residing in a village, Village Councils as informal bodies continue to serve as a venue for resolving disputes. Even though a vast apparatus of courts and police stations has been set up by the modern Indian state, villagers prefer, for reasons discussed below, to take their disputes for resolution before the traditional and informal Village Councils.[3]

The spread of literacy and modern infrastructure and encroachments by a modernized state have been associated with a gradual decline of traditional village institutions (CSE 1990; Gadgil and Guha 1992). Village Councils no longer discharge some of their traditional functions — including managing common lands and assisting poorer villagers with charity (Mukherjee 1923), functions which are now handled mostly though not very well through organizations sponsored by the Indian state. However, the Village Councils continue to provide, for the majority of villagers, an important venue for resolving conflicts and adjudicating disputes.

"More than 80 percent of people's disputes [in villages] get resolved by informal Village Councils, and no more than 20 percent find their way to the police." Even among the few cases that are taken to the police, "very many are resolved by *razinama* [mutual consent]. In most cases of disputes, the Village Council hears each side and its [informal] judgements are implemented because it has powers [to impose social sanction] like *gaon-se-alag-karna* [ostracism]. Customary law is still commonly practiced in villages."[4]

Other observers, including police officials and villagers themselves tended, by and large, to agree that the Village Council resolves many more disputes and conflicts than the formal machinery of the state. "Only very serious cases are brought before us [the police]. . . . most cases are heard in the village and some judgement is passed and it is settled there."[5]

Influences originating outside the village have affected the strength of Village Councils. The spread of a democratic ethos accompanied by the decline of the old feudal order has tended to strengthen participation in these councils.

> The voice of the *mukhiyas* [Village Council elders] has become stronger. . . . In olden days, everyone had to collect at *Thakursaab's* [village lord's] house whenever he gave the call. Whatever he said, we had to do. He would take supplies from merchants and not pay for them. He lorded it over all caste groups in this way. . . . Now things are very different. Now everyone has rights. . . . There are no big differences among people of the village. We all sit together and discuss and resolve things here.[6]

The rise of party politics, however, has had the opposite effect, leading in some villages to the rise of factionalism and the decay of Village Councils.

> There is a lot of party-*bazi* [factions aligned with opposite parties]. The situation is such that no one cares for anyone else. Everyone looks out only for himself. . . . Because of this party-*bazi*, there is less mutual affection in the village. . . . Everyone supports their own party and opposes the other party. No one listens to anyone [in the village]. People take their disputes to police stations and courts, where they fight for years on end without resolution.[7]

Most important, insofar as it concerns community peace and harmony, the salience and effectiveness of Village Councils have increased as villagers are finding it hard to obtain justice expeditiously from the formal system. Courts from the subdistrict to the national level have become bogged down in a huge backlog of cases — it takes an average of 20 years for any case to be disposed, according to one estimate.[8] Villagers unwilling to countenance these delays and unable to bear the huge expenses involved in hiring lawyers, obtaining documents, and traveling frequently to towns are increasingly seeking justice under the *peepal* tree in their village. City dwellers have begun to construct similar informal councils that help them resolve conflicts efficiently and fairly at the community level.[9]

Village Councils have gained strength as a result of influences emanating from outside the village,[10] and they are playing an important part in resolving conflicts and settling disputes. Social capital is also important: conflict is

averted in villages where social capital is high. Together, these two factors —
social capital and VC strength — help one to understand why levels of community harmony vary so widely among villages located within a relatively
small subregion and sharing a common framework of law and government
institutions.

Village-Level Differences in Community Harmony

On several different measures of dispute and disharmony, some villages
have markedly higher scores than others. Land is a frequent cause of disputes
in these agricultural societies, and much litigation revolves around disputes
related to land rights. Though the percentage of villagers engaged in agriculture is nearly the same in all villages, and though the distribution of land
is also fairly similar, the number of land disputes varies substantially from
village to village. More than four times as many land disputes per capita
exist in some villages that also exhibit other features common to less peaceful
communities.

Twenty-two court cases involving land disputes have been filed by the
residents of Palri village (population 1,681), but only four such cases have
been filed by the people of Nauwa (population 1,589). On average among
all 60 Rajasthan villages, 0.45 land-related cases are on record for every
hundred villagers. Sangawas tops the list among the 16 case-study villages,
with its score of 2.79 land dispute cases per hundred villagers. Hajiwas has
a score of 2.22, and Kundai, Palri, Ghodach, and Sare have scores of 1.67,
1.33, 1.11, and 0.97, respectively.[11]

In another group of case-study villages, however, these scores are much
lower than average. Nauwa has 0.25 land-related cases per hundred villagers,
and Balesariya, Sema, and Dantisar have scores of 0.24, 0.21, and 0.11,
respectively.[12]

Villages that have more land-related cases in the courts also tend to have
larger numbers of criminal cases registered with the police. Table 6.1 shows
the close correlation that exists among several different indicators of community harmony.

Communal discord has an evident local basis, these data suggest. Villages
that have fewer land disputes and fewer criminal cases per capita also show
up relatively better on the three other indicators of community harmony,
suggesting that there is a clear division among villages: residents of some

TABLE 6.1 Indicators of Community Harmony in Villages

	Instances of Public Violence in last ten years[1]	Land Disputes per hundred residents	Criminal Cases per hundred residents[2]	Percentage of Villagers who Celebrate Important Festivals with the Entire Village[3]	Percentage of Villagers who Feel Their Village Is More Peaceful than Other Villages[3]
(A) High Community Harmony Villages					
Dantisar	0	0.11	0.45	91%	90%
Balesariya	0	0.24	1.15	91	82
Nauwa	1	0.25	0.82	92	88
Sema	1	0.21	0.81	89	94
Khempur	3	0.44	0.97	91	84
(B) Low Community Harmony Villages					
Palri	4	1.31	4.55	73%	66%
Hajiwas	5	2.22	3.94	61	67
Sare	7	0.97	3.38	68	51
Kundai	10	1.67	3.11	61	54
Ghodach	11	1.11	1.97	84	74
Sangawas	17	2.79	3.94	67	57

[1] Data for this column are taken from interviews conducted with focus groups in each village. The core of the focus group was constituted in each case by the watershed Users Committee, but other villagers also joined in these discussions. An incident of public violence was defined as an occasion involving fights in public places, stone-throwing, or other violent incidents involving bloodshed in public.

[2] The 60 Rajasthan villages fall within the jurisdictions of 27 different police stations. I wrote to the officers in charge of all these police stations, and I visited as many of these stations as I could (14 in all). I could get information from 21 police stations, pertaining to 48 villages in all.

[3] Data presented in this column derive from opinions expressed by the random sample of villagers interviewed in each of these 60 villages.

villages are generally peaceful; and residents of other villages are litigious, fractious, and less peaceable by comparison.

What village-level features are significantly associated with high and low levels of community harmony? To facilitate comparison among 60 villages in the database, an *Index of Community Harmony* was constructed, relying on four measures of harmony for which data are available for all these villages. Information on two of these items was collected using individual surveys. For the other two items, information was collected with the help of a focus group organized in each village.

The two items included within the individual survey questionnaire are reproduced below:

- At festival times, say at Diwali (Hindus) or Id (Muslims), who do people in this village get together with to celebrate?

  - Their own immediate families [1]
  - A few neighbors [2]
  - Other people of the same caste [3]
  - Many people of different castes [4]
  - The entire village [5]

- Compared to other villages, is there more or less *ladia-jhagda* [fighting] in this village?

  - More [1]
  - The same [2]
  - Less [3]

Each village's scores on these items were derived by taking an average of scores reported by all persons interviewed in this village.[13] Information on two other items included within the Index was obtained with the help of focus group interviews. These items are as follows:

- Instances of Public Violence: In the last five years, how many times has public violence — such as fights in public places, stone-throwing, or other violent incidents involving bloodshed in public — taken place in this village?

- 10 times or more often [1]
- More than 5 but less than 10 times [2]
- 5 times or less [3]
- Not even once [4]

- Compared to other villages, is there more or less interpersonal conflict among people in this village?

  - More [1]
  - The same [2]
  - Less [3]

Although these two groups of items contain quite similar items, it was thought useful to triangulate villagers' individual opinions with information obtained collectively from a gathering of assembled villagers. Village scores on the four different items are closely correlated, as one would expect, and the four different items were combined after factor analysis into a single Index of Community Harmony (ICH).[14] The ICH has a range from zero to 100 points, and higher scores reflect fewer disputes and greater community harmony.

Village scores on these four items are also closely correlated with their record of land disputes and police cases. Data relating to land dispute cases (filed in the subdivisional courts) and criminal cases (registered with police stations) were available for only 48 of these 60 villages. The correlation coefficients between ICH and land disputes (per hundred villagers) is (−) 0.61, and that between ICH and criminal cases per hundred villagers is (−) 0.79, indicating once again that villages which are peaceful in any one respect are also likely to be equally peaceful in other respects.[15]

Mean village score on the ICH is 72.1 points, standard deviation is 12.2, while skewness is (−) 0.97. Eighteen villages get scores of 60 or fewer points on this index, including Palri, Hajiwas, Sangawas, and Kundai, among the 16 case-study villages. Fifteen villages have scores of 90 points or above, including Balesariya, Dantisar, Sema, and Nauwa.

It is observed that if one arranges ICH scores by district, villages of Dungarpur district achieve consistently high scores, indicating a higher than average level of community harmony for villages of this administrative district. Village scores for the other four districts (Ajmer, Bhilwara, Rajsamand, and Udaipur) are arrayed from high to low; however, villages of Dungarpur district are consistently high. Villages of this district are better performers than villages of the other four districts. More than 80 percent of the population of Dungarpur district belongs to Scheduled Tribes, and this might have something to do with these results, but it is hard to tell within the scope of the present analysis what precisely accounts for these observed differences. A dummy variable, DUNGARPUR (coded as 1 for Dungarpur villages, and as 0 for other villages), is included within the following regression tables, and it has a high and significant value in regression analysis.[16]

Scores on the ICH for all 60 villages are regressed against the agency, structural and social capital variables, described in chapter 4. Table 6.2 reports the results. Model 1 of table 6.2 tests all of the structural and agency variables in regression against the dependent variable, the 100-point Index of Community Harmony (ICH). The Social Capital Index (SCI) is not included here, and it is brought within the analysis in Models 2 and 3.[17]

Recall that the structuralist hypothesis holds that social capital does not matter, and that differences in village results can be explained fully by referring to structural differences among these villages, including differences that have to do with extent of modernization (represented here by the variable INFRASTR); relative resource endowments (the variables DRYLAND and PERCPOOR); and stratification and heterogeneity (measured here as N_CASTES, or the number of distinct caste groups in a village). Additionally, differences in literacy levels are also considered to see if these correspond in any way with the observed differences in community harmony.

Among variables associated with the structuralist hypothesis, only the variable N_CASTES achieves significance in Model 1, indicating that villages with more diverse and stratified populations tend to be less peaceful than others. However, this variable accounts for only a small part of the overall variation in communal harmony scores. The coefficient of this variable is −0.64. Among the 60 villages in the database, this variable takes values that range from a minimum of 5 to a maximum of 22. This range of 17 points multiplied by the coefficient of −0.64 amounts to a total of about 11 points on the dependent variable, the Index of Community Harmony. The lone structural variable that achieves significance in statistical analysis is not capable, thus, of explaining any large part of the variation in community harmony scores.[18] Other variables account for much a larger range of difference in the dependent variable.

The variable Str_VC, corresponding to the capacity of Village Councils, accounts for a more considerable part of the variance in ICH scores. The

	MODEL 1	MODEL 2	MODEL 3
Intercept	-56.84 (89.25)	-12.78 (42.7)	-13.32 (37.91)
INDEPENDENT VARIABLES			
(A) *Societal Variables*			
DRYLAND	42.05 (76.47)	0.24 (0.25)	
PERCPOOR	-1.94 (15.17)	-2.14 (13.17)	
INFRASTR	0.40 (1.14)	0.52 (1.21)	
N_CASTES	-0.64* (0.70)	0.44 (0.58)	
Literacy	-2.68 (34.62)	-2.87 (33.32)	
(B) *Agency Variables*			
Str_PCR	0.54 (2.47)		
Str_PANCH	-1.34 (1.78)		
Str_PARTY	-1.27 (1.64)	-2.8 (15.34)	
Str_CASTE	1.48 (1.89)		
Str_NEW	-1.44 (1.48)	-1.41 (1.53)	
Str_VC	11.01** (4.04)	8.23** (3.67)	7.26** (2.97)
(C) *Social Capital* (SCI)		0.35* (0.16)	0.39** (0.14)
(D) *Dummy Variable*			
DUNGARPUR	27.78* (11.01)	19.23* (10.9)	19.05** (6.65)
N	60	60	60
R^2	0.42	0.53	0.45
Adj-R^2	0.27	0.45	0.43
F-ratio	3.44	6.27	15.43
F-probability	0.0014	0.0001	<0.0001

Note: Standard errors are reported in parentheses. $^*p <= .05$ $^{**}p <= .01$ $^{***}p <= .001$

coefficient of this variable is 11.01 (in Model 1), and it takes values among the 60 villages that range from a low of 10.09 to a high of 13.80 points. This difference of 3.71 points multiplied together with its coefficient of 11.01 amounts to a total of almost 41 points on the ICH, which is about four times the variation that is accounted for by the structural variable, N_CASTES. The third variable that achieves significance in Model 1 is the dummy variable for Dungarpur district.

When social capital is brought within the regression model (Models 2 and 3), the coefficient of the agency variable, Str_VC, falls somewhat, and the coefficient of the dummy variable for Dungarpur district also falls in value. These two variables continue to remain significant, however, though the structural variable, N_CASTES, is no longer significant when social capital is brought within the analysis. R^2 improves to 0.53 for Model 2, and the F-ratio also improves, indicating that the inclusion of social capital within the model results in providing a better fit with the data.[19] It indicates also that when social capital is high, villagers are better able to tide over differences that arise on account of caste.

Overall, Model 3 shows, social capital and agency strength account separately for an almost equal range of variation in community harmony scores, i.e., each accounts separately for a range of variation amounting to approximately 30–35 percentage points on the Index of Community Harmony. The dummy variable for Dungarpur district corresponds with variation to the extent of 19 points.

None of the other variables is consistently significant among alternative specifications of the regression model. The variable N_CASTES, corresponding to the extent of heterogeneity in village population, is significant only in Model 1, but even here it accounts for a relatively small part of the overall variation in community harmony scores. When social capital is considered in the analysis, these differences arising on account of caste are no longer significant for the analysis of community harmony.

The agency hypothesis is substantially upheld by the data. Recall that the agency hypothesis (Hypothesis 3) maintains that agency capacity matters in addition to social capital. The appropriate agency in this case is revealed to be, not surprisingly, the Village Council. Both the Social Capital Index and the variable related to Village Council strength, Str_VC, are highly significant in alternative specifications of the regression model.

None of the other agency variables achieves any significance. Neither political party strength (Str_PARTY), nor strength of patron-client relations

(Str_PCR), caste associations (Str_CASTE), formal panchayats (Str_PANCH) or new development-oriented leaders (Str_NEW) is significant for explaining levels of communal harmony in these villages.[20]

Structural variables corresponding to Hypothesis 2 are also not very significant for explaining these differences. In addition to the variables specified in table 6.2, some other structural variables were also considered, including population size and proportion of population constituted by the dominant caste group (CASTEDOM), but none of these variables achieved significance in alternative specifications of the regression model. The nonsignificance of literacy and the infrastructure variable (INFRASTR) provide indications that villagers' relative familiarity with the formal legal system and their ease of access to this system also have little to do with the extent of peace and harmony in villages. Reasons why this should be so are examined in a following section.

Social Capital and Village Council strength — these are the two factors that the analysis reveals to be significantly associated with the level of community harmony in villages. Just as it was supported in the case of economic development, reviewed in the previous chapter, the agency hypothesis is once again upheld in the case of community harmony. Social capital matters for both these societal objectives, economic development as well as community harmony; in each case, however, the capacity of a specific form of agency has a significant bearing upon the results.

Different forms of agency influence result in different sectors. While the new village leaders activate social capital for purposes related to economic development, the old community leaders who sit on the Village Council have significant influence on the level of harmony in villages. How such influence works is illustrated below by considering examples from the 16 case-study villages.

Considering Cases of Low and High Communal Harmony

To keep the narrative brief, I will review the case of only two villages: Palri, where social capital and Village Council (VC) capacity are both low, and Dantisar, where both of these variables have a high level. Cases also exist where one of these variables is high and the other is low. These are, however, the intermediate cases. Social capital and agency strength have an additive effect upon communal harmony.[21] Where social capital is low, villagers cannot easily avert conflict, but high VC capacity enables them to resolve conflicts efficiently. In the reverse situation, where social capital is high and the VC is weak, conflict avoidance enables villagers to maintain relatively high communal harmony scores. Villages that are high in one of these attributes and low in the other have communal harmony scores that fall in the middle range. More interesting to examine, however, are villages that occupy opposite ends of the distribution.

Palri (Low Social Capital, Low VC Capacity, Low Community Harmony)

A settlement of about 300 households in Bhilwara district, Palri is among the least peaceful villages that I studied. It is also, without doubt, the dirtiest.[22] Residents of this village find it hard to agree upon almost anything at all.

Social capital is low. "Earlier there was more unity in this village," says Madhuram Jat, who is acknowledged by other villagers as the head of their barely functional Village Council. "Now there is [a great deal of] gootbazi [factionalism]. Every person thinks he is bigger and better [than everyone else]. No one listens to anyone any more. Every person belongs to some faction. . . . There is a lot of phoot [division]; people stay apart from each other; there is little prem-bhavna [mutual goodwill]."[23]

The Village Council is not effective here because people no longer heed its decisions.

> Earlier the mukhiyas [VC elders] decided things. Now no one listens to them because everyone belongs to some faction. . . . Everyone supports their own faction and opposes the other faction. . . . [Earlier when] matters were decided within the village, there was no factionalism, if there was any ladai-jhagda [conflict and disputes] then it would be resolved by samjhaish [persuasion and understanding], the community would levy penalties. . . . [Now] there is no such thing.[24]

Factions within Palri village are allied with competing political parties. Disputes that have a local origin within the village and that involve mostly personal rivalries among villagers become grounds for vicious political maneuvering. Factions become parties, and parties work to cement factions into solid voting blocks.

Party-*bazi* in our village does not go by caste . . . it goes by *man-mutaao* [personal grudges]. . . . There is no more any unity in the village as there was in times past. *Phoot* [divisions] have arisen . . . people keep themselves allied with different parties. . . . The main issue in this village is party-*bazi*. People of one faction maintain a distance from people of the other faction. . . . If people of one faction take up some issue, some development work, for instance, then people of the other faction will always oppose this work [no matter] if it is good or bad for the village [as a whole]. . . . Party leaders make people go to the police stations to fight. . . . *Nahin to unki roti kaise pakegi?* [Else how will their bread get baked, or their ends be met?][25]

Party politics in Palri has become a viciously competitive affair that feeds off people's insecurities and that fosters in-fighting within the village, and many old-time political leaders have withdrawn themselves from this fray. Makram Rebari is 55 years old and hereditary leader of the Rebari caste, of which there are 60 households in this village. He was sarpanch of the gram panchayat for several years, but now he keeps himself apart from village politics.

Love among men has ended in this village. . . . Earlier, there was *nyaya* [justice] in the village. . . . the *mukhiyas* [VC members] were concerned with justice, and they had no relation with parties. There was discipline, there was truth. . . . Now, the village is split into halves, and no one listens to the voice of the village, each half is a party. . . . Why did this happen? You tell me. You are the scholar. . . . Unity in the village has died out. . . . [VC members] do not decide any matter because no one listens to them. . . . Now people go to the *thana* [police station], there is no discipline, now all parties do everything only to serve their own ends. . . . Rightful and deserving representatives are no longer elected. . . . Earlier, untruths were fewer, now dishonesty and lies are the norm. Parties encourage people to tell lies, to stay disunited.[26]

Parties provide avenues for people to prolong their disputes by elevating them to a higher level. There are no caste, class, or ideological differences associated with party factions in Palri village. "Rebaris are split between the two factions, as are Jats and Balais."[27] Party differences reflect, instead, some pre-existing mutual animosities and personal feuds.[28]

By deepening and consolidating personal cleavages in the village, parties

build themselves bases, which they use to compete for votes. But such a
strategy is more viable in those villages where social capital is low.[29]

In high social capital villages, as we saw in the previous chapter, parties
are used by enterprising villagers to obtain development benefits for themselves and for other villagers. In low social capital villages, however, especially in those where the Village Council is also weak, people fall prey to
the divisive tactics of political manipulators. Parties use villagers in these
cases, and not the other way around. Development is low in these villages,
and community peace is also severely eroded.

Dantisar (High Social Capital, High VC Capacity, High Community Harmony)

Located in the south of Udaipur district, this village consists of 156 households, who live in comparative peace among themselves. 11 different caste
groups live within this village, exactly the same as in Palri, but community
peace is substantially higher by any account.

The reasons for greater interpersonal amity among villagers of Dantisar
are to be found in a relatively high level of social capital in this village and
also the continuing resilience of the Village Council.[30] Badan Singh heads
the Village Council in Dantisar.

> People here abide by the *mukhiyas'* [VC members'] decisions. If there
> is any *ladai-jhagda* [fighting or conflict], then the *mukhiyas* sit to-
> gether, they decide, [and] they impose penalties — feed so much grain
> to the pigeons, we say. We in this village have little truck with courts
> and magistrates. Still, if people are adamant, if they do not listen to
> the village, then they go to court. But even these people . . . we speak
> with them . . . and we convince them to return [their disputes for
> conciliation to the village assembly]. Despite the coming of the *voton-
> ki-rajniti* ["the politics of voting," or divisive politics], we are still united
> in this village.[31]

Unity among villagers does not extend to electing representatives, however,
and elections to the gram panchayat in Dantisar witnessed fierce rivalry between two competing candidates. One of these candidates, Anoop Singh, was
supported publicly by the patriarch, Badan Singh. But even though villagers

respect Badan Singh's decisions on social and community matters, which he makes in the company of other VC members, they are not in any way compelled to follow his lead on matters concerning politics. Anoop Singh won his election narrowly; he defeated his rival candidate by a mere 15 votes.

People in Dantisar have not come apart in competing factions, however, merely because they supported different candidates in the previous election. Unlike their counterparts in Palri, villagers in Dantisar are able to tide over these differences, which are forgotten once the election has passed. "There are two political parties in this village, but people are still united. Party differences come [into play] only at the time of elections. After that, people come together again. . . . There are few disputes. If any disputes arise, then we sit together and resolve them ourselves."[32]

Rather than undercutting the traditional basis of the Village Council, the introduction of a democratic polity has tended to strengthen this body in Dantisar. The decline of feudal power and the outlawing of the worst manifestations of the caste system have resulted in creating a stronger basis for unity within this village.

Rupaji Prajapat is 70 years old, leader of the Prajapats (potters), historically a backward caste. He has been a member of Dantisar's Village Council for the last 20 years.

> There is a big difference between the [old] days of the *rajas* [feudal lords] and the present day. People have become more knowledgeable. Understanding has increased, and unity has also increased in the village. The present times are much better. If there is any shortage of food, then the government provides . . . . *Begari* [forced labor by low-caste persons] has ended. Earlier we had to go with the pots [that we made] to *Thakursaab's* [the village lord's] house, we had to listen quietly to his *phatkar* [shouting and abuse], and we never got any money [for the pots we supplied]. . . . Now there is no such thing. There is more understanding, more unity. People talk freely to each other. . . . The *mukhiyas* sit as equals and decide matters. The voice of the *mukhiyas* [VC members] is strong in this village. Villagers continue to listen to them.[33]

High-caste persons in the village offer a similar view concerning the reinvigoration of the traditional Council following democracy and egalitarian reforms. Onkar Ba is 75 years old, hereditary leader of the Jain (trader) community in Dantisar, and member of the Village Council for 35 years.

Five years ago, the BJP was strong in this village; now it is the Congress Party. . . . This has made no difference . . . people follow the *mukhiyas* in this village. There is no *ladai-jhagda*. Party-*bazi* has made no difference [to peace] in this village. . . . People help each other in times of need. For [resolving] conflicts, for development work, we collect everyone in the village and we decide collectively. People contribute money according to their capacity. Everyone takes part in *shramdaan* [donating labor]. There is no violence here, no *goondagardi* [hooliganism].[34]

Developments originating outside the village — the rise of party-based political competition, the growth of government development expenditures, etc. — have produced different effects in different villages. In some villages, such as Palri and Hajiwas, for instance, party-based factions have arisen that feed off discord and disunity among villagers. In other villages such as Dantisar, Balesariya, Nauwa, and Sema, for example, the same developments have produced more positive effects. Peace and community harmony are highest in villages where social capital is high and where the Village Council continues to be legitimate and effective.

What factors account for the continued relevance of traditional Village Councils in modern times? Given that it is led by old men, and that women and younger villagers cannot usually attain leadership positions in these bodies, why do villagers not supplant the functions of Village Councils with the more democratic and more egalitarian machinery of the modern state? Why, in other words, do villagers continue to rely upon these Councils when they can go, instead, to the police and the formal court system? To address oneself to these questions, one must look at the manner in which the Indian villager relates to the formal systems of administering justice.

Justice and the Indian Villager

Imposed by the British colonial administration, the formal system of criminal justice has always been poorly understood and relatively inaccessible to the Indian villager. R. Carstairs, a British colonial administrator, writing at the dawn of the twentieth century, describes the situation prevailing at that time.

The system of criminal justice we had to administer . . . was modelled on, but differed widely from, the English system. The key to the difference was the fact that in England justice is a popular institution; in Tipperah [a rural district in Bengal] it was the business of the Crown. In England, justice goes to the people; in India, the people come to justice.

An Englishman with a grievance finds near his own door a magistrate to take his information and grant a summons. If it is a Police matter, he calls in the constable of the beat. If the case goes to trial, the tribunal is never far off. Everything is done under the vigilant eye of the strongest and fairest public opinion in the world. . . .

In Tipperah the law provided that, as in England, the case should be instituted before a magistrate, or before the Police. But in all this wide area, as large as Norfolk and Suffolk combined, there were only two magistrates. . . . An aggrieved person might have to travel any distance up to fifty miles over a roadless country. . . . A Police matter, again, involved a journey to the station, perhaps ten miles off. Trials . . . involved much hanging about, many journeys to and fro, and a constant spending of money.

Here there was no public opinion; no press; no official aid. . . . He [the villager] had to find his way to this strange tribunal in an unknown land as best he could, in charge of the police, whose tender mercies he dreaded, or alone.[35]

The situation of the villager in relation to the formal system of criminal justice has not changed a great deal in the century that has passed since this was written. While she no longer needs to travel an entirely "roadless" country, the villager still has to go a considerable distance — both physical and psychological — before she can avail herself of justice from the formal legal system.

Even after national independence, the system of justice is still administered by the state from above. It remains based on the Indian Penal Code (devised in 1860) and on other legislation of colonial origin[36] — and it is not derived from popular conceptions of right and wrong.

There is still a lot of hanging about involved in dealing with the police and the courts, many fruitless journeys to be performed, and large expenditures of money are associated with formal litigation, which most villagers can ill afford. The "tender mercies" of the police are still dreaded by most villagers (and many town people), and most Indians would quail at the thought of entering a police station for any purpose.

Even if these formidable obstacles of distance, distrust, fear, and expense are surmounted, however, there is still no reassurance that justice will, in fact, prevail. In addition to being expensive and hard to access for most Indians, justice in the formal system involves huge delays, sometimes spanning litigants' entire lifetimes. "You realize how appalling the state of our judicial system is [when you figure] that it will take our courts 324 years to clear the backlog of cases. . . . It takes an average of 20 years for a case to be disposed of in our courts — if it isn't land-related. If there is land involved, the story gets much grimmer. . . . Consider that the average Indian lives in a village and in villages most litigation involves land . . . [and] you realize how hopeless the judicial system [is] in rural India."[37]

More than 100,000 cases are pending in the Rajasthan High Court alone, and hundreds of thousands remain to be decided by its subordinate district courts.[38] Ravi Dangi, a leading lawyer of Bhilwara city, informed me of a court case concerning the eviction from a landlord's property of a tenant who had refused to pay rent for ten years. "Even when ownership of the property was not in dispute, even when a lawyer was the plaintiff [and was thus knowledgeable about court procedures] and even when most witnesses were lawyers and other city persons and [so were relatively] easy to find and summon to the court, it took all of 17 years [for the courts to decide this matter]." "Normally," he added, "it takes decades, generations [to decide any case]. . . . Thousands of cases from the 1960s are pending decision in the courts. . . . Nothing is sure but the expenses."[39]

The number of courts and magistrates has increased greatly since the time described by Carstairs, but justice remains very much a distant affair for most Indians. Among villagers, consequently, the formal court system is often regarded not so much as a venue "for settling disputes, [as] for furthering them" (Weiner 1963: 130).[40] "Today there can be little doubt," concludes Moog (1997: 49–50), that "courts are often of little or no value in dispute settlement. For many people they have effectively lost their legitimacy in the performance of this function . . . much of what these courts are doing is not 'meaningful' dispute resolution at all. Many of the cases filed with them are grounded in illegitimate claims, and in legitimate cases the judgments themselves are often worthless, or nearly so, due to the time lapse involved, changed circumstances, or simply the unenforceability of the decisions. . . . The winner in name may, in fact, turn out to be the loser, financially and otherwise."

The situation of the police has also not changed appreciably; in fact it has regressed in many respects in the decades following national independence. While the government has been keen to plow ever increasing funds into programs of rural development, and while international aid agencies have paid to build new offices and buy new vehicles for new development programs, such as women and children's welfare, watershed development, and adult education, the backbone of civil administration — the police and the magistracy — remain confined to poorly appointed offices and primitive facilities — especially in the rural areas.

"There are 12 constables on average in a rural police station, of whom generally two will be found away on leave; two are in the office (they are the 'station writers'); one functions as the *dak* messenger [he carries letters back and forth between the police station and senior police officials and the courts]; and between three to five constables work full-time as process servers [they serve summonses received from the courts]." This leaves between one and three policemen, on average, for patrolling, investigating, and controlling crimes in an area that may serve up to a hundred thousand people. "The SHO [Station House Officer, or police station in-charge] has to try hard to catch hold of some constable for getting crimes investigated."

"Earlier we [the police] had very regular contacts with the village. There was a *gasht* [beat constable] chart, and all villages were visited regularly. Now the police are under much greater pressure [to do other things], and we go to the village only after there has been a serious enough crime and hardly at all before. . . . Preventive policing is no longer possible. By and large, we are not *pro*-active now; we are *reactive*."[41]

New duties, including protecting city-based VIPs and dealing with frequent law and order situations in the urban areas, have taken a severe toll on the resources available with the police in rural areas.[42] Several techniques of evasion are utilized to cope with the increasing workload of complaints and investigations. To register a case, the police must have before them a *written* report, which is hard enough for most villagers to provide. Further, unless the crime is of a very serious nature, involving murder, rape, or armed robbery, for instance, the police prefer, if they can, to ignore the complaint and drive away the complainant. "To show a higher registration of cases is not good . . . our objective is to reduce the number of registrations . . . and to increase the percentage of solved cases."[43]

Resources available with the police force have not increased much to keep pace with their increasing duties. And the methods employed by them have not changed much either, especially in the rural areas.

Incidents of police "atrocities" are frequently reported by the Indian media, and allegations of torture and corruption keep alive an image of the police force that was born during or even before the time of colonial rule. Brass (1997a: 331) describes in detail a contemporary incident in a village in Uttar Pradesh which "reveals the local police in a characteristic mode — implicated directly in local conflicts, open to bribery, [and] capable of loot and harassment of innocent persons."

Villagers in Rajasthan share a similar image of policemen. "The old image of the *Thanedar* [colloquial term for police station officer-in-charge] remains alive in the minds of villagers — a drunken lout, who will beat you, speak roughly, and demand money. The reality is very different today, but this image remains."[44]

And so most people prefer to stay away from the police and the courts. Where social capital is high, villagers are able to avert conflicts. Where Village Councils are strong, they are able to resolve the conflicts that arise. It is only in the remaining villages, where both social capital and Village Council strength are low, that villagers' disputes take the form of police registrations and cases in courts. Such inhospitable venues are successfully avoided by other villagers.

Incentives associated with a modernizing state — the spread of education, a huge increase of public expenditure in rural areas, and rising two-party competition — have provided ground, as we saw in the last chapter, for the emergence of new development-oriented leaders in these villages. Another set of incentives, also given birth by the structures and processes of the Indian state, help to keep alive the traditional Village Councils. Because the police and the courts are slow, costly, and relatively inaccessible, and because the processes followed by these bodies have little in common with popular conceptions of justice and fair play, informal and traditional institutions are kept alive in the rural areas.

What can one say, however, about the future of these Village Councils? Will they continue to function as before? Should they be strengthened further by devolving formal legal authority to these bodies? Or will they simply wither away as modernization advances further into the countryside? It is useful to view the historical context.

Village Councils in Historical Perspective

Early British administrators observed how justice was traditionally dispensed in villages in India.

> A committee of elders for settling disputes is assembled in every form and condition of village, whether in the north or south [of India], and quite independently of what the village constitution is. It was, and still is, to some extent, the universal Indian mode of settling caste, social and land cases, and especially boundary disputes. . . . It is not a mere occasional assembly of elders, called together when there is a dispute, but the continuing and ordinary governing body as opposed to a single "headman," or the oligarchy of a few chiefs and officers (Baden-Powell 1899: 13).

This informal panchayat or Village Council, remains today, as it was in ancient times, a body "composed of different caste-peoples, representative of all communities . . . [and dealing] with things that pertain to the whole village" (Mukerjee 1923: 261, 264). Though it may be an exaggeration to imply that there is or ever was "implicit faith in the justice of the [Village Council], and implicit obedience to its decrees," the Council in most villages still today "hears every side of a case, has men to advocate each side and does not give its judgements until they are unanimous. . . . The democratic procedures of these bodies is [also] obvious. In many [Councils], the headman is elected, and is dismissed if he is found wanting. Partiality will be sufficient ground for dismissal. . . . Ex-communication follows the refusal [of any villager] to obey the [Council's] decree. . . . The strength and the efficacy of the [Council] depend upon the active co-operation of each caste" within the village (ibid.: 271–272).[45]

Village Councils were born, it is claimed by Mukerjee, in times when the central state had a sparse presence in the countryside, and when villagers had only themselves for regulating their common affairs. That such Councils continue relatively unhindered is an indication that in the Indian countryside, at least, modernizing influences are unevenly distributed among different societal domains.

Every single village among the 69 that I visited in Rajasthan and Madhya Pradesh has a functioning Village Council — and accounts from other parts of Rajasthan and India indicate that such councils may be widespread over large parts of the country.[46] Elders from each of the caste groups in the village sit on the Council, and the number of representatives from each caste group is roughly proportional to its share in the village population.

The courtroom for these occasions is constituted by some public space, either a platform built under a large and ancient tree, or a courtyard adjoining the village temple. The Council meets usually once every quarter or whenever some complaint is put before it by an aggrieved villager. Evidence is taken from both sides to a dispute, witnesses are heard, and judgment is pronounced in this open assembly of all villagers. Proven wrongdoers are punished, and the penalties imposed upon them usually involve fines that are either paid into a village common fund or which are scattered as grain to feed birds in the vicinity.[47]

Elements of continuity with the past combine with features that have changed considerably since national independence. Village Councils are no longer exclusively dominated by the upper castes. Even as historical accounts have attested to a form of egalitarian functioning,[48] villagers of different castes commonly perceive greater equity in recent times in the process and decisions of Village Councils. *Panchas* (representatives) of all caste groups sit as equals on the central platform. Though representatives of the scheduled castes (previously known as untouchables) sit some distance apart or even at a lower level from other panchas, they have equal say in the decision, particularly when a person from their own caste group is involved as a party. Meetings of the Council are never organized in somebody's house or in spaces that might belong exclusively or primarily to a particular caste group. Participation in the Village Council has become more democratic and egalitarian. As a result, VCs in most villages have grown in strength.

Egalitarianism does not, however, cross gender or age boundaries. Representation on the Council is an all-male affair: the representative of each caste group is a hereditary leader of that group, and his eldest son succeeds to this office, unless he shows himself incapable of villagers' respect, in which case he is replaced by another male member of the same caste.[49] Women and younger men attend meetings of the Council, and they contribute to its discussions, but the mantle of decision belongs to the elderly men.

Though blemished in this regard, the Village Council still provides the only forum where villagers can have their disputes resolved expeditiously and at low cost. Its standard of judgment and its conceptions of appropriate behavior derive from everyday life in village India, while medieval England and ancient Rome provide exemplars for the post-colonial system of formal jurisprudence. Should traditional and informal Village Councils be strengthened, therefore, or should they be superseded by making the formal court system more effective and more accessible?

What Can be Done?

The most numerous classes of disputes in the countryside involve relatively petty matters, such as boundary disputes, damage to crops by stray cattle, theft of small property, destruction of fences, and altercations between individuals leading to minor injuries. More than 80 percent of such cases are being resolved informally by the Village Council, and less than 20 percent reach the police and the formal courts.[50]

Should Village Councils be granted formal legal powers to decide such matters? To elicit their preference in the matter, the following question was put to 1,898 villagers in Rajasthan and 334 villagers in Madhya Pradesh:

> In all villages there are some disputes among individuals, such as disputes about land boundaries, about animals straying into other people's lands, about people abusing or insulting one another, and so on. In some villages, such minor disputes are resolved within the village itself, by the village council of elders, perhaps. In other villages, people take such minor disputes to the police. What do you feel: should the authority for settling such disputes and punishing wrongdoers vest with the police, or with the village council of elders?

Three options were listed, along with an open fourth category:

- Option 1: Such authority should vest with the police alone
- Option 2: Such authority should vest with the village council of elders alone
- Option 3: The police and the village council should both have authority

Table 6.3 reports the results of this inquiry.

1,515 Rajasthan villagers (80 percent) selected Option 2, preferring to have formal judicial authority rest exclusively with the Village Council. Only 61 villagers (3.2 percent) prefer the current arrangements, where formal authority vests with the police alone, and they selected Option 1. The remaining 17 percent selected Option 3, i.e., they wanted to see such authority exercised simultaneously by both the Village Council and the police, but not by the police alone.

These proportions were fairly similar in Madhya Pradesh, even though this state has a separate police force, reporting to a Director General based in its state capital, and a separate system of district courts, which reports up to the separate Madhya Pradesh High Court. Of the villagers interviewed in

TABLE 6.3 Percentage of Villagers (Rajasthan and Madhya Pradesh) Who Prefer Formal Legal Authority for Dispute Resolution to Vest With the Police or the Village Council

	Only VC	Only Police	VC and Police Equally
All Villagers	79.9	3.2	16.9
By Age			
Ages 45 and over	79.4	3.4	17.2
Ages18 to 44	80.6	3.0	16.4
By Gender			
Male Villagers	85.8	1.3	12.9
Female Villagers	75.4	5.1	19.5
By Education			
No education	78.7	4.0	17.4
Some education	83.4	1.3	15.3
By Caste			
Upper/ Middle Castes	77.4	2.6	20
Backward Castes	76.2	3.1	20.7
Scheduled Castes	78.5	4.9	16.6

Madhya Pradesh, 82.6 percent selected Option 2, and only 2.4 percent expressed themselves in favor of Option 1.

The proportions do not vary significantly even when villagers are categorized by age, gender, education, or caste. In general, three-quarters or more villagers of any category prefer that authority for adjudicating disputes reside exclusively with Village Councils. Less than five percent are in favor of continuing with the present system.

The present system, where the police have exclusive authority and Village Councils have no formal authority at all, is *not* the preferred choice of the vast majority of villagers, more than three-quarters of whom would prefer a system in which the informal Village Councils are given formal legal recognition.

Would the rural majority in favor of such devolution be able to have its way? Most likely not. Laws and systems of governance are devised in India (as in other developing countries) by people who live in cities. Systems at the grassroots that do not mesh with structures at the top — and which fit poorly with the image of a "modernized" state — are likely to be viewed with extreme disfavor by city-based policymakers. No matter how valuable these systems are for people who live in villages, traditional modes of social organization can hardly be admitted within the formal apparatus of a "modern" state. And so a gulf remains that separates the written-down world of laws and state organizations from the lived world of ordinary villagers.

Some agency is required that enables rural residents to meet their demands for a just, peaceful and developing society, and which enables them to gain the benefits of governance for themselves. The state sends down myriad tentacle organizations — gram panchayats, village cooperatives, *mahila mandals*, etc. — but these organs of the state fail to bridge the gaps adequately. They are not designed for making representations upward, from the village to the state, and so they remain merely implementing agencies of a central state, useful for the state, but not very helpful to people.

Villagers need to devise bridging mechanisms of their own. Where interaction with the state is profitable, agents emerge who bring the village closer to the state. A set of young, development-oriented leaders has emerged who enable villagers to interact productively with development agencies of the state. In other domains, however, where interaction with organs of the state is likely to have costs more than benefits, domains such as justice and conflict resolution, as we have seen in this chapter, another set of agents help to keep the village insulated from the state.

It is a tribute to the inventiveness of villagers to recognize the diversity of mechanisms they have developed to cope with the inroads of a modernizing state. Preferring to engage with the state in some domains and to withdraw from its embrace in other domains, villagers have fashioned responses in each area that match best with their needs and their capabilities. These capabilities — and the fact that they vary significantly from village to village — are rarely admitted in policy discourse. Academics' and policy formulations usually regard villages as a more-or-less homogeneous mass, something to be developed, to be administered, to be policed. This examination of social capital serves as a corrective to this homogenizing vision. Villagers' capacities matter as much as state policies, and it is a limited vision which ignores the former for the sake of the latter.

7 Democratic Participation in Rural North India: Social Capital and New Political Entrepreneurs

We have seen in the last two chapters how social capital matters for economic development and community peace. Social capital is important for each of these outcomes, we observed, but agency is needed in each case for mobilizing the stock of social capital and obtaining a flow of benefits.

One other societal outcome remains to be investigated in this book. Proponents of social capital maintain that participation in democracy will also be higher — and more people will be involved actively in a larger range of political activities — in communities where the stock of social capital is high. "Citizens in civic communities," it is claimed, "demand more effective public service, and they are prepared to act collectively to achieve their shared goals" (Putnam et al. 1993: 182). We have investigated this claim before by examining *outcomes*, such as economic development benefits, that villagers derive by acting collectively. In this chapter, we will examine their involvement in the *process* of governance and public decisionmaking.

While superior institutional outcomes are no doubt useful for reinforcing faith in the democratic process, people's involvement in this process is also important for the health of democracy. Wider participation helps entrench democracy by reducing the appeal of alternative, violent and nondemocratic options. Prospects for stability become enhanced as increasing numbers of individuals and groups "buy into" the democratic system and out of nondemocratic alternatives (Bunce 1996; Przeworski 1991). It is important, therefore, to investigate separately the breadth and quality of participation in democratic processes.

To judge the quality of participation, political scientists have distinguished between procedural and substantive democracy (Diamond, Linz and Lipset 1995). In the context of India, Sabharwal (1997: 137–140) claims that while procedural democracy is fairly well established, including "a Constitution, a differentiated party structure, and periodic acts of choice, between parties, by an electorate for elections to legislatures," the practice of democracy is substantially frail. "By and large, the formal structures have been instituted readily; but there has been only limited awareness of the complex range of skills, values, ideas, motivations and practices necessary for their satisfactory operation." Participation in the substance of democracy is low in this estimation; consequently, he expects, "violent practice will increasingly invade the democratic routine."

Additional reasons to worry about the future of democracy in India are provided by other analysts. The decline of the Congress Party, regarded by many as a crucial component of democratic stability in this country (Weiner 1967, 1989); unstable coalitions and frequent elections (four elections to Parliament and numerous state assembly elections were held in the 1990s); and slow economic growth, averaging less than one percent per annum in real per capita terms have gone together with mobilization by diverse groups seeking to gain particularistic benefits for themselves (Brass 1994; Rudolph and Rudolph 1987). This combination of circumstances is a potent mixture that can lead, according to Huntington (1968) and O'Donnell (1973), to a breakdown of democratic rule and a crisis of governability.[1]

Different reasons have been offered to explain why democracy survives in India, against the odds, as it were, and diverse formulations are proposed for strengthening democratic stability in the years to come. Building strong reformist parties (Kohli 1987, 1997); recognizing and upholding the roles played by local leaders (Mitra 1991, 1992); and decentralizing power to village *panchayats* (Crook and Manor 1998; Kurien 1999; Mathew 1994) are offered by analysts as competing explanations and alternative programs of action.

No comparative analysis has been provided so far, however, that helps to evaluate these competing explanations against each other. Which particular type of agency — political parties, village leaders, or *gram panchayats* (village government) — or caste associations or patron-client links — provide a viable means for expanding participation in democracy, particularly among poor and low-status Indians? To what extent does caste throw its divisive shadow upon political participation by villagers in India? How has long-term structural change — rise in literacy, modern infrastructure, and growth of mass media — influenced patterns of participation in the Indian countryside? And how do community-level features, such as social capital, influence the level and quality of participation?

The examination in this chapter is intended to provide some answers to these comparative questions, particularly for two Indian states, Rajasthan and Madhya Pradesh, that have a combined population of more than a hundred million persons. In particular, we will assess the utility that social capital might have for enhancing participation in democracy, and we will test the alternative views about social capital that were presented in chapter 2.

Comparing Political Participation Levels in Villages

In order to evaluate the alternative hypotheses, we need a standard for comparing political participation among villages. Because it needs to reflect participation in the substance (and not merely the routine procedures) of democracy, our standard of comparison cannot rely solely on voting percentages.

A methodology for comparing participation in democracy is available, which has been developed over long years of use in many different countries, both industrialized and developing. A number of works, including Almond and Verba (1965), Rosenstone and Hansen (1993), Verba, Nie and Kim (1978), and Verba, Schlozman and Brady (1995) have helped to refine this methodology, which measures political participation with the help of a survey administered among a random sample of the concerned population. Reflecting our interest in substantive democracy, political participation is understood in these works as involvement in "all those activities by private citizens that are more or less directly aimed at influencing the selection of government personnel and/or the decisions that they make" (Verba, Nie and Kim 1971: 9). "Involving far more than voting in elections, it includes election campaigning, collective action around policy issues, contacting political representatives, and direct action like protests and demonstrations" (Bratton 1999: 552).

Two works that have applied the survey methodology quite recently — Verba, Schlozman and Brady (1995) and Rosenstone and Hansen (1993) — were consulted for designing the survey instrument that was administered in 1999 among 2,232 villagers, equally men and women, in 69 villages of Rajasthan and Madhya Pradesh. Items of the survey questionnaire, reproduced below, were adapted from these two works, after making changes to take account of differences in language and political system.

Voting

- In talking to people about elections, it is found that they are some-times not able to vote because they are not registered, they don't have time, or they have difficulty getting to the polls. Think about the *Vidhan Sabha* (MLA) elections since you were old enough to vote. Have you voted in all of them, in most of them, in some of them, rarely voted in them, or have you never voted at all in a MLA election?
- Now thinking about the local (*Panchayat*) elections that have been held since you were old enough to vote, have you voted in all of them, in most of them, in some of them, rarely voted in them, or have you never voted at all in a panchayat election?
- Think back to the recent *Vidhan Sabha* elections held last year in winter. Did you happen to vote in that election?

Campaign Work

- We would like to find out about some of the things people do to help a party or candidate win an election. During the last *Vidhan Sabha* (MLA) election campaign, did you talk to any people and try to show them why they should vote for one of the parties or candidates?
- Did you go to any political meetings, rallies, speeches or things like that in support of a particular candidate?
- Did you do any (other) work for any one of the parties or candidates during that election?
- How much did your own work in the campaign contribute to the number of votes the candidate got in your village — a great deal, some, very little, or none?

Contacting

- How often in the past one year have you gotten together with others in this village and jointly petitioned government officials or politi-cal leaders — never, once, a few times, or quite often?

- What about the local *panchayat* leaders? Have you initiated contact with such a person in the last twelve months?

Protest

- In the past two years, have you taken part in any protest, march or demonstration on some national or local issue?

Responses to these questions were scored from high to low depending upon how often or how widely the respondent participated in the concerned activity. In relation to the first question reported above, for example, a response of "voted in all MLA elections" was given a score of 5, "voted in most of them" and "voted in some of them" were scored 4 and 3, respectively, "rarely voted" was scored 2, and "never voted at all in a MLA election" was scored 1. The scores that individual citizens received on each of these questions fall into a quite distinct pattern, as discussed below.

Voting, campaigning, contacting and protesting cover a wide range of activities associated with involvement in democratic decisionmaking, and they represent different means by which citizens seek to influence the choice of policy as well as the selection of policymakers. However, not all citizens take part equally in each of these activities. Increasingly higher costs must be borne by citizens who participate in the more proactive forms of self-expression. Citizens who take part in protests must expect to devote significant amounts of time; there is also a possibility that they might be placed under arrest or that lawsuits might be filed against them. Contacting does not usually involve the possibility of arrests or prosecution, but it does require a significant expenditure of time and may also involve travel expenses, as when villagers travel to district headquarters to meet with government officials or party representatives. Campaigning is likely to be less costly than protesting or contacting, but it is more costly than voting, which is the cheapest and least proactive of all forms of political participation. Because of these relative costs, many more citizens take part in voting, and progressively fewer citizens are involved in campaigning, contacting, and protesting.

Ninety-one percent of villagers said that they had voted in the last-held election to the state legislature.[2] However, only 25 percent of respondents said they had campaigned actively on behalf of a party or candidate; 33 percent said they had personally contacted a public representative at least once during the past year; and only 11 percent said they had taken part in any protest or demonstration.

It would appear from these figures that only a small fraction of rural Indians are actively participating in the process of democracy. As table 7.1 below shows, however, these participation rates are not dissimilar to those observed in other democracies where similar surveys were conducted at about the same time.

These national variations are interesting because they provide some preliminary indication that participation rates may not be sensitive to level of wealth: rates observed in the United States are not much higher than those seen in India and Zambia, and the figure for campaign work is considerably lower in the United States than it is in the other two countries. However, these national-level comparisons are at best only indicatory.[3] Whether or not wealth makes any difference to political participation in rural India and what other factors are associated with high participation rates will be verified below through a comparison of village-level data.

To compare political participation rates among the 69 Indian villages, an Index of Political Activity is constructed from responses to survey questions related to the three activities of campaigning, contacting, and protesting. Voting figures are not very reliable, as we saw earlier. Additionally, participation in voting does not seem to respond to the same set of factors as participation in the other three activities. Factor analysis conducted on the opinions reported by north Indian villagers shows that the three survey items, which correspond to voting, all load highly on a single common factor. A

TABLE 7.1 Political Participation in Three Countries

Percentage who said they had participated in:	United States (n= 2,517)	Zambia (n=421)	India: Rajasthan and MP (n= 2,232)
Campaign Work	8%	25%	24%
Contacting	34	38	33
Protest	6	7	11

Sources: For United States data: Verba, Schlozman and Brady (1995). For Zambia data: Bratton (1999).

separate common factor is associated, however, with the other seven survey items related to campaign work, contacting, and protest.[4] Voting forms one dimension of political activity; and campaign work, contacting and protesting — the more voluntary and less socially obligatory acts — constitute a separate dimension. Because we are interested in substantive and not merely procedural participation, it helps to confine our attention to the second of these two separate dimensions.

Factor analysis indicates that individual respondents who have high participation scores on any one of the seven survey items related to campaigning, contacting, and protesting tend, in general, to have high scores on each of the other six items. Villagers who are active in respect of one form of political activity, say campaign work, are likely to be equally active in the other two forms, contacting and protesting. A single underlying quality or set of attributes seems to be at work that makes some villagers participate more actively than others. To identify these attributes and to distinguish more active from less active villagers, an *Index of Political Activity* is constructed by taking a simple sum of scores of these seven items.[5] The least active individuals achieve a score of zero points on this index, while the most active respondents score a full 100 points.[6] Village scores are calculated for the purpose of this analysis by taking a simple average of scores over all respondents of each particular village. Since a random sample of respondents was interviewed in each village, the sample mean is an unbiased estimate of the mean score for the entire village population. Village scores range from a low of 10.8 points (village Dholpuriya) to a high of 54.5 points (village Kucheel). This difference in scores between these two villages, amounting to about 44 percentage points, provides the range of variation that must be accounted for by the alternative hypotheses that were presented in chapter 2.

Explaining Differences in Political Participation Scores

Why are political participation scores higher in some villages compared with others? Recall the three competing hypotheses that were presented in chapter 2. According to the social capital hypothesis (Hypothesis 1), differences in political activity levels across villages should be accounted for substantially by their respective levels of social capital. Hypothesis 2, the structuralist hypothesis, regards differences in relative modernization and factors such as caste differentiation to be critical; while Hypothesis 3 suggests that agency matters in addition to social capital. These hypotheses are tested first with the help of statistical analyses. Case-study data are examined next to explain the statistical results.

Variables corresponding to the three competing hypotheses are examined in table 7.2 below with the help of regression analysis conducted on survey data aggregated at the village level. Village scores on the Index of Political Activity provide the dependent variable for this analysis.

Model 1 considers variables corresponding to the structuralist hypothesis, and among these only DISTMKT (distance to market in kilometers) is found significant in statistical analysis. This variable has a negative coefficient, indicating that all else being the same, villages located further away from the market are likely to be sites of comparatively less political activity. The size of this coefficient is quite low, however, ranging between minus 0.05 and minus 0.07 in alternative specifications of the model. The maximum distance to market among villages in the sample is 44 kilometers and the minimum distance is 4 kilometers. This difference of 40 kilometers, multiplied by the coefficient of this variable (-0.06), accounts for a total of only 2.4 points on the Index of Political Activity, or about five percent of the observed variance.[7]

None of the other structuralist variables — NCASTES (number of distinct caste groups), CASTEDOM (percentage of village population belonging to the numerically dominant caste), or PERCPOOR (percentage of village population below the poverty line) — is significant in alternative specifications of the regression model. Variables corresponding to the structuralist hypothesis are mostly not significant for understanding differences in political activity. R-squared for Model 1 is just 0.24 and adjusted R-squared is a bare 0.13. The F-ratio is 2.24, which is quite small when compared with the corresponding figure for other specifications of the regression model.

Model 2 introduces social capital within the analysis. R-squared rises to 0.54, and the F-ratio rises to 6.80. In addition to DISTMKT, which remains significant as before and with nearly the same size of coefficient, another variable, the Social Capital Index, also achieves significance. The coefficient of the Social Capital Index is 0.27. Village scores on the Social Capital Index vary from zero to 100 points. This variable helps account, thus, for variation to the extent of 27 points on the Index of Political Activity, which is quite considerable, given that the entire variation in the dependent variable occurs within a range of 44 percentage points.

TABLE 7.2 OLS Regressions on Political Activity (Village-Level Analysis): 100-point Index of Political Activity is the Dependent Variable ($n = 60$)

	MODEL 1	MODEL 2	MODEL 3
Intercept	25.38 (35.91)	-19.35 (27.8)	-25.36 (31.32)
INDEPENDENT VARIABLES			
(A) *Societal Variables*			
POPULATION	0.0005 (0.002)	0.002 (0.002)	
DISTMKT	-0.05* (0.02)	-0.07* (0.03)	-0.07* (0.03)
INFRASTR	0.27 (0.69)	0.41 (0.55)	
NCASTES	0.65 (0.46)	0.48 (0.28)	0.38 (0.22)
CASTEDOM	-0.35 (0.84)	-0.31 (0.86)	
PERCPOOR	0.72 (6.09)	0.62 (5.77)	
LITERACY	4.40 (14.8)	5.47 (11.61)	7.40 (9.95)
(B) *Agency Variables*			
Str_PARTY			0.58 (2.19)
Str_CASTE			0.52 (1.33)
Str_PCR			-0.47 (2.26)
Str_VC			0.35 (0.74)
Str_NEW			0.64* (0.31)
(C) *Social Capital* (SCI)		0.27**** (0.04)	0.13*** (0.04)
(D) *Interaction*			
(SCI*Str_NEW)			0.02**** (0.004)
N	60	60	60
R^2	0.24	0.54	0.72
Adj-R^2	0.13	0.45	0.64
F-ratio	2.24	6.80	9.88
F-probability	0.03	0.0001	0.0001

Model 3 introduces the agency variables. Variables related to the capacity of six different forms of agency are considered here, including political parties (the variable Str_PARTY), caste associations (Str_CASTE), patron-client linkages (Str_PCR), the informal Village Council (Str_VC), and the new, younger, educated and non-caste based village leaders who have emerged within the last two decades (Str_NEW). Only the last of these six variables achieves significance in regression analysis. None of the other five agency forms are significant for political activity levels in villages. Though social capital continues to be significant, the coefficient of the Social Capital Index is lower compared to Model 2.

The capacity of the new leaders (Str_NEW) is significant both by itself and also in interaction with village social capital. An interaction variable — constructed by multiplying together each village's scores on the Social Capital Index with its scores on the variable Str_NEW — is highly significant.[8] R-squared rises further in Model 3 and it has a value of 0.72. Adjusted R-squared is 0.64, and the F-ratio is 9.88, implying that Model 3 provides the best overall fit with the data.

Result: Social capital is significantly associated with high political activity by villagers, this analysis indicates. The effects of social capital are multiplied, however, by the capacity of new village leaders. The agency hypothesis (Hypothesis 3) is substantially upheld by the data on political participation — just as it was before for the cases of economic development and community harmony. Social capital matters for political participation by villagers, and the capacity of new leaders adds to (and also multiplies) the effects of social capital. No other variable is equally significant for political activity at the village level.

Variables related to the strength of caste associations (Str_CASTE) and of patron-client links (Str_PCR) are not significantly associated with the extent of political activity by villagers. Neither do any of the other variables related to caste — N_CASTES and CASTEDOM — achieve significance in this analysis.

Differences in political activity levels among these villages cannot be explained with the help of any caste-related variable. Even when these data were analyzed at the level of the individual villager, high caste rank was neither highly nor significantly correlated with the Index of Political Activity. Upper and middle caste persons are not likely to participate any more actively in diverse political activities compared to backward and scheduled castes, these data show. Campaigning, contacting, and protesting — the three activities included within the Index — are not undertaken to any greater extent among upper compared to lower castes.

Voting also does not appear to be greatly influenced by considerations of caste. No more than 405 of 2,232 respondents (18 percent) in Rajasthan and Madhya Pradesh said that they voted once or more times as their caste fellows had advised. On the other hand, 1,688 respondents (75 percent) said they had never voted at the say-so of their caste brethren. These preferences might be colored by a need to appear socially and politically correct. Even when the question was asked in the abstract, however, and not in terms of the respondent's personal preferences, very few villagers regard caste leaders as commanding any considerable influence on voting. Only 352 of 2,232 villagers (16 percent) felt that candidates to electoral offices would do well to contact caste leaders for mobilizing votes in their village. Almost three times this number, (54 percent) felt that candidates would gain larger numbers of votes through contacting the new political entrepreneurs (*naya netas*).

The rise of these new non-caste-based entrepreneurs, described in chapter 3, marks a qualitative change in political organization at the local level. It has the effect of neutralizing to some degree the advantages for political participation that were possessed earlier by high-caste and relatively wealthy villagers.

Neither caste nor wealth is any longer closely associated with high individual scores on the Index of Political Activity. As measured by landholding — an appropriate measure of wealth in these rural areas and also one for which data are relatively easy to compile — wealth seems to have little to do with high levels of political activity. The correlation coefficient between landholding (measured in hectares) and the Index of Political Activity is only 0.08, and it is not statistically significant, implying that poorer villagers are as likely as richer villagers to have high political activity scores.[9]

Analyses dealing with other parts of India have also shown that upper caste and greater wealth may no longer be significantly associated with higher political participation. "The odds that a *dalit* [scheduled or backward caste] will vote are much higher today than that of an upper caste. This has been accompanied by a significant rise in their sense of efficacy and their involvement in more active forms of political participation. . . . The textbook rule about political participation is that the higher you are in the social hierarchy, the greater the chance of your participating in political activity. Contemporary India is perhaps the only exception to this rule" (Yadav 1999: 2397).

Wealth and caste rank do not matter much, but some other individual-level attributes that do have high and significant correlation coefficients with the Index of Political Activity include gender, information, and education.[10] Gender has a high and negative correlation with the Index. The correlation coefficient is (-0.61),[11] implying that women participate relatively less than men. Women score, on average, 16.5 percentage points less than men on the Index of Political Activity. The gender differential is considerably lower, however, among women who are educated.

Education has a high positive correlation with political activity level. Every additional year of school education is associated with scoring an extra 2.1 points on the Index of Political Activity, as shown by regression analysis using individual-level data. Education and information both add separately and substantially to individuals' political activity scores. A variable, Information, was constructed by considering seven different sources of information commonly consulted by villagers, and it was found that every additional source of information helps add, on average, an additional four points on this index.[12] Adding six extra years of education and three additional sources of information helps to make up for the quite considerable disabilities that are associated with being a woman in rural Rajasthan and Madhya Pradesh.[13]

Education, Information and New Political Entrepreneurs

Political activity based on caste affiliation and caste rank is becoming less common, and social and political relationships in these villages are being transformed as education and information are spreading in the countryside. A new type of political entrepreneur has emerged in these Indian villages, and these new agents help mobilize villagers to act collectively for multiple purposes. Political participation is high in villages where social capital is high *and* where new political entrepreneurs are more capable, as we saw from the statistical analysis presented in the previous section.[14] This section discusses in more detail how and why these agents are important for activating social capital.

The new political entrepreneurs have come up in villages mostly within the last two decades. The rise in educational achievement in the countryside is important for explaining the advent of these new political entrepreneurs, as we saw in chapter 3. However, the role of party competition is also relevant. In Rajasthan and Madhya Pradesh and in most other Indian states, political parties have no permanent grassroots-level organization in rural areas.[15] Party offices do not exist in even one of the 16 villages that I studied in depth. The nearest party office is usually located at the district capital, which is more than a hundred miles distant from some villages. There are almost a thousand villages in each district on average, so district-level party officials have little time for or motivation to attend to each village individually. District-level party offices are bare-bones operations in most cases; thinly staffed, barely financed, and poorly led, they are incapable of conducting hundreds of separate negotiations with the dozens of government officials who function at the district-level (Kohli 1990, 1994; Kothari 1988).

A local level of government — the village *panchayat* — is in existence, but most villagers regard the *panchayat* as being responsive more to the central government than to themselves. *Panchayats* are mostly seen to function as implementing agencies on behalf of the central government, and they are not considered to be very useful for making upward representations on behalf of villagers (Bagchi 1991; Jain 1993). Hardly any villager thinks of turning to *panchayat* representatives for assistance with any activity related to contacting, campaigning, or protesting. Table 7.3 presents some comparative statistics in this regard.

Because few institutional links, such as parties or local government or trade unions, are either available or useful for these purposes, villagers turn to other kinds of intermediaries for handling their interaction with state agents. Historical accounts, such as Cohn (1969), Frykenberg (1969) and Spear (1973), have usually identified richer and upper caste villagers as providing the crucial linkage between the state and ordinary villagers. However, these caste- and patronage-based personalities can no longer effectively represent villagers' demands before government officials. The nature of tasks requiring mediation has changed, and higher caste does not by itself furnish the abilities, such as education, information, and knowledge of rules and procedures, that have become essential for the new purposes.

The 197 caste- and patronage-based village leaders interviewed for this exercise were found to have only 3.5 years of education on average. Nearly one quarter of these leaders are entirely illiterate. The new set of younger leaders who have emerged in villages in the recent past, mostly within the past two decades, have almost three times as much education — 9.6 years of education on average. They are much better informed than the old leaders, and they have regular contacts with government officials and party politicians, more than twice as often as the old leaders, as seen from Table 2.2, which provides these and other comparative statistics.

This new group of non-caste-based political entrepreneurs now provides

TABLE 7.3 Demand for Mediation by Villagers[1]

Number of villagers who said they would approach each type of leader for help related to:[2]	TYPES OF AGENCY (Leadership)				
	Party	PCR	Panch	Caste	New
(a) Dealing with the police or the *tahsil*	114	72	101	372	1,172
(b) Getting a bank loan or an insurance policy	92	317	166	146	1,118
(c) Learning about agricultural technology	107	49	313	203	1,149
(d) Replacing a non-performing school teacher	84	25	332	215	1,218
(e) Getting wage employment	87	64	274	156	1,431

Party = Political Party Officials
PCR = Leadership based on Patron-Client Relations (the old *Jajmans*)
Panch = Elected Village Panchayat Officials
Caste = Leaders of Caste Groups
New = New Village Leaders (*Naya Netas*)

[1] Leaders were identified in each of the 69 villages following a positional and a reputational approach, as explained in Appendix A. First, all those persons were identified who held leadership positions in official and unofficial organizations, including the village panchayat, the village cooperative agency, in the different caste groups, and in relations based on patronage. Next, people were asked about other persons in the village who exercised leadership on behalf of villagers, whether or not they were part of any formal or informal organization. The new leaders were identified mostly from the second set of questions. They are, in this sense, a residual category, but also one that corresponds to a fairly distinct profile—they are younger, more educated, better informed, and better connected outside the village than leaders of any of the other categories.

[2] Numbers in the table reflect the preferences expressed by a random sample of 2,232 villagers. Row totals may not add up to this total number because some villagers did not respond to a particular question or selected a residual "other" category.

the crucial mediating link between villagers and the state. A majority of villagers seek the assistance of the new village leaders in matters related to contacting, campaigning, and protesting. When they need to make contact, for instance, with banks and insurance companies, with the police or the *Tahsil*, with district-level party officials, or with any of a huge number of extension agencies and other government departments that implement development projects and employment-generating works, most villagers seek assistance from the new leaders.

More than 2,000 residents selected by random sampling among 69 villages were asked which type of leader they would consult if they needed to make contact with a specified list of government departments and market-based organizations. They were asked to select between five different leader types — including party politicians, old patrons, *panchayat* representatives, caste leaders and the new village leaders. Table 7.3 reports the results. In each of five different situations, involving mediation with different government or market organizations, no fewer than 60 percent of villagers selected the new leaders as their first choice.

Their higher levels of education give younger villagers a distinct advantage in dealing with agencies of the state. Even though it is a necessary condition for exercising the new leadership, however, education is hardly sufficient for this purpose. A great deal of hard work is also required — to scurry around from office to office; to fill forms and lobby government officials; to work on their behalf supervising construction labor; to fill forms and keep accounts; arrange elaborate "site visits" when officials or politicians come to the village. To do all these things and also to attend to villagers' everyday concerns — to take a sick person to hospital, often in the middle of the night, and to keep up one's contacts among doctors; to have someone's government pension approved and paid out in time (to know the associated rules and the people in charge in the *Tahsil* and Block Offices); to get someone a loan sanction from a bank — to badger, pester, entreat, implore, threaten, cajole and bribe, if necessary — and to do these things day in and day out — this is not an easy life.

Persons born to comfort and privilege find it hard to tread these paths. And the new leadership is drawn disproportionately from educated youngsters belonging to middle and lower segments of the caste hierarchy. Backward castes constitute 41 percent of the population, but 49 percent of new leaders (103 of 211 new leaders in 69 villages) belong to this caste group. Scheduled Castes — previously marginal to village politics — now contribute more than their share of the new leadership. They constitute 22 percent of these villages' population, but 26 percent of new leaders hail from these castes. Proportionately fewer new leaders are drawn from among the upper and middle caste groups.

The great demand for their services among fellow villagers gives the new leaders positions of influence within the village. Unlike the old village patrons, however, the new leaders cannot easily use their special connections with the state to benefit at the expense of other villagers. The spread of education and information among other, especially younger, villagers has given rise to a more widespread capacity for independent action. Leaders, young or old, can no longer easily deceive a significant percentage of villagers. Leadership exercised in the spirit of service is more likely to create a fund of obligations. And new leaders who have political ambitions or who aspire to higher social status are careful not to overcharge villagers for the services they provide.[16]

Not all new leaders behave in these laudable ways, but there is a significant percentage — more than half, as far as I could make out — who are in it for the long haul and who invest in institution building at the grassroots. Instead of dividing villagers by caste or religion, these new leaders build wide-ranging social networks that bring together villagers of different castes. The larger and more cohesive this network, the more successfully a new leader can negotiate with government officials and party politicians; and the more successful these negotiation, the larger the benefits that follow, and the stronger the appeal of the new leader in his village. Larger networks promise greater collective benefits, and greater benefits help new leaders consolidate their position in the village. There is little incentive, consequently, for new leaders to confine their activities to members of a particular caste or religious order.

The Changing Relation Between Caste and Political Activity

Hardly any new leader in these Rajasthan and Madhya Pradesh villages has built their network on a caste or religious basis. Jabbar Khan, a Muslim and prominent new leader of Chitakhera village in Ajmer district, counts Phoosalal, a Hindu, as his principal lieutenant. Their political action group includes people of different castes and religions.[17] Other new leaders, including Logar Lal Dangi of Nauwa, Khivaram of Sangawas, and Goverdhan

Gayari, also do not build caste-based constituencies. The example of Vishnu Suwalka, another new leader who I met, is illustrative in this regard.

> My father had a tiny business, making and selling illegal liquor. I am the second of six children. There was no money in the house, but it does not cost too much to study in these times. . . . I walked to the high school ten kilometers away from our village. Then I did a bachelors degree in 1985 and I got a law degree in 1988. I stayed with my relatives at that time. I got two hundred rupees a month [about ten dollars at that time] from home for all my expenses. In 1989 I started working as an independent criminal lawyer. . . . I had to develop a new client base, so I worked harder than other, more established lawyers. I found my clients among poorer villagers who can be found hanging about the courts, lost and unknowing. I asked these villagers what brought them here, and I went with them to the police station, to the Tahsil, to other offices, wherever their work lay. I learned the ropes and I got to know the personalities in these offices. Slowly villagers developed faith in me. I helped Kalals [his caste fellows] but also poor persons from other castes — there are many poor Brahmins, you know — as well as poor Regars, Rebaris and Rajputs. It was never my intention to serve any particular caste. I wanted to work among all those persons, regardless of caste, who were denied justice because they did not have enough money or approach. . . . I have a good practice in Gangapur by now, and people have elected me unopposed to the position of sarpanch of my village. Even twenty years ago, it was not possible to imagine a Kalal becoming a lawyer and a leader.[18]

Non-caste-based political entrepreneurs in these villages are more successful than others in delivering economic benefits and providing avenues for greater political participation, and villagers associate with these entrepreneurs regardless of caste or religion. It is not clear, however, whether a similar pattern will be replicated all over India.

Analyses of national-level survey data provide some indication of a declining association between caste and political activity. Interpreting a range of recent national surveys, conducted by the New Delhi-based Center for Study of Developing Societies and other organizations, Oldenburg (1999) observes that:

Citizens now do not vote according to the orders of caste leader, political patron, or even husband; nor are their votes typically "bought"
in any direct way. There is a genuinely secret ballot. . . . The survey
data reveal some important facts that run counter to the conventional
wisdom on voter behavior. . . . In 1996, 75 percent of the sample said
they were not guided by anyone in their voting decision; only 16 percent of the men admitted to being guided by someone else (p. 97).
Of the 25 percent who sought advice, only seven percent sought it
from caste and community leaders. . . . that is, less than *two* percent
of the electorate got direct advice on how to vote from caste and community leaders. . . . The most important survey data show the change
over time. In 1971, 51 percent of the respondents agreed that it was
"important to vote the way your caste/community does" (30 percent
disagreed), but in 1996 the percentages were reversed: 51 percent disagreed with that statement (29 percent agreed). . . . In 1998, "caste
and community" was seen as an issue by only 5.5 percent of the respondents in one poll (*Frontline/Centre for Media Studies* poll of January 1998; *Frontline*, March 6, 1998) and ranked last of nine issues in
another (*India Today/ORG-MARG* poll; *India Today*, January 5 1998).
All the evidence points to the fact that these respondents are correct:
members of particular castes (and especially members of the large
caste groupings such as "Dalit" or "Other Backward Classes") can be
found voting for every party. . . . In India as a whole, moreover, political polarization along social cleavages has declined. It is less and less
true that knowing the caste of a voter lets you reliably predict the party
he or she will vote for. If there are two parties competing in a constituency it does not necessarily mean anymore that they represent two
distinct social groups.

Some other analyses show, however, that caste is being reconstructed by
ambitious political entrepreneurs, who build constituencies for themselves
by promising economic gains and political efficacy to others of the same
caste. Caste-based associations have been erected and strengthened for delivering these types of benefits in some parts of India, and people in these
regions have mobilized for political action together with others of the same
caste group.[19]
    In other parts of India, however, caste has lost ground as a unit of political
activity. Reporting on *panchayat* elections in the state of Uttar Pradesh held

in summer 2000, for example, Pal (2000: 3289), observes: "the caste factor, which has been considered the bedrock of Indian politics, was pushed to a secondary position. . . . In fact, caste character has, to some extent, been [replaced by] group character, comprising different castes and communities having almost similar socio-economic status in rural society and economy."

Development is the primary concern of more than 85 percent of villagers, as we saw in chapter 1, and leaders who help uphold their development-related aspirations are valued and supported far more than leaders of any other types. Different forms of political association have been created in different places to answer to citizens' economic and political needs. Caste has been reconstructed in some places to respond to these needs. But in other parts of India, as in the Rajasthan and Madhya Pradesh villages studied here, different forms of political organization have arisen that are not based on caste or religious linkages.

Diverse dynamics are in place in different parts of India, it appears, and it is necessary to observe new and emergent forms of political organization that are gaining ground in different parts. Political organization in terms of caste or any other category cannot any longer be assumed. Rather, it will need to be explained in terms of finer and more localized levels of analysis.

Decentralization and Fragmentation

New, non-caste-based forms of political organization have emerged in Rajasthan and Madhya Pradesh villages studied here, and parties have had to adjust their electoral strategies. The locus of public decisionmaking has changed as a consequence, becoming more localized than before. In this section and in the concluding part of the next chapter, I will review how these changes have arisen and how they are likely to affect the future course of democracy in these regions.

The new village leaders — commonly known as *naye neta* (new leaders) or *naye karyakarta* (new social workers) in these Rajasthan and Madhya Pradesh villages — represent villagers' collective and individual demands to the state. But they also mediate in the reverse direction, performing important agency functions on behalf of government officials and party politicians. Government officials need to assemble large numbers of villagers to participate in departmental programs — else they are unable to achieve their targets of work. Politicians need to pull villagers together for voting or for participating in rallies organized by their party. Because they lack any independent means for contacting individual villagers — and because villagers will hardly turn out at the behest of someone they do not know and cannot trust — officials and politicians both look to individuals in the village who are well known and frequently contacted by villagers in need.

Parties are not distinguishable from each other in terms of programs,[20] and they do not usually have any permanent organization at the local level, so all parties are driven to seek alliance with men of influence in the village.[21] Where they previously contacted traditional patrons in the village — landed, upper caste and older males — officials and politicians are increasingly striking bargains with other villagers whose influence in the village has become relatively stronger, especially over the past three decades. "In each village we try to find out — who are the persons who help villagers in need. Who takes them to the hospital when they are sick or wounded? Who goes to the police station with them? Who helps them to get bank loans? . . . Most important, who gets them wage employment and who makes sure that wages are paid in time. . . . these persons we contact in each village."[22] Parties compete among themselves to attract such persons into their fold, and government patronage in the form of development benefits is bartered in return for promises of allegiance.

Instead of reaching out to relatively large territories controlled by regional satraps or high-caste patrons (Migdal 1988), parties are increasingly forced to compete at the localized level of an individual village. Their electoral fate depends in large part on how many villages they can attract into their fold — and each village must be competed for separately and individually. Political competition has fragmented in this manner. There are multiple webs in which party organizers are entangled at any time — and the new village leaders are the spiders in these webs. They mediate between villagers, on the one hand, and parties, on the other; and the majority of villagers believe that parties can gain more by contacting new leaders compared to anyone else in the village community.

One would expect parties and new village leaders to have symmetrical relations based on mutual dependence, for each has some resources — followers and votes in the case of village leaders, and access to development benefits in the case of parties — that the other side covets. But relations between parties and new leaders are hardly symmetrical in practice, especially in villages where the community is bonded together by strong structural and cognitive bonds — where social capital is high — and where village leaders are more knowledgeable and skillful at brokering deals.[23] One new leader recounts an interesting experience in this regard.

We belonged to the BJP at that time, but just before the *panchayat* elections [in 1997], we had a dispute with the BJP district organizers about who was to be the candidate for *sarpanch* [*panchayat* chief] from our village. So we [my followers in the village and I] decided to switch over to the Congress party. The Congress people gave their ticket [party nomination] to all ten people that our group nominated [replacing their own regular candidates], and we won nine of ten seats in the panchayat election. . . . In 1998, when the MLA [state assembly] elections were being fought, Shanti Lal Chaplot [BJP leader of Udaipur district and Speaker of the State Assembly at that time] came to the village and asked us to support the BJP candidate. He got us [funding for] a new water supply scheme, a new community center, and also for a new *anganwadi* [child care center] opened in our village. In return, we gave him our votes, and we campaigned for his candidate in neighboring villages.[24]

Parties compete among themselves to attract villages into their fold. And the new village leaders use these occasions as opportunities for obtaining higher state development benefits for their village.

Communities that are more close-knit and better led mobilize more often and in larger numbers — and they also set the terms for these engagements. The new leaders' capacities to mobilize villagers and to deliver collective benefits are influenced critically by the level of *social capital* in a village. Villagers who have a tradition of acting together for mutual benefit and who expect to act collectively in future are more likely to forge a united front and work together for mounting political pressure on party candidates and government officials. Villagers torn apart by distrust and jealousy are less likely to act collectively for mutual benefit, and their leaders have to work with a smaller resource pool.

Much lower level bargains are struck by leaders who are not backed by a united village, and collective action is more sporadic and low-key in villages with low social capital. Political activity is muted also where the new leadership is less capable. Leaders known to lack bureaucratic know-how are unlikely to achieve much on their behalf, so villagers will rarely act to their direction.

High social capital assists with the tasks of political mobilization. And capable leadership is required for rewards to be achieved with high probability. The strengths of caste associations and patron-client links are not significant for explaining political participation at the village level. Differences in structural attributes such as caste stratification and relative poverty are also not significant. The level of social capital and the relative capacities of the new political entrepreneurs account, however, for a substantial part of the variance in political activity levels. Social capital and the capacity of new leaders are two critical factors that help direct participation into channels — such as campaigning, contacting, and protesting — which are normal and healthy and which weave dissent into the fabric of democratic rule and legitimate process.

8 Conclusion

Social capital matters significantly for achieving diverse societal objectives, as we saw in the previous chapters, but those communities achieve the best results where capable agents are available along with high social capital. Social capital represents a potential — a propensity for mutually beneficial collective action. Potential needs to be mobilized, however, and directed toward carefully selected ends. Agents assist in these tasks, and they help enhance the productivity of social capital. To conclude this book, I will briefly revisit the evidence that supports this view.

I will also enlarge upon the crucial role being played in rural Rajasthan and Madhya Pradesh by a newly arisen group of village agents. Efforts by ordinary villagers have become more productive because of program information and tactical advice provided by these new agents. New forms of political organization have come up in these villages that cut across caste and religious boundaries. Educated, self-made, and not dependent upon caste rank or feudal lineage, the new village leaders are restructuring political relationships. Ordinary villagers are asserting their rights, and parties are reconstructing electoral strategies in order to deal with these changes. As these effects come to fruition in the years to come, some basic changes will be seen in the workings of Indian democracy. It will become stronger, as I discuss in the second half of this chapter, and also more locally driven.

I. Social Capital and Societal Performance: The Role of Agency

Three principal objectives — economic development, community peace, and democratic participation — were examined in this book. Outcomes related to each of these objectives were assessed for a group of 69 village communities located in two Indian states, Rajasthan and Madhya Pradesh (see Appendix A for methodology and site selection). Fairly significant differences were observed among these villages in terms of their economic, social, and political achievements, even though they are all located within a fairly small and relatively homogeneous region.

Several bodies of theory were consulted to account for these differences (chapter 2), and case study as well as statistical analysis were employed to evaluate the alternative hypotheses. A locally relevant scale for measuring social capital was developed in chapter 4, and variables corresponding to other competing and complementary explanations were also made operational. The following results were derived from this analysis.

Economic Development

We saw in chapter 5 that no matter which development activities one considers, some village communities tend, by and large, to perform better than other village communities. Village performance was assessed with respect to four quite different development programs. It was found that villages that outperformed others in respect of any one of these programs also performed better, on average, in each of the other three programs.

Some villages are high development performers, by and large, and others are low performers. The nature of individual programs does not matter so much for development performance; some villages possess a particular quality which enables them to achieve superior performance across multiple programs. Agencies concerned with promoting development would do well to identify and support this village-level attribute.

Alternative factors associated with different bodies of theory were examined to assess which of them might matter for development performance at the village level. Social capital was found to be significant for explaining differences among village communities, but social capital does not by itself account for a substantial part of the observed variation. Agency capacity matters in addition to social capital, and it is the capacity of a particular type of agency — the newly emerged set of younger and more educated village leaders — that matters most for development performance.

Many high social capital villages do not have commensurately high scores for development performance. Some villages with lower social capital achieve higher development scores. Agents are more capable in the latter set of villages. Consequently, their lower stock of social capital is more productively employed. Why this should be so is examined theoretically in chapter 2, illustrated by case studies in chapter 5, and discussed briefly in the following paragraphs.

Village communities with high social capital have a greater propensity for mutually beneficial collective action. People in such villages can more easily get together to launch collective action. They can surmount free-rider problems more readily than villages that have low levels of this resource.

But collective *action* is not the same as collective *achievement*. To achieve higher benefits, social capital must be harnessed and directed intelligently toward incentives available in the external environment. Strategies must be adopted that are capable of achieving success. Undirected social capital might end up achieving nothing more than a lot of collective inputs. For high outputs to be obtained, however, something more is required in addition to high social capital. Capable agency helps provide the missing ingredient.

For achieving economic benefits, villagers must know how to get the best deals from state organizations and market operations. To sell their crops at the highest price, they need to know, for instance, what prices are currently being offered for different grades of the same crop, on what basis traders differentiate between these grades, what stratagems traders adopt to undervalue crop quality (or underestimate its quantity), and how these ruses can be countered effectively. High social capital villagers can act collectively to put pressure on grain merchants, but without being well informed about price trends and market practices they can hardly achieve very much. Agents play the role of information providers and they help make the contacts required by the village community.

Similarly, in dealings with the state, collective action is likely to be more effective when villagers are well informed about which government departments provide program benefits, how applications are made to these departments, whose support is likely to help one's case, and how such supports can best be assembled. Social capital helps villagers mobilize more readily for these efforts. But agents provide the information and access that can help make collective action effective in terms of its aims. By assisting people to select goals that are achievable and adopt strategies that can work in their environment, agents help to enhance the productivity of social capital. They reduce transaction costs, and they help villagers select suitable targets for collective action.

Political parties have traditionally performed these roles in Western contexts, but parties are only very poorly articulated at the grassroots level in India (Kohli 1990; Weiner 1989). Regardless of how well they might connect with each other thus, people in Indian villages — particularly poor people, the majority — face severe difficulties when they try to connect with officials of the state. Political parties have not made it easier for the majority of Indians to make contact with public officials, a theme I develop further in the second half of this chapter. And local governments in rural north India, the village *panchayats*, are also not very useful to villagers for making contact with government officials.[1]

To gain access to officials of the state and to avail themselves of the benefits of government programs, villagers must take recourse to other agents. Individual as well as collective efforts are made fruitful through the actions of the new village leaders, who have come up in the last twenty years in response to this vacuum of upward representation, and who help villagers make beneficial linkages with state organizations and market operations. The rise of these new village leaders over the past twenty years has occurred alongside vast increases in educational achievement, the spread of mass media in rural areas, a huge increase in the government's outlay for rural development programs, and intensified two-party competition (chapter 3).

Another type of village agent is associated, however, with collective action in the domain of community peace. There are costs to collective action — in terms of time spent, alternatives foregone, and resources devoted — and agents are preferred who can maximize the benefits that can be achieved after incurring these costs. Different agent types have comparative advantage for different societal domains. While the new village leaders are important for achievements related to economic development, another type of local agency, the traditional Village Council, matters more for the goal of community harmony, examined below.

Community Peace

Even though they are all located within a relatively small geographic area, and even though they are all exposed to the same formal structure of legal administration, villages differ considerably among themselves in terms of numbers of unresolved disputes and recorded instances of public violence. Villagers' subjective assessments of harmony and peaceful co-habitation also vary considerably (chapter 6), and these differences tend to compound one another. Villages that have fewer land disputes and fewer criminal court cases per capita are also the ones in which residents feel more at peace with one another and where they get together more often to celebrate festive occasions with the entire community. Such villages are peaceful and harmonious, by and large, but there are some other villages that are more prone to conflicts, violence, and disharmony.

A host of alternative village-level features were examined in chapter 6 to account for these differences. We looked at whether remotely located villages were more or less peaceful than those located closer to major market centers. Does the caste composition of a village have anything to do with its record of violence and disharmony? Does literacy or relative poverty have any bearing upon these results?

It was found that none of these factors matters very much for explaining differences in community harmony. Differences in their stocks of social capital matter a great deal, however, along with differences in the capacity of a specific agency type.

Conflicts and disputes get *averted*, the analysis reveals, in communities where social capital is high. And conflicts are *resolved* more efficaciously where the traditional Village Council (VC) is more effective. Together, these two village-level attributes, social capital and VC capacity, explain a considerable part of the observed variance in community harmony scores. No other agency type matters, and no other village-level attribute is significant for these results. Only social capital and VC capacity differ systematically between peaceful and violence-prone villages.

Working to enhance social capital and to strengthen VC capacity will help to bolster community peace in general, and separate policies will be required to address each of these characteristics. While social capital is a *collective* attribute of villagers, i.e., it is a product of the relationships that exist among members of a village community; agency capacity is an *individual* trait. High social capital and high agency capacity do not always go hand in hand, as we saw in chapter 4. Where they do, however, in such villages and at such times, community harmony exists at a relatively high level. The same is true of economic development and of political participation (examined below): agency capacity is independent of social capital, and it is the combination of these two separate elements that associates most closely with superior results.

Participation in Democracy

More than 70 percent of Indians live in villages, and the quality of democracy in India depends in large part on how well people in its rural areas are integrated within mainstream political activities. Different political activities — including voting, campaigning, contacting, and protesting — were examined in chapter 7. Very large numbers of villagers participate regularly in voting, but there is also a considerable number, comparable to other democracies, who take part in campaigning, contacting, and protesting. Differences between villages are quite pronounced for the latter three activities — voting percentages fluctuate relatively little across villages — and an Index of Political Activity was constructed by combining together each village's scores for campaigning, contacting, and protesting.[2] Village scores on this Index differ considerably from one another. Some villages are quite active politically, and others are quiescent, by and large.

According to its proponents, social capital should matter a great deal for explaining these differences in political activity scores. Citizens in high social capital communities "demand more effective public services," it is claimed, "and they are prepared to act collectively to achieve their shared goals. . . . their counterparts in less civic regions more commonly assume the role of alienated and cynical supplicants" (Putnam et al. 1993: 182).

Factors corresponding to different hypotheses were examined to understand the observed difference in political activity scores. In addition to social capital, a number of other village-level features — including membership in political parties, relative poverty, caste composition and caste leadership, literacy, and distance from urban centers — were also examined.

Social capital is significantly associated with political activity scores, it was found. However, differences in agency capacity tend to multiply the effects of social capital, and it is the combination of these two factors that is most closely related to political activity scores. No other factor matters as much, not party membership, not caste composition, and not degree of modernization.

The new village leaders, who help villagers achieve collective economic benefits, also help facilitate their participation in democratic governance. Their activities are assisted when there is a high stock of social capital; it is easier to mobilize villagers in such communities. But high social capital is most productive where capable agents are also available. It is the interaction of these two variables — social capital and agency capacity — that is crucial for distinguishing between high-participating and low-participating villages.

Agency matters in Rajasthan and Madhya Pradesh villages because information about state institutions and government programs is not widespread among villagers and also because few channels are available that enable villagers to connect effectively with market and state institutions. Communications between villager and state and villager and market are weak. This does not have to do merely with illiteracy and poor-quality infrastructure, though these features certainly do make a difference. Villagers' ability to benefit from government programs and market incentives is limited as well because of the weakness of middle-level institutions, those that stand between the grassroots and the national levels.

Parties are weakly organized in the Indian countryside, and local governments serve merely as implementing agencies of a centralized state. No other institutionalized forms of mediation are available that can help villagers make connections with state officials and party politicians. Consequently, villagers face a large gap in the middle — between individual and community groups, on the one hand, and the state, on the other — which they find hard to bridge by themselves. "In contemporary India," as Yadav (1999a: 2399) concludes, "the chain that links peoples' needs to their felt desire to their articulated demand to its aggregation and finally to its translation into public policy is impossibly long and notoriously weak."

High social capital is not enough by itself to make up for weak middle-level institutions. Members of a community having a high level of social capital are more willing and more able to act collectively for mutual benefit. But to what ends should they target their collective efforts, and what strategies should be adopted? What tactic will succeed, for instance, in getting an employment-generation project allocated to their village? Should they apply and wait their turn, or should they become more proactive and petition some official (which one?), should they meet with some politician (who?), or should they be even more active still, mounting demonstrations and blocking roads? Which is the most effective use of collective resources, including time and money? Which route promises the most efficient conversion of social capital into mutual benefits? And which routes will result in wasted efforts and high costs and should be avoided?

Weaknesses in middle-level institutions produce large gaps in information and access, and these gaps make it difficult for citizens to take full advantage of the opportunities for self-development that are made available by state organizations and market operations. Agency becomes important when middle-level institutions are weak, a situation that seems to be quite common in developing and transitional countries, as revealed by accounts from contemporary Russia,[3] Uganda,[4] Bolivia,[5] and Central America.[6]

The role that middle-level institutions play is depicted schematically in figure 8.1. The top half of figure 8.1 represents the formal institutions — of state and market — that generate incentives and disincentives for individual and collective action. Structuralists — whose views we examined in chapter 2 — believe that these incentives and disincentives determine the quality of societal performance. The broken arrow leading from incentives to results represents their view.

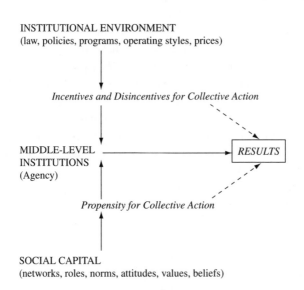

INSTITUTIONAL ENVIRONMENT
(law, policies, programs, operating styles, prices)

Incentives and Disincentives for Collective Action

MIDDLE-LEVEL
INSTITUTIONS
(Agency)

RESULTS

Propensity for Collective Action

SOCIAL CAPITAL
(networks, roles, norms, attitudes, values, beliefs)

FIGURE 8.1 Structure, Social Capital, and Middle-Level Institutions/Agency

Proponents of social capital believe, on the other hand, that societal performance is shaped by the propensity for mutually beneficial collective action which exists within community groups and local organizations. This bottom-up view of societal performance is represented in the lower half of figure 8.1.

While both the structural and the social capital view attest to important influences, neither is sufficient by itself to account fully for institutional performance. High social capital helps produce better results in a high-incentive environment. And appropriate institutions are more rewarding in situations where social capital is high. However, incentives and propensities must be *connected* for obtaining the best results — and middle-level institutions or capable agents are required for making these connections.

Middle-level institutions, such as parties, unions, interest groups, trade associations, etc., help citizens make connections with state and market organizations. When these institutions are weak — and when no other capable agency is available — social capital and institutional incentives remain disconnected, and societal performance suffers.

National-level institutions and community-level social capital can both be made more productive in these contexts through policies that reduce the width of the missing middle or which help build strong bridges over the existing gap.[7] What is important to examine in each situation are the pathways that citizens can use to connect with — and to bring their social capital to bear upon — opportunities made available by the state and by markets.

The value of a social capital examination lies not so much in the fact that different communities are found to be differently endowed with this asset. So much could have been expected, given Putnam's and Coleman's path-breaking work on this subject. What is more valuable for policy is the uncovering of pathways through which social capital has its effects in any particular context and for any particular purposes.

Conduits and pathways were not thought important when social capital was examined in the contemporary Italian context (Putnam et al., 1993). But such pathways are found to matter in India and in other countries. A possible explanation for this observed difference can be sketched as follows. Agency does not show up as a separate factor in the analysis of contemporary Italy because middle-level institutions are reasonably strong in this context and they provide the necessary agency. Political parties were quite strongly organized, and regional governments were actively strengthened through a policy of decentralization, implemented at the start of Putnam's study. Social

capital could flow relatively unhindered into institutional performance because such middle-level institutions were already reasonably strong.[8]

But middle-level institutions were weak in the case of Weimar Germany,
where "parties had little in the way of formal organization, especially at the
grassroots level, and were really active only at election time. . . . National
political institutions and structures proved either unwilling or unable to
address their citizens' needs" (Berman 1997a: 410–411). Social capital did
not translate into good results, and it had quite the opposite effect in this
case.

The similarity with contemporary rural India is remarkable: parties in
India usually have no organization at the village level, and citizens find it
hard to have their problems addressed adequately by the government machinery (chapters 3 and 7). Middle-level institutions are weak in India, as
they were in Weimar Germany, and independent agency has an important
role to play in both these cases and also in similar cases elsewhere.

Because the supply of mediation services is weak from institutional
sources, villagers in Rajasthan and Madhya Pradesh have developed their
own solutions to the problem of the missing middle. They have strengthened
one type of agency — the traditional Village Council — to deal with issues
related to community harmony (chapter 6). Another type of agent — the new
village leader — has emerged spontaneously and in response to modernizing
influences, particularly the growth of literacy (chapter 3), and these agents
help villagers deal with matters related to economic development and political participation.

Improving performance in these contexts will require paying attention to
two factors — level of social capital and agency strength — that were found
to be consistently associated with high performance in different domains.
Performance should improve, this analysis indicates, if the levels of social
capital and agency strength are both enhanced through purposive action.

Social capital may or may not be easy to build up over the short term.
The evidence in this regard is mixed and so far inconclusive. Putnam et al.
(1993) propose that social capital is accumulated only very slowly. "History
determines," they claim, and "historical turning points . . . have extremely
long-lived consequences" (1993: 179).

Work by other analysts indicates, however, that social capital may not
be a historically fixed endowment, that it might be possible to build up
stocks of social capital within relatively short spans of time (e.g., Hall 1997;
Schneider et al. 1997). The issue is far from resolved, however, and resolving

it with any reasonable conviction will require undertaking careful analysis of longitudinal data. This kind of analysis has not been undertaken so far. The concept of social capital has gained popularity relatively recently, and social scientists have utilized mainly cross-sectional data to make their cases for and against its putative effects.

Though what causes social capital to rise or fall cannot be determined precisely using these data, investigations conducted in the Indian setting give reason to doubt the thesis of historical determinacy. Krishna and Uphoff (1999) compared social capital scores among households and villages in four different districts of Rajasthan state. Because of their different historical legacies, villages in the two northern districts, Udaipur and Rajsamand, should be expected to have higher levels of social capital compared to those of Ajmer and Bhilwara districts.[9] We found that, on average, a difference of eight to ten percentage points separated households in these two groups of districts (table 8.1). But average scores conceal the vast differences that exist among households and villages within each district. Variations within districts are several times larger than the observed variations in average levels across districts, so history cannot account fully or even in large part for the large intra-district variations that we observed.

History does not determine social capital levels, but what other influences

TABLE 8.1. Social Capital Scores by District

District	Average Score	Maximum Score	Minimum Score	Variation *within* District (Maximum– Minimum)
Ajmer	54	97	30	67
Bhilwara	53	88	27	61
Rajsamand	63	93	38	55
Udaipur	62	97	33	64
Variation *across* Districts (Highest–Lowest)	10	9	11	

Source: Krishna and Uphoff (1999)

are at work is hard to tell within the scope of such cross-sectional analyses. Evidence from rural development programs undertaken in different parts of the world does suggest, however, that social mobilization programs and others that demonstrate the value of cooperation have helped set up structures and inculcate attitudes which promote collective action for mutual benefit.[10] More careful long-term analyses should help to identify with more precision factors responsible for the rise and fall of social capital.

While additional analysis is awaited regarding the causes of social capital, experience shows that agency strength can grow quite rapidly even within relatively short intervals of time. We found in chapter 3 that new development-oriented village leaders have come up and gained capacity and influence mostly within the past twenty years. Influences identified by modernization theory — including the spread of education, mass media, and voting, and rising state expenditures in rural areas — have been responsible for adding to agency strength at the local level.

Economic development and political participation in villages have benefited as these new agents have arisen and gained strength. Participation in politics is no longer only a preserve of rich and high-caste villagers. Political parties, which earlier banked upon feudal strongmen for organizing vote banks in villages, are increasingly turning toward the newly emerged loose networks of poorer and lower-caste villagers, assembled by new non-caste-based leaders. All parties have reached out to these networks, and the annual subvention for anti-poverty programs has increased by more than 700 percent (in inflation-adjusted terms) within the past fifteen years, even as the growth in per capita income was less than one percent a year. The increasing political role of poor Indian villagers has resulted in changing the strategy and the composition of ruling coalitions. It is important to reflect upon what exactly these changes have meant for Indian villagers and how the future of democracy in India might be affected when these changes deepen and gain ground.

II. Inverting the Pyramid: Reorganizing Democracy From the Grassroots Up

Democracy was installed in India fifty years ago, but few enforceable rights were available to most Indian villagers. Holding public officials to account was — and to a large extent still is — well near impossible for the ordinary villager.[11] Political parties, which should have provided linkages between citizens and public officials, were mostly poorly organized in the countryside. Building party organizations is a long and tedious affair, requiring toil without reward for several years. And leaders of major political parties were only too glad to take the easy way out.

Party leaders struck deals with village strongmen, mostly upper caste land-owning elites, who could deliver blocks of votes by dint of their traditional domination over other villagers. In exchange for bringing in the vote, these village strongmen were provided with privileged access to state officials. State and party leaders recognized only the strongman and hardly any other villager. When ordinary villagers needed to make contact with government officials, they would go with a note from the local strongman, so few villagers dared to cross their strongman or vote against his preferred candidates.

It was a convenient and mutually advantageous bargain. The ruling party got its votes with relatively little effort; investment in organization building could be deferred or avoided altogether. And strongmen in villages increased their hold over other villagers. By delivering the vote, they preserved their dominant positions (Frankel 1989; Hasan 1989; Kothari 1988; Migdal 1988; Narain et al. 1976; Singh 1988).[12]

Many villagers who grew up in earlier times still continue to follow the lead of their erstwhile feudal lords. "How do you vote in elections?" I asked Gangaram Prajapat, 65 years old and of the potter caste. "As Thakur Sahib tells us," he responded promptly and quite unselfconsciously, referring to the upper caste landlord of his village.[13]

However, while Prajapat and other older villagers continue to follow the lead of the village Thakur, many younger villagers, including Prajapat's son, have started to hew a different path. Until the Congress Party remained the single dominant force in Rajasthan, however, it proved very hard for these youngsters to dent the Thakur's influence. The Thakur delivered villagers' votes to the Congress Party, and in return he held undisputed sway over government officials of the area. "Police officials came to my house first when they visited this village," he recounts,[14] and villagers were cowed sufficiently to keep their dissent muted and in the background.

Two factors were at work, however, that combined to provide a democratic opening for these villagers. First, education was spreading rapidly among younger villagers, and mass media had started to penetrate the rural interior. Newspapers, radio, and then television started to appear in villages, carrying images of progress, change, and equality; and submitting to the dictates of the Thakur began to feel irksome, particularly among younger, more educated, and more traveled villagers. At about the same time, starting in 1977, non-Congress parties started to win state elections in Rajasthan and Madhya Pradesh, and party alternation provided an opportunity for villagers to express their discontent, without suffering the risk of being permanently cut off from power and from patronage.

Over the past twenty years — as education has become more common in these villages, and as parties have alternated frequently in power — these changes have worked themselves deeper into the fabric of village society. The Thakur is still powerful in Kundai village, but he competes for influence with other villagers. Thirty years ago — though governments were democratically elected even at that time — few people in Kundai village would have dared to challenge the Thakur so openly and consistently.

Democracy is by itself not enough to produce equity and equal participation. Self-assurance among ordinary citizens is also necessary if democracy is to be enjoyed equitably by all. Self-assurance and awareness of democratic rights have increased substantially over the past twenty years. A new generation has arisen in these villages that is markedly better educated than its forebears, and self-perceptions are quite different between younger and older villagers, as the following vignette illustrates.

Palri village is located about a hundred kilometers north of Kundai. Fateh is a young leader of this village, and it is difficult to meet him undisturbed, for large numbers of villagers are always around requesting his services. I got a chance to see him on my third attempt, and we sat on a string cot in an open courtyard next to his house. His old father sat beside us on the cot, but he did not speak much. Fateh and his father belong to a scheduled — i.e., a formerly untouchable — caste, the Balais.

The interview was beginning to get interesting — Fateh was telling me about a protest he had organized against the Forest Department — when Surja Jat, an upper caste man of the village, walked by. Fateh Balai invited Surja Jat to come and sit with us, to talk, he said in dialect, with "this strange man from America, who spends entire days doing nothing but asking questions." Surja smiled, shook hands with Fateh, and sat beside us on the cot. Meanwhile, Fateh's father had slid down from the cot to sit in the dusty ground at our feet.

Surja invited him to come and sit on the cot along with us, but the old man declined. "I'm OK where I am," he murmured. And he was, I saw, quite comfortable in his assumed station, sitting *below* the level of an upper caste man. His son was equally comfortable sitting *beside and equal* with the upper caste man. And the upper caste man was equally comfortable with the separate attitudes of the father and the son.

I wish I had photographed this tableau because it depicts so much of what is happening in these villages. A huge increase in educational achievement has gone together with the spread of egalitarian attitudes among younger villagers. Education has increased rapidly in the past 20 years, as we saw in chapter 3. While only 22 percent of villagers aged over 55 years went to school for five years or more, 70 percent of younger villagers aged 18–25 years have attained this level.

Educational achievement has more than *tripled* in the space of a single generation, and it has also spread equally among different caste groups in these villages. Younger villagers belonging to scheduled and backward castes are almost at par with upper caste villagers in terms of basic education, and they are no longer held back, as their parents were, by the drag of ignorance and illiteracy. Older villagers may continue to pay heed to the old prejudices and iniquities of caste, but younger villagers are much less willing to abide by these traditions.

Change at the margin has powerful effects, as the economists inform us, and the marginal rate of education in rural India is far above the average rate (see tables 3.1 and 3.2). In addition to their higher education, younger villagers are also much better informed than older ones, as table 8.2 shows, and young villagers from lower and backward caste groups are about as well informed as their counterparts from upper and middle castes.

With their superior education and with more and better information at hand, younger villagers can deal directly with state and market agencies, without seeking the support of upper caste patrons. Neither because of higher birth nor on grounds of superior capacity are upper castes able any longer to maintain their previously exclusive relationship with the state.

A new cohort of village leaders has sprung spontaneously from among young villagers of different caste backgrounds in these villages. Political parties have not been directly involved in nurturing and developing the new leadership in most cases, nor, in most cases, has any other organization come to their aid. These young village leaders, through dint of their own doggedness and sheer hard work, have independently acquired program information and contacts with government officials.

Devendra Singh, a new leader of Ghodach village, had the following

TABLE 8.2 Percentage of Villagers Who Regularly Consult
Newspapers and Radio/Television[1]

Caste Group	Age-Group		
	Above 55 years	35–55 years	Less than 35 years
Upper	51%	72%	81%
Middle	39	61	73
Backward	33	61	72
Scheduled Tribe (ST)	7	37	54
Scheduled Caste (SC)	14	53	77

[1] Constructed from responses given by a random sample of over 2,000 villagers who were consulted for this study.

experience to relate, which is not dissimilar to the experiences narrated by other new leaders.

> After getting primary education in the village school, I rented a room in Udaipur [the district capital] to study in a high school there. After completing high school, I applied for many jobs and I spent a lot of money on these applications, but I did not have "approach" anywhere so I could not get a job and I returned to the village. I just idled away my time for the first two years. I was sitting by the village well one day when Bhola Balai asked my help to fill an application form for getting an old-age pension from the *Tahsil*.[15] He asked me to go with him to the *Tahsil*. "You wear pants [and not a dhoti like other villagers], you can speak without fearing the *babus* [clerks] — you read and write," he told me.
>
> So I went to the *Tahsil* with him and the *babus* there ran circles around me. They ignored me and said they were too busy to help . . . [but] most of the time they were sitting around drinking tea and gossiping. I came back home, tired and humiliated. Bhola came for me again the next day. He would pay my fare, he said, and I was doing nothing anyway, so I went back to the *Tahsil*. This time I pleaded with the *babuji*. I sat at his feet and I said I would not leave until my work

was done. I waited the whole day, and people laughed at me. I returned again the next day. The *babuji* asked for some money and I gave it, not much, just a little bit. . . . He taught me how to complete the file. . . Bhola's pension started two months later. . . .

Other villagers then asked me to help with their work in the *Tahsil* — to get copies of land records, for registration of land sales, to deal with rent notices, etc. I kept going back to the same *babuji*. Then one day I had to do some work in the *Panchayat Samiti* [another subdistrict office that deals with development programs], so I asked the *Tahsil babuji* if he had some friend who worked in that office. . . . Now that friend is also a regular contact.

I have contacts in many government offices now and also in political parties. . . . If anyone falls ill, I take them on my motorcycle to the Udaipur hospital. I know all the doctors there. I don't charge anything for these services, only what I have to pay from my pocket. Not all government officials ask for money, but there are other expenses — bus fares, tea. . . . [16]

People like Devendra Singh, Fateh Balai, and Prem Prajapat have emerged almost everywhere in the 69 villages where I studied these trends, and these young leaders are changing the practice of politics in these villages. Relations between different caste groups are being overhauled as a result.

Khivaram is 27 years old, of the Meghwal (a scheduled) caste. His village, Sangawas, lies within Rajsamand district, north of Udaipur. Together with Sawai Singh, a Rajput, and other villagers from different castes, Khivaram has successfully struggled against the dominance of a group led by Girdhari Singh, the traditional strongman of this village and the one to whom all political parties earlier went for votes.

They registered false police cases against us when we started agitating against their corrupt practices in the *panchayat* [village government]. Girdhari Singh would use his political connections to pressurize the police and the local administration.[17] But Sawai Singh and I are educated. We went and met the Collector [the head of the district administration] and we told him that we had been falsely implicated. I produced *written* proof that panchayat funds had been stolen. I told him there was only *hearsay* evidence against us, the police had nothing firm to go on. We went many times . . . [finally] the cases against us

were closed. . . . We kept up our community work in the village. We
collected funds from among our group, and I went back to the Collector to ask for a matching grant under the *Apna Gaon Apna Kaam*
scheme to erect an additional building for our village school.[18]. . . We
invited the Collector and the Superintendent of Police to inspect the
new building. . . . I have got to know many government officials. Our
group has taken up other development projects with funding from the
government. Nearly all villagers are with us now, and not even five
percent are with the other group [led by Girdhari Singh]. Many political leaders meet us first when they come for votes to this village.[19]

One fairly sure indication of political influence in a village can be assessed, I found, by asking the following question: "When the jeep carrying
a party candidate or organizer comes into a village, to whose house does it
go first?" Jeeps belonging to the BJP continue to go to Girdhari Singh's
house, but those of the Congress Party make straight for Khivaram's more
humble dwelling. Within the passage of a single generation, a Meghwal has
come to occupy political influence comparable to that of a Rajput landlord.
Education has bolstered self-assurance among ordinary villagers, and party
alternation has provided them with opportunities for competing as equals.
    Similar trends are visible in other villages in the region. Other lower- and
middle-caste village leaders have arisen who are challenging the monopoly
of political power long enjoyed by some upper caste men. When they come
to Sema village, Congress party organizers — including C. P. Joshi, elected
representative from this area and at the time of writing Minister for Rural
Development in the Rajasthan government — drive their jeep to the house
of Goverdhan Gayari, a 24-year old, backward-caste man, educated to the
high school level. The BJP organizers and their jeeps are more commonly
seen at the houses of two long-dominant Shrimali Brahmins.
    The old leadership continues to have influence in some villages, but
overall its influence is on the decline. A new dynamic of competition has
emerged that undercuts the old bases of village politics.
    Neither Gayari nor his political rivals in the village build their support
bases on the basis of caste affiliations. While party politicians visit his village
only at election time, Gayari continues to labor on behalf of villagers through
all the months that separate one election from the next. His sources of
support in the village are built among Bhils, scheduled castes, and other
poorer households, including some that are upper caste. "I help Kalals, peo-

ple of my own caste," claims Vishnu Suwalka, a new leader of Bhilwara district, "but also poor persons from other castes. There are many poor Brahmins, you know, as well as poor Regars, Rebaris, and Rajputs."[20] Khivaram, Logar Lal Dangi, and other new leaders, whom we have met in the previous pages, similarly do not confine their activities to villagers of any particular caste. Their upper caste rivals must match this strategy to survive in the village, so they, too, reach out to villagers of other castes.

Parties have had to adapt their strategies to take account of these changes at the village level. "The criterion for voting was earlier *jati* (caste), now it is *vikaas* [development]. Development work done in a village has the most effect on voting."[21]

Villagers, particularly young villagers, have become increasingly assertive in demanding services and economic benefits from political parties, and it is only rarely that a politician will rely primarily upon feudal strongmen to deliver the vote. "Ordinary village people want a bus to come to their village, they are no longer willing to walk five kilometers. They want electricity to run their pumps [for irrigating fields]. . . . They want schools. . . . if they have a primary school, they want a middle school . . . [then] a high school. They have seen these things [available] in other villages, so why not in their village? Anyone who can get them these things will have their [political] support."[22]

It is not just poorer villagers, however, who demand economic development benefits from the state. More than 90 percent of villagers selected at random in Rajasthan and Madhya Pradesh (2,078 of 2,232 villagers interviewed for this study), including both richer and poorer villagers, mentioned roads, schools, teachers, health centers, water supply, electricity connections, and employment generating and other similar projects among their five principal demands from the state.

Larger and larger state expenditures are being channeled into rural areas. The annual subvention for rural development programs was increased by 700 percent (in constant rupees) since 1985, even though per capita incomes grew by hardly one percent during this time.[23] Parties are promising even higher development benefits to attract villagers' votes, and the manifestos of the two major parties for the 1999 elections to Parliament were virtually indistinguishable in this regard.[24]

Parties and candidates respond to villagers' demands by promising ever larger development benefits to all villages, but these promises are nearly always forgotten once the election is over. "First the Congress candidate came to our village [during the 1999 election campaign]," recounts Gyarsi Bai of Balapur village in Ajmer district, "and he promised a new school building for the village. Then the BJP team came and they said they would give us a new water tank if they came to power." Politicians promise with unfailing regularity — to abolish unemployment, to eradicate illiteracy, to provide health for all by 2020 — and similar promises are repeated from year to year.

Villagers, both rich and poor, are no longer impressed by these promises. What concerns them more are actions taken at the village level: who does what to bring the promised services and benefits to *their* doorsteps?

Parties themselves function poorly for these purposes. With virtually no organization at the village level, they are forced to rely upon other agents at the local level. Landed and upper caste strongmen are no longer exclusively or even primarily useful for electoral purposes. Their monopoly of access to state officials has been challenged successfully by younger men, and most villagers prefer to seek assistance from these new village leaders. Whenever they have any work requiring intervention with government officials (or with dealers in the market), a majority of villagers — more than 65 percent in any given case — prefer to make contact with new rather than old village leaders (see table 7.3). Because of their higher education and because of the efforts they have invested in gaining familiarity with the procedures and developing contacts with the officials of the state, these new leaders are more valuable to villagers for a host of different purposes.

New leaders who are skillful in dealing with the world outside the village and who use these skills to work for the greater advantage of the village community — men like Logarlal Dangi of Nauwa, Goverdhan Gayari of Sema, Babulal Bor of Kundai, Khivaram of Sangawas, and dozens of others — are elevated by fellow villagers to the status of spokesperson. Assistance that is provided at times of great need — taking a sick person to the district hospital in the middle of the night, helping another escape lightly from a rapacious policeman, getting old-age pension approved for someone else — creates a fund of personal obligations that new leaders can bank upon. Especially when such assistance is provided willingly and without regard for immediate personal gain, it helps elevate the new leader to high status in his village.

Parties are increasingly seeking to cash in on the bank of obligations accumulated by new leaders. "We look for persons of influence in each village," one party chief told me. "Those persons are gaining most influence

. . . who are able to get villagers' day-to-day work done in government offices. Persons who take a sick villager to the hospital and who can get doctors to attend properly are remembered by the patient's family for long afterward. Those who can [liaise effectively] with the police, with the *Tahsil*, with banks — these are the persons who matter in the village today. They can get the most number of votes, especially if they are personally honest and not out to make money from these activities."[25] The head of the other major party in this region advocates a similar strategy. "We catch hold of these worker-type persons in every village, and we know that the other party will also do the same, so we try to get to them first at election time."[26]

Villagers who are united and who are led by capable young leaders can successfully play off political parties against each other. In the bargain, they are able to derive higher development benefits for their village. Political parties, on their part, have been only too glad to go along, and they have found new means to support larger numbers of such local-level bargains.

Starting from fiscal year 1993–94, elected members of parliament and state assemblies have approved new budgetary allocations that they can use at their discretion to finance community infrastructure projects in villages of their choice, as reported in chapter 3. Simultaneously, the annual allocation for regular programmatic expenditure on rural development programs has increased several times in per capita terms.

Government funds are being directed in increasing quantities toward rural areas, and an informal decentralization is simultaneously in progress. Villagers rather than state bureaucrats are selecting development projects. And politicians are providing them with the wherewithal to implement these projects. Power is flowing into the hands of villagers in this manner, and they are learning to participate actively — and to considerable effect — in the politics of their nation.

Alternative avenues for political expression have become available, and people in villages, especially poor and lower caste people, are asserting their rights. The caste composition of the new leadership in these Rajasthan and Madhya Pradesh villages reflects the recent dispersion of power. Scheduled castes, the former untouchables, constitute 22 percent of population in the 69 villages that I studied, but 26 percent of new leaders hail from these castes. Other backward castes also provide more than their share of new leaders (these castes account for 41 percent of village population and 49 percent of new leaders).

The relationship between caste groups is being overturned here in a largely peaceful revolution. Who speaks for whom is very different today than it was forty or even twenty years ago. Upper caste strongmen no longer speak on behalf of entire villages. And regional caste leaders have little influence over villagers who care less for *jati* (caste) and more for *vikaas* (development). Parties are turning to new people and adopting new ways for attracting villagers' votes. Multi-caste village networks are on the rise, led by non-caste-based younger leaders, and politicians are increasingly directing their appeals toward such networks. Different types of political networks might be emerging in other parts of India, as discussed in chapter 7, but the relationship between high caste and political efficacy is no longer as neat as it might have been forty or even twenty years ago. Localized forms of political expression are on the ascendant, and analyses of Indian politics in future will need to be more fine-grained, tracing carefully the emergent microfoundations of new alliances and new networks.

The rise of new village networks in Rajasthan and Madhya Pradesh has been accompanied by an expansion of democratic participation at the grassroots. "Twenty years earlier when we [party workers] went into any village, we thought it enough to speak to the *Mukhiyas, Patels, and Lamberdars* [headmen, caste leaders, and feudal strongmen]. . . . Now every villager has to be contacted individually. People get upset if we contact only these leaders. They say, 'Why did he only meet *Ba-saab* [the old gentleman] and not me? Have I not got a vote to give?' "[27]

With the electorate getting atomized in this manner, parties and candidates will need to work harder than before, assembling majorities village-by-village and villager-by-villager. As *jati* becomes less important for voting and *vikaas* gains ground, parties will compete to offer larger and larger offerings of development benefits to villagers. Power will pass away from the center as villagers decide increasingly for themselves which dams they will build and which benefits they will forego.

Fragmentation, decentralization, and atomization of public decisionmaking will change the ways in which majorities get assembled and governments are formed in India. Unstable coalition governments might rule at the center. At the periphery, however, we will continue to see distinct improvements in the quality and breadth of India's democracy.

The new set of younger, more educated, and non-caste-based political entrepreneurs are democratizing politics at the village level, and they are helping make established socioeconomic and political structures more accountable to the ordinary villager. The old caste-bound leaders monopolized narrow conduits of influence with the state. The new leaders are opening up multiple avenues for profitable interaction, and villagers' engagements with the state and with markets are becoming more widespread than ever before.

Growing agency capacity will enable villagers to access and activate their stocks of social capital more effectively. Both development and democracy will improve as a result.

Appendix A: Methodology

The database for this dissertation combines an intensive eleven months' long study of 16 Rajasthan villages with an extensive survey of 69 villages, including the 16 that were studied intensively. Appendix B provides the details relating to these villages.

In the extensive survey, questionnaires were administered among villagers and leaders, while the intensive phase involved more probing and open-ended conversations with a cross-section of villagers, including both leaders and other villagers. Separately, I sought out city-based professionals who were in regular contact with these villages. I interviewed 105 such professionals, including lawyers, doctors, bankers, government officials, and party politicians in the districts of Bhilwara, Rajsamand, and Udaipur.

All 16 villages selected for intensive study belong to these three districts. Two more districts, Ajmer to the north and Dungarpur to the south, were added to this lot of three districts for conducting the extensive survey. A wide cross-section of population and villages, including Scheduled Tribe areas in Dungarpur and villages with considerable Muslim population (in Ajmer district), were covered by this selection.

Villages for study in Rajasthan were selected on the basis of data provided by the state government's Watershed Development Department. I relied upon these data for a particular reason. Figures for comparing levels of communal harmony and political participation among villages seemed relatively easy to obtain.[1] Village performance in respect of the third objective, development performance, was difficult to scale, however, without having some reliable and comparable indicators. I had to select villages that had started off at a roughly similar level, and I had to find some venture or program that all or a majority of villagers valued equally. Selecting villages that had participated in the Watershed Development Program served both of these purposes.

I had known the Watershed Development Program previously, having set it up and managed it between 1991 and 1993. To participate in this government-supported program, villagers were required to contribute collectively a part of the resources (mostly in the form of labor or locally available raw materials). Activities were planned and implemented on behalf of villagers by Users Committees that were elected annually. Villagers implemented the program collectively through the committees that they had elected, so collective action could be compared — and hypotheses related to social capital tested — by comparing program results. Watershed development also served a very important need of most or all villagers, as I learned in the course of a previous investigation.[2] By helping them to secure their livelihoods more assuredly in an environment where drought occurs every two years out of five, watershed development had served an important common need.

Villages participating in watershed development among the five selected districts of Rajasthan — from north to south, Ajmer, Bhilwara, Rajsamand, Udaipur and Dungarpur — were ranked High, Middle, and Low in terms of their achievements within the watershed development program, and I randomly selected an equal number of villages from each of these three categories. Both the smaller sample of 16 villages and the larger sample of 60 villages were selected in this manner.

Within villages, individuals to interview for the extensive survey were selected randomly from the official list of voters for that village. Sometimes villages were divided into wards, and these ward lists had to be compiled and renumbered before submitting them to the random number generator.

The larger sample was surveyed with the help of a set of questionnaires that I designed after spending an initial period of fourteen weeks in the field. Living for between one and two weeks in each of eight villages, I was able to get a better idea of how the variables of interest could be operationalized to be relevant for the local context. The questionnaire was pilot-tested in four villages, refined further, and then administered to a group of 1,898 individuals, selected by drawing random samples from the electoral rolls for each of the 60 selected villages in Rajasthan. This questionnaire has 114 items in all, and it took, on average, about one hour to complete in interview with the respondent. Separately, another and shorter questionnaire was developed that was administered among village leaders. A third set of interviews was conducted among focus groups in each village. Interested readers can write to me for copies of these questionnaires.

I administered the questionnaire in a few villages, but the major part of this survey was undertaken by eight investigators, four men and four women, who are themselves village residents, who belong to the local area, who wear what the villagers wear, and who speak the same dialects. Some of these investigators I have known for many years (though they had never before "investigated" anything) and others I recruited from the villages where I lived for the first fourteen weeks of my field study. These investigators and I trained together for a month before going our separate ways, they to conduct the survey and I to the next group of eight case-study villages. We met each other once every week for the first six weeks of the survey to discuss issues of approach, methods and logistics. For twelve weeks after that, the investigators, operating in groups of four, were comfortable running the survey by themselves, and they contacted me infrequently, mostly if they needed to replace some name on the survey list. Some people had died, eloped or migrated since the electoral rolls were compiled, in 1995, and some (roughly one to two percent) never existed.[3] About five percent of the sample needed to be replaced with other names, which were drawn as a reserve list at the time of initial sampling. Villagers were interviewed mostly in the security of their own homes. Male investigators interviewed the men, while female investigators spoke with the women of the village.

A separate questionnaire was administered among 408 leaders who were identified by the villagers. Village leaders were identified following a reputational, a positional, and most important, a functional method. We asked villagers to identify the following types of individuals in their village: (a) those who occupied official positions (including within *panchayats* and cooperative societies); (b) others who did not occupy any governmental position but who were still regarded as leaders (e.g., caste leaders); and (c) persons to whom villagers would go when they needed assistance in connection with one or more indicated subjects (related to economic development, community peace, and political participation). The functional approach proved most useful, for it helped to identify individuals who, though not normally regarded as "leaders," are nevertheless still prime movers of events in the village.

The need for cross-checking in another region arose as I began to analyze the Rajasthan results. Caste could surely not be so unimportant for political mobilization, I thought, as the Rajasthan data seemed to indicate? I went out to Madhya Pradesh in the summer of 1999 and I spent three weeks' time among nine villages there. Together with a small team of field investigators, I interviewed a random sample of adult villagers (a total of 334 persons) along with village leaders and district-level government and party officials. Both large and small villages were selected among this sample, as well as villages that are located along major roads and others that are more remotely situated. Villages voting predominantly for the Congress Party were selected, on information provided by local party leaders, and also those that were regarded as bastions of the other major political party, the BJP. This sample of nine Madhya Pradesh villages was selected among rural areas of district Mandsaur.

Appendix B: Details of 60 Villages in Rajasthan

Village	District	Area (hecs.)	Percent Irrigated	House-holds	Number of Caste Groups	Population (1991)	Percent SC	Percent ST	Literacy (1991)	Households below poverty line (%)	Animals (Cowunits)[1]
Ararka	Ajmer	1,504	0.08	215	22	1,385	0.17	0.00	0.30	0.34	1,595
Chachiyawas	Ajmer	1,367	0.04	254	14	1,516	0.27	0.00	0.33	0.19	2,000
Deendwara	Ajmer	2,032	0.08	411	23	2,553	0.19	0.00	0.22	0.21	1,700
Dhanipurohitan	Ajmer	140	0.09	6	8	39	0.00	0.00	0.44	0.37	825
Dholpuriya	Ajmer	799	0.06	178	10	956	0.29	0.00	0.24	0.19	975
Gegal	Ajmer	936	0.05	244	8	1,530	0.04	0.02	0.29	0.10	300
Gurha	Ajmer	604	0.07	178	8	1,110	0.02	0.00	0.15	0.13	2,375
Khandach	Ajmer	1,317	0.08	196	20	1,110	0.13	0.00	0.34	0.16	1,750
Kucheel	Ajmer	2,233	0.08	450	20	2,875	0.16	0.00	0.21	0.11	3,250
Narwar	Ajmer	926	0.20	288	22	1,699	0.41	0.00	0.32	0.20	4,750
Sarana	Ajmer	362	0.15	216	13	1,223	0.07	0.00	0.35	0.31	688
Udaipurkhurd	Ajmer	701	0.02	143	14	670	0.10	0.09	0.27	0.71	1,300
Balesariya	Bhilwara	946	0.11	243	12	1,011	0.11	0.08	0.13	0.33	850
Bankakhera	Bhilwara	1,969	0.10	475	17	2,407	0.12	0.03	0.17	0.16	2,000
Borda	Bhilwara	687	0.03	179	9	843	0.10	0.07	0.23	0.52	425
Chawandiya	Bhilwara	1,121	0.08	263	8	1,324	0.17	0.05	0.28	0.22	963
Dantra	Bhilwara	1,586	0.02	382	11	1,894	0.26	0.06	0.24	0.55	700
Gehuli	Bhilwara	478	0.12	179	10	855	0.16	0.01	0.25	0.30	1,425
Gothra	Bhilwara	877	0.05	178	7	904	0.21	0.00	0.07	0.54	600

Village	District	Area (hecs.)	Percent Irrigated	House-holds	Number of Caste Groups	Population (1991)	Percent SC	Percent ST	Literacy (1991)	Households below poverty line (%)	Animals (Cowunits)
Hajiwas	Bhilwara	598	0.06	174	8	916	0.26	0.00	0.22	0.35	498
Jharol	Bhilwara	949	0.10	174	9	881	0.27	0.04	0.16	0.40	525
Mansha	Bhilwara	1,039	0.15	246	10	1,443	0.09	0.12	0.22	0.41	1,863
Palri	Bhilwara	896	0.05	311	11	1,681	0.12	0.05	0.23	0.25	1,650
Redwas	Bhilwara	1,108	0.11	294	12	1,510	0.10	0.08	0.18	0.51	538
Barod	Dungarpur	534	0.05	195	7	1,088	0.01	0.86	0.19	0.77	700
Chautra	Dungarpur	339	0.03	134	4	747	0.00	0.48	0.05	0.44	700
Dooka	Dungarpur	1,572	0.02	551	8	2,942	0.07	0.81	0.15	0.92	10,500
Gadamoraiya	Dungarpur	209	0.03	79	10	402	0.01	0.56	0.33	0.84	153
Garamalji	Dungarpur	306	0.01	111	1	662	0.00	1.00	0.09	0.84	1,050
Kesharpura	Dungarpur	199	0.03	111	1	560	0.00	1.00	0.15	0.88	85
Khemaroo	Dungarpur	506	0.00	216	4	1,342	0.02	0.97	0.15	0.86	550
Pakhroon	Dungarpur	292	0.01	120	1	724	0.00	1.00	0.23	0.55	750
Piplada	Dungarpur	501	0.04	164	6	959	0.03	0.55	0.23	0.74	1,375
Sadariya	Dungarpur	788	0.01	288	4	1,531	0.00	0.30	0.07	0.56	475
Takari	Dungarpur	426	0.04	134	2	703	0.07	0.93	0.17	0.46	1,200
Vasua	Dungarpur	383	0.01	188	1	1,047	0.00	1.00	0.20	0.85	1,050
Dadmi	Rajsamand	445	0.05	115	5	503	0.12	0.44	0.16	0.23	425
Goadach	Rajsamand	1,359	0.08	406	10	2,003	0.14	0.22	0.22	0.58	1,875
Koshiwara	Rajsamand	1,098	0.06	403	10	1,822	0.05	0.16	0.23	0.44	750
Kunda	Rajsamand	517	0.06	127	7	591	0.11	0.49	0.07	0.78	750

Village	District	Area (hecs.)	Percent Irrigated	House-holds	Number of Caste Groups	Population (1991)	Percent SC	Percent ST	Literacy (1991)	Households below poverty line (%)	Animals (Cowunits)
Nedach	Rajasamand	747	0.08	324	11	1,443	0.10	0.34	0.13	0.66	450
Negdiya	Rajasamand	1,010	0.06	297	12	1,533	0.03	0.29	0.27	0.58	800
Sakroda	Rajasamand	1,113	0.06	375	11	1,792	0.12	0.07	0.19	0.37	600
Sangawas	Rajasamand	397	0.06	139	11	761	0.16	0.03	0.32	0.55	375
Sema	Rajasamand	822	0.05	482	12	2,193	0.05	0.18	0.22	0.85	1,500
Sodawas	Rajasamand	190	0.02	123	5	668	0.02	0.00	0.24	0.16	300
Sundarcha	Rajasamand	718	0.05	230	9	1,185	0.06	0.21	0.37	0.36	900
Ushan	Rajasamand	1,326	0.04	252	6	1,516	0.02	0.53	0.15	0.63	1,450
Bhesrakhurd	Udaipur	583	0.04	210	5	1,045	0.02	0.41	0.26	0.51	900
Dantisar	Udaipur	526	0.03	156	11	731	0.06	0.12	0.13	0.23	950
Dholimagri	Udaipur	394	0.03	198	9	982	0.10	0.07	0.23	0.37	2,125
Kailashpuri	Udaipur	376	0.03	279	5	1,201	0.00	0.43	0.48	0.28	413
Khamkimadri	Udaipur	880	0.06	219	9	1,187	0.04	0.28	0.30	0.56	2,675
Kharbaro ka Guda	Udaipur	421	0.06	178	9	940	0.05	0.16	0.23	0.29	2,500
Kherighasa	Udaipur	273	0.01	155	9	745	0.06	0.21	0.15	0.32	1,300
Kundai	Udaipur	644	0.11	145	12	770	0.16	0.28	0.30	0.48	300
Nauwa	Udaipur	1,061	0.03	327	12	1,589	0.04	0.38	0.22	0.55	2,000
Odwariya	Udaipur	472	0.05	241	9	1,304	0.09	0.16	0.18	0.32	2,125
Sarekala	Udaipur	1,330	0.01	373	4	1,656	0.07	0.63	0.17	0.28	1,575
Sinhara	Udaipur	342	0.12	161	12	881	0.23	0.26	0.21	0.08	225

[1] The number of small animals (goat, sheep) is divided by four before adding it to the number of large animals (cows, buffaloes, camels).

Appendix C: Map of Village Balesariya

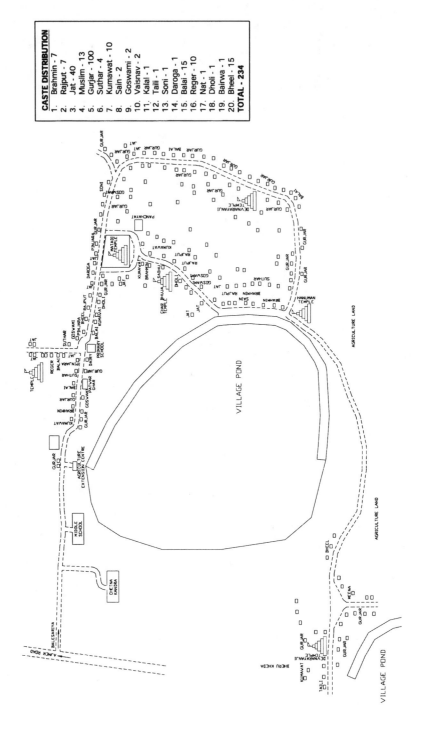

CASTE DISTRIBUTION

1. Brahmin - 7
2. Rajput - 7
3. Jat - 40
4. Muslim - 13
5. Gurjar - 100
6. Suthar - 4
7. Kumawat - 10
8. Sain - 2
9. Goswami - 2
10. Vaisnav - 2
11. Kalal - 1
12. Taili - 1
13. Soni - 1
14. Daroga - 1
15. Balai - 15
16. Reger - 10
17. Nat - 1
18. Dholi - 1
19. Bairwa - 1
20. Bheel - 15

TOTAL - 234

Notes

Chapter 1

1. Forty-seven percent of all Indians, i.e., almost half a billion people, continue to be classified as poor according to this definition. The corresponding proportion is as high as 85 percent in Zambia, 72 percent in Madagascar, 69 percent in Uganda, and 53 percent in Guatemala, indicating that poverty continues despite global growth to be one of the foremost problems afflicting a considerable part of the world's population (World Bank 1999).

2. Esman and Uphoff (1984) provide one of the earliest and most widely cited arguments in this regard. Also see, for instance, Chandhoke (1995); Cohen and Arato (1992); Kothari (1988); and World Bank (1997, 2000). The literature on democratization also emphasizes the roles that organizations of civil society play in installing as well as safeguarding democracy, for instance, Hipscher (1996); Linz and Stepan (1996); O'Donnell and Schmitter (1987).

3. If increasing the number of formal and registered associations were to translate directly into enhancing levels of social capital, then it should be rather easy to accumulate social capital rapidly. The state could simply pay citizens to enlist, and it could open its offices to register their associations in the hundreds. But this solution is hardly promising because it seems unlikely to have any positive impact on attitudes or practices related to cooperation and collective action.

4. "In much of the developing world, especially in the countryside and rural areas," observes Varshney (2001: 368), "formal associations do not exist. This does not mean, however, that civic interconnections or activities are absent... Cities tend to have formal associations; villages make do with informal sites and meetings." Because of such everyday engagements, he finds, "villages con-

stitute a remarkably small portion of communal rioting." A similar conclusion about the conflict-averting role of informal village associations is upheld in chapter 6 of this book.

5.   Differences in density of associational membership might reflect as well the relative ease and facility with which citizens in different countries can have their associations registered. In rural north India, at least, registering a formal organization requires spending days, often months, dealing with complex and complicated procedures, which are virtually impassable for the average villager. "It took us two years' time to complete the procedures involved in registering our organization," reported Ganesh Labana, Director of a small NGO I visited in Rajsamand district. "We had to make fourteen visits to this office, each one costing us more than three hundred rupees [ten dollars at that time, equal to ten days wages] in bus fares and hotel charges." Formal associations are, in consequence, mostly initiated by the state in these contexts.

6.   Even twenty years ago, economic development needs had acquired great importance for villagers. As observed by Robinson (1988: 264–65) during elections held in 1981, "These are signals of an important change. . . . These ideas are taking root. People who never dreamed of rights to clean drinking water, a site for a house, credit for agricultural inputs, or subsistence wages now demand them. . . . Ideas about wages, houses, and access to water [have] trickle[d] down well. The voters listen, vote, judge and vote again. The candidates know this and they try to deliver some form of economic development to their constituents."

7.   Notable exceptions include Bailey (1960), who provides early signs that a new form of village leadership might be emerging, based on linkages external to the village community. Mitra (1991, 1992) provides indications of a movement away from caste-based and toward opportunity-based leadership in villages in Gujarat, Orissa and Madhya Pradesh. Reddy and Hargopal (1985) similarly report the emergence of leadership dispersal in Andhra Pradesh. This trend has gained ground rapidly in Rajasthan, especially over the past twenty years, and the pace of change might be as fast if not faster elsewhere in India.

8.   On average, villagers of the 69 villages studied had regular dealings with 18 agencies of the government and at least seven different market agencies. Contrary to what has sometimes been supposed, villagers do not shy away from these encounters. Contact with state and market agencies is initiated frequently by villagers who seek economic benefits for themselves and for other co-villagers.

9.   This issue of limits is illustrated, for instance, by the following question, which was raised at a workshop where I presented some of these findings: "Could an Indian village community with a reasonably high level of social capital conceivably become a mini-Singapore in the near future?" I regard this question

to be serious and important, and I attempt to provide a reasonable answer in this book.

10. Provisional figures from 2001 Census of India, as reported at www.censusindia.net/results/provindia1.html.

11. "Agent" is interpreted here "in its older — and 'grander' — sense as someone who acts and brings about change, and whose achievements can be judged in terms of her own values and objectives, whether or not we assess them in terms of some external criteria as well" (Sen 1999: 18–19).

12. The analysis by Putnam et al. (1993) of social capital in Italy is incomplete, according to some critics, because they fail to consider the role that political parties have played not only by way of aggregating and representing citizen's demands but also by helping citizens articulate and organize in support of their demands. This contention is reviewed in the following chapter.

13. Tarrow (1977) demonstrates the mediating roles played by mayors and other local officials in France and Italy.

14. Members of Parliament and State Assemblies in India do not have available to them any statutory funding as, for instance, American Congressmen are given (Fiorina 1977), which can enable them to maintain and pay for the upkeep of district offices.

15. Among these three variables — strength of traditional village councils, level of social capital, and effectiveness of village development agents — none is correlated to any significant extent with any of the others (chapter 4). Agency strength derives from factors in the *external* environment while social capital hinges upon stable social arrangements *internal* to the village.

Chapter 2

1. For instance, Grootaert (1998), Morris (1998), and Narayan and Pritchett (1997). Woolcock and Narayan (2000) provide a useful review of this literature.

2. Aggregation is inherently assumed in this argument. Why social capital existing at the level of small groups should always and automatically aggregate to result in better performance for entire regions or countries is not problematic for Putnam and other writers in this school. Some critics of the social capital position regard aggregation to be a considerable problem, as I will discuss later in this chapter.

3. Morlino (1995), O'Neill (1996), and Tarrow (1996), for instance, are all highly critical of the selective interpretation employed by Putnam. "History," in Putnam's version, "has been nicely rounded to fit the argument," claims O'Neill (1996: 6).

4. Similarly, in the context of British local governments, Lowndes and Wilson

(2001: 641) stress "the importance of the institutional design variable in shaping the creation and mobilization of social capital."

5.   "Sports clubs, choral societies, cooperatives and cultural associations have been organized by and for two major political parties, the Communists and the Christian Democrats," claim Foley and Edwards (1996: 42) for the Emilia-Romagna region. Tarrow (1996) enlarges this claim to include other regions as well.

6.   Scott (1976) discussed in Bates (1990) and more exhaustively and critically in Popkin (1979).

7.   Norms are not always or even usually so homogeneous or homogenizing. Culture provides "a tool-kit of symbols, stories, rituals and world-views, which people may use in varying configurations to solve different kinds of problems" (Swidler 1986: 273). Norms are varied and contested, and any "excessive emphasis on a process of norm internalization [is a product] . . . of an oversocialized conception of human action," which accords poorly with human nature and social experience (Portes 1998: 7).

8.   Evidence from other developing countries also indicates that intermediate agencies required for citizens to cooperate in one issue area are different from those required for other issue areas (Esman and Uphoff 1984). Not all such intermediary agencies are likely to be equally effective. In the six Central American countries she studies, Amber Seligson (1999) finds, for example, that compared to other intermediary agencies, such as unions or school-related support groups, agencies which perform broad-based community development functions are more effective in enforcing government accountability. This research and other bodies of evidence suggest that social capital is brought to bear upon different objectives through different routes and transmission mechanisms. Some among these mechanisms may be more effective; other channels may be blocked or constrained. The effects of social capital will be evidenced unequally, thus, in different issue-areas or social domains.

9.   One other possibility needs to be taken into account. This relates to the suggestion that there may be different types or varieties of social capital, each associated with some specific issue area (Coleman 1990: 302). An observation of high performance in one social domain co-existing with low performance results in another is fully compatible with this view of sector- and issue-specific social capital. Instead of bringing in sector-specific transmission mechanisms, all one needs to do in this case is to adduce sector-specific social capital. The question of whether social capital is one thing or many revolves, however, on concept-specification and definition. In this book, I follow the definition made popular by Putnam, which considers social capital as a community asset. Communities that have high levels of social capital, defined in this way, are expected to act collectively for mutual benefit across multiple societal domains. An alternative definition that is used, for example, by Lin (2001) regards social capital

as resources embedded in social networks accessed and used by actors for actions. Different types of social capital become possible when we consider that people belong to different networks that they use for different purposes. These and other issues related to definition, measurement, and contextualization are taken up in chapter 4.

10. Baden-Powell (1899 [1970]) and Mukherjee (1923) are useful for tracing the historical lineage of these indigenous Village Councils. Indications that such traditional leaders and their informal councils continue to be salient at the present time, i.e., even after the introduction of formal and elected local government bodies, are provided for Tamil Nadu and Andhra Pradesh by Srinivas (1987); for Uttar Pradesh by Foster and Simmons (1978); and for Rajasthan by Census of India (1961, 1981); Purohit (1974); and Saxena and Charan (1973).

11. On the changing role of the post-colonial state in India, see, for example, Bardhan (1984, 1992); Brass (1994); Frankel (1978); and Rudolph and Rudolph (1987). Khilnani (1997), especially chapters 1 and 2, provides a succinct summarization of the contending views. Few of these authors are concerned, however, with the transformations these changes in state structure and functions have induced in village-level patterns of authority and influence. Rudolph and Rudolph provide evidence of new regional groupings, but they do not track these changes down to the village level. Béteille (1996) and Weiner (1989) hold out a hope that economic and political development would bring about changes in authority patterns at the village level but neither author specifies the nature of changes that can be expected. Village studies by Bailey (1960, 1963) do, however, provide some early indications of change in village leadership following upon these macro-level changes.

12. The emergence of such new forms of village leadership not based on ascriptive or economic status constitutes a relatively new phenomenon. Life in Indian villages in the past has been mostly "dominated by powerful minorities within village societies. The kinds of people one finds in dominant roles barely changed over the decades" (Manor 1997: 263). Similar statements regarding patterns of leadership inherited from the past are made for villages in Uttar Pradesh by Hasan (1989) and Singh (1988); and for Rajasthani villages by Fisher (1997); Kuhn (1998); Patel (1994), Mitchie (1979); and Narain et al. (1976). Indications that the nature, functions and social background of village leaders are changing are provided by Bailey (1960), by Mitra (1991, 1992) and by Reddy and Hargopal (1985). The trends reported by these authors have gained momentum in the recent past, as I will discuss in chapter 3.

Chapter 3

1. Processes wherein parties garner votes by relying upon caste and extended patron-client links in the countryside have been described, for example, by Migdal

(1988), Kothari (1988), and Weiner (1986). Popular conceptions have followed these academic formulations in regarding caste as the appropriate unit of political mobilization in rural India. "As is common in Indian villages," an article in the *New York Times* (May 3, 1999) asserts, "politics is dominated by caste-based voting." "Caste," concurs the *Economist* (October 16, 1999), is "the most decisive influence over the average voter." While this might still be true, it is no longer the only (or even the most important) mode of political mobilization in the 69 villages that I studied. New forms of collective action have emerged, in these villages, and considerable collective action, especially within the economic and political realms, is organized on non-caste and non-patron-client lines, as discussed in this chapter.

2.   In earlier times, too, Indian villages have provided to outside observers the picture of a community "with a strong sense of identity and with institutions which regulate internal affairs and allow the village to act as a corporate unit" (Bailey 1963: 112). Suggesting "a sort of microcosm. . .in many ways a reflection of the macrocosm which is the outside world" (Béteille 1996:232), villages constitute "the lowest level of the political system . . . [with] a considerable measure of autonomy from higher levels" (Srinivas 1987:30). Programs of rural development and community infrastructure building launched by the Indian state since the late 1970s have provided additional incentives for collective action organized along village lines, and the newly arisen non-caste-based leaders have helped to promote this trend.

3.   Social legislation by a proactive state has also helped to diminish differences in privilege among high caste and low. Legislation is never automatically transformed into action on the ground, however, and without the enhanced ability among lower caste persons to deal competently with the machinery of the state, social legislation might have remained, as so much legislation does in India, merely a statement of intent, meant to pacify through symbolic action. Chapter 7 revisits this discussion.

4.   "Power within the village community is achieved not only in the relationships which exist inside that community," Bailey (1960: 114–15) observed forty years ago, "there is now an additional resource in the hands of the ambitious man: the relationship which he can establish with the Administrators. He can use this relationship to achieve his ends within the village." Leadership based on such *outside* connections has gained further importance over the last twenty years, overshadowing, in many instances, other forms of leadership deriving from ethnic or religious groupings *within* the village.

5.   There were 34,565 inhabited villages in Rajasthan in 1961, and there are 37,889 villages at the present time (GOR 1997). While population has more than doubled in this period, the number of villages has gone up by only 11 percent. New villages have come up mostly in the western part of the state,

particularly in previously uninhabited regions that were opened up for agriculture after the construction of the Indira Gandhi Canal and its numerous tributaries. The rest of the state, including the southern part studied here, has remained largely unaffected by new settlements.

6. Families of hardly three percent of the random sample of 1,898 villagers who were interviewed for this study had migrated to their present place of residence; 94 percent of respondents mentioned that neither they nor anyone else in their family had lived away from the village at any time for a period longer than one year. Rural-urban migration is large in absolute numbers, but it is confined to a small minority of villagers, less than 10 percent at most.

7. In 1991, 629 million rural Indians lived among 580,781 villages, making an average of approximately 1,100 persons per village. The corresponding figures for Rajasthan state are 34 million village inhabitants and 37,889 villages (GOI 1999; GOR 1997).

8. Neighborhoods are more dispersed in the tribal areas of southern Udaipur and Dungarpur districts. Bhils (a scheduled tribe) prefer to build their houses on isolated hilltops located above their fields. There is a central settlement in these villages too, and it is inhabited mostly by non-tribal villagers.

9. In addition, agricultural and pastoral systems are linked through various energy subsidies. Animal manure is a rich source of nutrients for crops, and crop residues provide food for animals. Farmers induce itinerant herders with money and with food to overnight sheep in barren fields. Sheep droppings are a rich source of manure (Agrawal 1999). Integrating crop- and animal-husbandry is thus more than just a question of risk management. I am indebted to Bob Fisher for reminding me of this feature.

10. The private sector has yet to make any substantial inroads into these and other rural parts, comprising more than three-fourths of all of rural India, where multiple cropping and commercial agriculture are not widely practiced and where they are not ever likely to become viable concerns. Chapter 5 discusses these and other details related to economic development in this region.

11. Caste and state power have had a mutually constitutive relationship historically. "Traditional India was not a rigid society," asserts Bayly (1988: 156–58), "it was British rule which made it so. . . . Hierarchy and Brahmin interpretation of Hindu society which was theoretical rather than actual over much of India as late as 1750 was firmly ensconced a century later. . . . The British indirectly stimulated these changes. Early officials began the process of ranking and grading the Indian social order in an attempt to understand and control it." In Rajasthan and other parts of India where native rule survived, albeit under the tutelage of paramount British power, caste distinctions were similarly hardened and ossified as rulers found in them a means to exercise local control. As the state changed hands a few centuries later from British to Indian administrators,

and as the rules of the game changed once again, village social organization has changed further in response to the new imperatives of survival and power. For an excellent short overview of the evolving relationship between caste relations and state power, see Sheth (1999).

12. The historical relation of caste with authority at the village level is narrated in some detail in the pre-independence *Report on the Political Administration of Udaipur, 1903–1904* (Udaipur State Archives).

13. *Report on the Political Administration of Udaipur, 1903–1904* (Udaipur State Archives).

14. Interview with Bhanwarlal Mahajan, 85 years of age, and Chairman, Village Cooperative Society, Village Palri, District Bhilwara (July 22, 1998).

15. Sunderlal Paliwal, a leader of the Brahmin community and *sarpanch* of Sunderchha *panchayat* from 1964 to 1978, mentioned that "Whenever the Maharana's entourage used to pass anywhere near our village, we were responsible for ensuring its safety. We used to gather together large groups of Bhils and other lower caste persons, and days before the event we would secure every hilltop and every crossing in the road. No one paid us anything for this work, it was our duty, and we did not pay the Bhils, except by punishing those who did not obey orders." Interviewed in Sunderchha village, District Rajsamand, Rajasthan (June 2, 1998).

16. Chakravarty (1975), Fisher (1997) and Narain and Mathur (1990) provide evidence that a similar strategy was adopted by the Congress Party in other parts of Rajasthan; while Frankel (1989), Hasan (1989), Migdal (1988), and Kothari (1988) indicate its widespread utilization in other parts of India.

17. Name disguised at the request of the respondent. Interviewed in Village A, District Udaipur, June 14, 1998.

18. A *patwari* is a field-level government official responsible for keeping the land records of a small group of villages. He reports to the *Tahsildar*, the chief of the sub-district (or Tahsil) office. Because land is the most important asset in rural India, because villagers have been mostly unlettered, and because land records like all other government documents have been zealously kept secret from the public, the villagers have bestowed *patwaris* with almost mythical powers. *Oopar karta, neeche patwar* — "Like God is above, the *Patwari* is below" — is one popular saying. For a sweeper to become a *patwari* is consequently a considerable elevation in social status.

19. A similar conclusion for other parts of India is reported by Sheth (1999: 2504): "A brahmin dealing in leather or an ex-untouchable dealing in diamonds is no longer looked upon as a social deviant. . . . Today, households within a single caste have not only been greatly differentiated in terms of their occupations, educational and income levels, and lifestyles, but these differences have led them to align outside the caste, with different socio-economic networks and

groupings in society — categories which cannot be identified in terms of the caste system."

20. "Backward" caste is a category consisting of all those caste groups that are neither upper caste nor listed as a Scheduled Caste by India's constitution. Historical discrimination is claimed by these caste groups as a ground for special treatment by the state. Mostly, members of these caste groups are small and marginal farmers.

21. Figures on education or land ownership subdivided by caste do not exist for all of Rajasthan or all of India. The figures presented in these tables are representative for all adults of this area, subject, of course, to some inevitable sampling errors.

22. It is curious to observe the quite striking differences between middle castes and backward castes. One reason why middle castes have invested less in education has to do, I suspect, with the fact that middle castes own more land per capita. Middle castes can support larger numbers of their sons and daughters on the land, and they are comparatively less pressured to seek alternative avenues for gainful employment. Middle caste women are among the least educated persons in these villages among all age groups, suggesting that sociological as well as economic reasons might account more fully for lower educational achievement among this group of villagers.

23. 1991 Census criterion and figures, reported in GOR (1997).

24. "If democracy in Kerala works better than in the rest of India," claims Heller (2000: 497–99), "it is in large part because individuals have been equipped with the basic human capabilities required of citizenship. Literacy in Kerala has reached 91 percent, compared with 49 percent for India as a whole. . . . As a direct result, traditionally marginalized groups, most notably women and dalits [SCs and backward castes] have acquired the basic social skills required for informed participation. . . . Caste and community in Kerala continue to be a powerful basis of social identity and civic engagement. But in the realm of politics and in the expression of public authority, these forms of association have been subordinated to broader aggregations."

25. Because villagers have few means for holding schoolteachers accountable, the quality of teaching in most village schools remains quite low. To the extent it enables a student to become functionally literate, however, attendance at even such low-quality schools has a salutary effect on personal and political efficacy. Interestingly, "private" schools, run unofficially by some unemployed local youth, have started operating in some villages, and parents willingly pay up to a hundred rupees each month to have their wards educated by such locally accountable schoolteachers. Improving the quality of education, perhaps by decentralizing decisionmaking in the public system, can help accelerate the ongoing expansion of participation in democracy. I am thankful to Atul Kohli for bringing this point to my attention.

26. A fairly significant gender gap continues to persist, however, despite this overall increase in educational achievement. While 84 percent of all male villagers between 18 and 25 have five or more years of education, the corresponding percentage among women is only 70 percent. Education is growing among women of most caste groups, however, though at a somewhat lower rate among middle caste and ST women.

27. Sisson (1972: 315, 323), in his magisterial study of the Congress Party in Rajasthan, had anticipated some of these features. "While participation in the [Congress] party organization [in the 1950s and 1960s] has not been extensive among Scheduled Castes and Tribes," he reported, some "representatives of these groups have enjoyed [greater] access . . . [particularly] recent recruits who were of higher educational achievement and less dependent upon high-caste patrons than their forefathers." "New and more assertive leadership from among these groups will no doubt arise," he predicted, who "will be less responsive to the paternal cues that have customarily emanated from well-intentioned, high-caste patrons."

28. Urban jobs have been hard to procure for all young persons with school and college degrees, and a large pool of educated and unemployed youth can be found in almost every village of Rajasthan, Madhya Pradesh, and probably all other Indian states. 819,362 persons were seeking jobs in Rajasthan in 1996, and another 294,164 persons registered with employment exchanges in this year, but jobs could be found for only 11,483 of them (GOR 1997). These figures are most likely to underestimate the true extent of unemployment as many educated persons do not register for jobs with the official employment exchanges.

29. Including two from the Supplies Department, two from the *Tahsil*, two from the Labor Department, one from the Electricity Board (if he wants an electric connection), one from the Public Health Department, and one from the *panchayat*. Of course, not everyone takes the trouble to accumulate all these licenses and permits. It is preferable in most cases to bear the risk of inspection, harassment, and demands for bribes.

30. This is not to say that state intervention is either effective or welcomed by citizens. Despite intervening over such a wide scale, however, "the state is far from supremely effective: it regularly fails to protect its citizens, it does not provide them with welfare, and it has not fulfilled its extensive ambitions to transform Indian society" (Khilnani 1997: 59).

31. While expenditure on the 16 schemes classified together as Rural Development was Rs. 1,008 million in Rajasthan in fiscal year 1992–93, it was more than double this amount just four years later. In fiscal year 1996–97, Rs. 2,315 million were provided for these schemes (GOR 1999).

32. Employment-generating schemes of similar scope have also been introduced

in other Indian states. In Maharashtra, the Employment Guarantee Scheme generated "nine days of employment for each worker in the rural labor force" in the late 1980s (Echeverri-Gent 1993: 94).

33. Interview with L. K. Laddha, Range Forest Officer, Udaipur, July 12, 1998.
34. Interview with H. K. Sharma, Assistant Engineer, Irrigation Department, Udaipur, July 17, 1998.
35. Interview with M. K. Singh, Assistant Engineer, Soil Conservation Department, Udaipur, July 10, 1998 (name disguised at the request of the respondent).
36. Interviewed in Nauwa village, Udaipur district, June 25–26, 1998.
37. Interview with N. K. Singhvi, Deputy Manager, State Bank of Bikaner and Jaipur Zonal Office, Udaipur, July 10, 1998.
38. "We do not have frequent contact with villagers like we did ten or even twenty years ago. When we go to the scene of a crime we ask first for individuals with whom we are in constant contact. These are the persons who bring cases to us from the village. We help them at that time, and they help us when we go to the village" (Interview with Saubhagya Singh, Police Station Officer-In-Charge, Bhilwara, March 21, 1999).
39. "Family planning is the most important activity for the staff of a [government] health center in the rural area. We cannot achieve our targets unless we have good relations with important villagers. We look after these fellows when they bring patients to us at the hospital, and we go to them when we need cases for family planning targets" (Dr. K. C. Tak, Bhilwara, dated July 23, 1998). Dr. Tak profiled these intermediaries as being "about 25–35 years of age, who are educated and understand the [official] procedures. They come to us directly, but sometimes they get senior party leaders to call us on the telephone before they come."
40. "Newspapers give prices in different markets. Educated villagers are asked by others about where they can get the best prices. They also bring these educated fellows along to check that the merchant does not cheat them. We cultivate these educated villagers ourselves for they have become an important link between us [merchants] and our clients [villagers]" (Interview with Ramesh Chaudhury, President, Udaipur Chamber of Commerce and Industry, and three other grain wholesalers. Udaipur, March 13, 1999).
41. In village Ghodach, the rivals have achieved peaceful coexistence by informally allocating different government departments among themselves. One leader deals exclusively with the Public Works and Irrigation Departments on behalf of all villagers, another deals with the Soil Conservation and the Irrigation Departments, and a third has uncontested jurisdiction for all matters concerning the police and the Tahsil. In most other villages, however, including Losing, Sema, Nauwa and Kundeli, rivalry among the new leaders gets manifested as alliances with different political parties. Political party affiliations reflect per-

sonal rivalries, as they most often do in these villages and as I shall discuss in chapter 7, and hardly ever are these based on programmatic or ideological differences.

42. Leadership of particular caste groups is acquired by heredity and not in any other manner. New leaders can aspire only to positions that are subordinate to these hereditary leaders, and they lose their independence of action in the process.

43. An interesting parallel is reported for rural Maharashtra. Examining why rural cooperatives have worked comparatively well in Maharashtra (and Gujarat), even though their record in most other states has been quite dismal, Attwood (1992: 292–93) observes that "sources of constructive leadership in the country-side . . . seem to depend on two factors: how rural leaders (including both old elites and new entrepreneurs) interact with village people, and how they interact with urban elites. . . . What seems distinctive about Maharashtra is that rural leaders tend to identify with their village roots and act on problems found in that environment. . . . [These] politicians build support through development patronage — that is, through ensuring that projects such as roads, banks, percolation tanks, schools and clinics reach their constituents. . . . Wherever there are local leaders or groups of seasonally unemployed farmers who want an [employment generating] project, they know how to pressure political representatives and state officials to create one, forthwith. Thus the range of demands and responsibilities placed on the political system has expanded significantly. Furthermore, this demand is specifically for the poor, since the non-poor are not interested in breaking rocks to build roads" (pp. 295–97).

44. A few of these new leaders have some notable influence in a wider area. However, acquiring influence in neighboring villages is contingent upon first developing a firm base of loyalty within one's own village.

45. Interviewed in Kundai village, Udaipur district, June 16, 1998.

46. Interview with Bhanwarlal Garg, Congress Party worker for 25 years, presently the Chairman of its Block Committee for Suvana Block of Bhilwara District, and also *Pradhan* (President) of *Panchayat Samiti* Suvana. Bhilwara, July 25, 1998.

47. Strengthened two-party competition has had important results in terms of widening political participation, claims Lodha (1999: 3348), "movements for subaltern assertiveness are more fruitful [now] within the framework of the BJP-Congress balance of power." "Consolidation of two-party system in Rajasthan" is noted as well by Yadav (1996: 97).

48. "Even nominal reference to ideology and policy are nearly absent from the [appeals of] mainstream parties" (Dreze and Sen 1997: 99). "Membership and party support," says Kuhn (1998: 275), speaking of southern Rajasthan, "are not characterized by adherence to programs or ideologies, but to the purpose of

establishing connections" to derive economic benefits. A comparison of parties' election manifestos in Chapter 8 also reveals the lack of any major programmatic differences, at least insofar as rural areas are concerned.

49. Interviewed in Udaipur, July 9, 1998.

50. Interviewed in Udaipur, July 12, 1998.

51. One exception is provided by Sunderchha village in Rajsamand district. This village is composed of three caste-segregated hamlets, located a few kilometers apart from each other, over difficult and rocky terrain. The primary school of this village is located in the upper caste hamlet, which is closest to the main approach road, and scheduled caste children need to walk for almost an hour in order to attend school. Not surprisingly, most scheduled caste parents have kept their children away from school or they have waited until these children are older and more capable of walking such distances by themselves. In no other village among the 16 that I observed closely over extended periods of time or even in the remaining 53 which I visited for shorter periods were lower castes faced with the same kind of obvious disability.

52. Even before these discretionary funds became available to national- and state-level politicians, they were being used to considerable effect by politicos in the capital city. Oldenburg (1976: 72) reports: "The Delhi [Municipal] Councilor, because of his 'constituency fund,' can do a fair amount for his constituents in terms of material benefits as well as in terms of access and influence in the bureaucratic system. Fifty thousand rupees per year of the zonal budget is reserved for projects designated by the councilor . . . [who] can designate specific galis [lanes] for improvement (new paving, a sewer line, etc.) as well as determining which projects should be done first."

53. An MLA's constituency is about one-eighth the size of an MP's constituency, so these allocations are roughly equal in per capita terms. Inflation, which ran at under 10 percent during this time, did little to dent these huge step-ups in MPs' and MLAs' discretionary financing.

Chapter 4

1. There is another group of studies, not reported here, that deduce the existence of social capital from values of the dependent variables. A profusion of social capitals has erupted consequently that are related to different outcomes but that bear little relationship to one another (Baron and Hannan 1994; Woolcock 1998).

2. "The denotation of a word is the totality of objects indicated by that word; and the connotation is the totality of characteristics anything must possess to be in denotation of that word" (Sartori 1970: 1041).

3. To be sure, Putnam et al. (1993) combine four separate measures for construct-

ing their Civic Community Index. Along with density of formally registered civic associations, measures are also used that relate, respectively, to electoral turnout, preferential voting, and newspaper readership. Among these measures, however, only the density measure appears valid in terms of the definition that they provide for social capital. The measure for preferential voting is used to reinforce the distinction between horizontal and vertical organization, which is redundant considering that only horizontally organized networks were included in the measure of density. The other two measures — electoral turnout and newspaper readership — are also questionable. Higher social capital leads to more political participation — such is the claim — so electoral turnout is arguably an effect of social capital and not one of its constituents. Newspaper readership may add to the value of activities that citizens undertake, but it is difficult to make the connection between this factor and either norms or networks. One is left, therefore, with the measure of density computed over all formal organizations (but not informal ones). No independent measure of norms is included within the CCI, on account of the assumption, most likely unfounded in actual practice, that only cooperative norms will prevail within such horizontally shaped networks.

4. "Intense horizontal interactions . . . are an essential form of social capital," it is claimed for the Italian context. "A vertical network, no matter how dense and no matter how important to its participants, cannot sustain social trust and cooperation" (Putnam et al. 1993: 173–74).

5. Analysts have also disagreed on what to regard as a horizontally-organized network. "The Boy Scouts . . . are a hierarchically organized group, yet they are" favorably regarded by most social capital analysts. On the other hand, "militias and other nationalist organizations," excluded in most accounts, "do not appear to be much more vertically or hierarchically organized than other types" that get added within the usual measures of social capital (Berman 1997b: 567).

6. "Since the strengths [and types] of sentiments that exist between individuals is so difficult to measure apart from actual behavior — and is likely to be mercurial to boot — it is hard to conduct empirical research about it. One simply cannot explain variations in the solidarity of given groups without using an operational definition of the term" (Hechter 1987: 19).

7. "Actors do not behave or decide as atoms outside a social context, nor do they adhere slavishly to a script written for them by the particular intersection of social categories that they happen to occupy. . . . While social relations may indeed often be a necessary condition for trust and trustworthiness, they are not sufficient to guarantee these and may even provide occasion and means for malfeasance and conflict on a scale larger than in their absence" (Granovetter 1985: 487, 491).

8. Eastis (1998), paraphrased in Edwards and Foley (1998a: 132–33).

9.   "Many analyses that attempt to quantify social capital concentrate on formal networks and groups with an assumption that the quality and quantity of social life can be used as a proxy for social capital," states Lyon (2000: 677). However, "formal associations may only be a small factor in the production of trust or social capital. . .[and] the links between networks, norms and trust [need to be] made clear."

10. In many Third World countries, and particularly those where modernization efforts have been launched from above, formal associations are mostly creatures of the state, intended to reconfigure social relations in the villages. In parts of West Africa, "peasants were urged to participate in organizations established by a government organization. . . . Any organization that showed signs of autonomy was unacceptable to governments" and disallowed (Lecomte and Krishna 1997: 810). In India "as in many parts of the developing world, cooperatives were promoted as tools of the state bureaucracy . . . [and there is] no democratic participation" (Baviskar and Attwood 1995: 4–5).

11. Government-sponsored organizations in other parts of the Third World have also been attended mostly by richer and better connected residents and mostly also with the limited objective of deriving economic benefits cheaply. Savings and credit associations have been widely promoted by government and donor agencies in Tanzania, but not all villagers have enjoyed equal access to organizations that have been perceived chiefly as sources of cheap money. "Government officials and employees of the project agency got first claim to these resources, along with some relatively better-off villagers. . . . [Most] villagers perceived these schemes as not for ordinary farmers. They came to these projects mostly with a cynical attitude, hoping to gain access to subsidized credit or to some other cheaply available resources." (Zoetelief 1999.)

12. This hypothetical example is discussed along with other real-world cases in Krishna (2000).

13. With further refinements made on account of differences in culture and lifestyle, this scale has proved valid and useful also in other developing country contexts (Grootaert and van Bastelaer, forthcoming). Suggestions for further refinement and a methodology for field application are presented in Krishna and Shrader (2000).

14. A bigha is a local unit for measuring land. One bigha is roughly equal to one-sixth of a hectare.

15. A scree plot has a distinct elbow, i.e., it flattens out between factors one and two. The conclusion about a single common factor is reinforced also by observing that root mean square off-diagonal residuals are equal to 0.104, which is well within the acceptable limit of 0.126 as indicated by Harman's criterion for a sample size of 64. Kaiser's Measure of Sampling Adequacy: Overall MSA = 0.828. Communality = 3.81.

16. Individual correlation coefficients are all significant at the 0.0001 level with a value of 0.65 or higher; Cronbach's Alpha coefficient = 0.91.

17. Correlation coefficients are all 0.85 or higher, and significant at the 0.01 level.

18. Each item is given an equal weight within the Index, which is obtained by summing across the scores after first dividing each variable by its range, so that each item has a maximum range of one. A further transformation results in an index that has a range from zero to hundred. This latter transformation is useful at a later stage for interpreting regression results. An alternative index was constructed by weighting the individual items with their factor scores. The two indices are highly correlated with one another (0.98), indicating that this index is robust against alternative weighting schemes, and there is no special merit in preferring one index over the other.

19. Alternative indices of social capital can be constructed employing these variables instead of or in addition to the six variables that I use for the Social Capital index. Three alternative indices of social capital were constructed, combining different sets of variables. These alternative constructions are highly correlated among themselves, as can be expected. Moreover, there is no change in the regression results reported in the following chapters in terms of which variables are statistically significant if instead of the Social Capital Index any of these other indices is considered.

20. Skewness = 0.68.

21. MLAs (Members of the State Legislative Assembly) and MPs (Members of the national Parliament) are also elected, but they have constituencies that usually span approximately 200 and 1,000 villages, respectively.

22. One other local agency that could be considered in this regard is the village cooperative society, which has also been formed by the government, and which has multiple activities, though not as numerous as the *panchayat's*. However, 1,661 of 1,898 Rajasthan villagers (87.5 percent) said that they had never attended any meeting of these societies. The proportion of nonparticipants is relatively constant, varying between 84.5 and 93.1 percent among all 60 villages. It is even higher on average (91 percent) among the nine Madhya Pradesh villages, so cooperatives are a uniformly weak type of agency in these villages. Cooperatives in these states have been instituted mostly from the top down. Discussions with villagers revealed that they thought of these state-controlled bodies quite as investigators in other parts of the country have regarded them to be — "uniformly wasteful, inefficient, corrupt, unproductive, and even moribund" (Attwood 1992: 302).

23. The term Village Council is mine. Villagers themselves refer to these bodies as *Gaon-ki-Panchayat*, or villagers' *panchayat* as opposed to the other one that is *Sarkari*, or the government's, *panchayat*. Persons who sit on these bodies are spoken of as *purana netas* (old leaders).

24. Notice that the same question was asked in respect of caste associations, new

leaders, and also Village Councils. A clear distinction is apparent, however, among items in this question for which villagers answered "Yes" in respect of different types of agencies. "Yes" responses were received usually for the top half of items when this question was asked in respect of New leaders and for the bottom half when the same question was asked in relation to Village Councils, which indicates that duties are quite clearly divided between these two types of village agencies. A similar division of labor is indicated by table 2.2. Very few "Yes" responses were received when the same question with all its items was asked in respect of caste associations, political parties, *panchayats*, and patron-client relationships.

25. Regression analysis was conducted to uncover the factors that might be associated with each of these agency strength variables. Except in the case of STR_VC, however, the Social Capital Index was not significant as an independent variable. The results of these analyses are reported in the following chapters where I examine likely causes for high agency strength, more particularly for Str_NEW and Str_VC that are revealed to be particularly important for one or more of the three objectives I consider.

26. How effective new leaders are in obtaining economic development benefits for villagers depends, for instance, on their ability to strike deals with party politicians and government officials. Similarly, political parties' and *panchayats'* effectiveness depends upon how well they can relate to their external environments. Even in the case of Village Councils (VCs), the agency form that is most closely associated with social capital, effectiveness is a variable that responds to structural influences, which are not related to social capital. VCs are more effective, by and large, in villages that are located a greater distance from the market or where literacy is lower. Social capital is not responsive to the same influences.

27. In addition, this variable is also relevant for assessing claims related to homogeneous versus heterogeneous groups.

28. Government offices are also located usually at these market centers, so in addition to measuring distance to commerce, the variable DISTMKT also provides a measure of the physical distance that villagers must traverse in order to meet with government officials.

29. Census 1991 data report the level of service available in each village related to these facilities. These data were updated with the help of personal observations in each village. Gradations related to level of service were adopted from Census classifications.

Chapter 5

1. 1,450 of 1,898 respondents contacted in 60 Rajasthan villages reported cultivation as their primary source of income, and another 294 reported agricultural

labor. In the nine Madhya Pradesh villages, 304 of 334 villagers interviewed had cultivation or agricultural labor as their principal occupation.

2. Famine relief programs are mounted that provide wages to people, and drinking water is transported at great expense.

3. Maize is the principal crop of Udaipur, Rajsamand and Dungarpur, and more than 60 percent of the gross cropped area in each of these districts is planted to this crop. *Jowar* and *Bajra* (two different kinds of millets) are important crops in Ajmer, and together these account for more than two-thirds of gross cropped area in this district. Bhilwara, which lies between Ajmer and Udaipur, has maize and *jowar* for its principal crops.

4. Five-year plans were suspended for the three-year period between 1966 and 1969 and again for the year 1979–1980. In the table below, these two periods have been combined together with the preceding Five-Year Plan period.

5. 2,563 of India's development "blocks"—the entire country is divided into slightly more than 5,000 such units of development administration—are covered under drought-prone areas and watershed development programs that are intended to "drought-proof" the economies of these areas (GOI 1998).

6. Pretty (1995) and Chambers, et al. (1990) make the general case; Saxena (1994) discusses the importance of livelihood stability in the context of large parts of India; Rosin (1994) describes traditional livelihood strategies and management systems in Rajasthan.

7. Sustainable livelihoods and sustainable food security for the poor, including regeneration of environmental resources, constitute two of five principal goals professed by UNDP. The other three goals include gender equality, pro-poor governance, and fostering an enabling environment for pro-poor economic growth (UNDP 1998: 20). The Food and Agricultural Organization (FAO) has an entire division devoted to helping people attain Sustainable Livelihoods.

8. Of these 27.9 million persons, 19.4 million or nearly 70 percent are government employees.

9. Figures reported in this paragraph are taken from GOI (1998).

10. Other than what they make from their crops and their cattle and sheep, the majority of households in Rajasthan and Madhya Pradesh, 76 percent, derive no regular income from any other source. The other 24 percent of households usually have one person working in a government undertaking or a private-sector concern. Many of these persons send some part of their (usually meager) wages home to the village.

11. GOI (1998), chapter 17, page 1.

12. The District Rural Development Agencies (DRDAs) maintain an updated list of poor households in each village. The poverty cutoff was defined at the time of writing as annual income below Rs. 11,000 ($260), which is calculated as the income with which a person can just about afford to eat the minimum requirement of 2,400 calories per day.

13. Of the total of 30 million blind persons in the world, six million are in rural India (GOR 1998).
14. Hardly any privately owned health facilities are located in these rural areas. Where they exist, these facilities are staffed usually by government doctors and nursing staff, who supplement their incomes by moonlighting in these facilities. Private educational facilities have only recently started being set up in these villages, and more than 95 percent of village children continue to be educated in government-run schools. Water supply is a state monopoly, as is electricity, public transportation (private buses are allowed to operate on routes that the public sector considers nonviable for itself), and bank credit (which was nationalized in 1971).
15. Between 1989 and 1997, 720 million man-days of employment were generated by a single state program, the *Jawahar Rozgaar Yojana* (Jawahar Employment Scheme, or JRY), which amounts to six days of employment for every worker in the rural labor force (GOR 1999). Additional employment opportunities are provided by other state programs — the Drought Prone Areas and the Desert Development Programs, the Employment Assurance Scheme, the Million Wells Scheme, and others — that are intended, just as JRY is intended, as much for constructing community assets as for providing wages to those who might otherwise starve to extinction.
16. I was the founder Director of this program and of its implementing agency, the Rajasthan government's Department of Watershed Development. For a more detailed account of this program and of its numerous achievements, both dismal and outstanding, see Krishna (1997).
17. The government's program expanded at the rate of almost a half-million hectares per year, which was huge and often hard to handle, but this was still too slow to cover an area of more than 20 million hectares in this state where these kinds of treatments are necessary and beneficial. Subsidies were later cut to 80 and then 70 percent of program cost, reflecting a growing apprehension that the government effort would be more sustainable over the long term if it was accompanied by increasing public contributions. On this point, see Kerr et al. (1999).
18. The four different variables have the following factor loading scores on the single common factor: 0.72, 0.81, 0.84 and 0.85. Communality is 2.76, implying that the underlying factor accounts for about 70 percent of the combined variance of the four individual items. Kaiser's overall MSA = 0.79; RMS off-diagonal residuals = 0.11. A scree plot has a distinct elbow and it flattens out between factors one and two.
19. This index was constructed by taking a simple sum of scores over these four items, after first standardizing them by re-scoring their values so that each has a maximum range of one. Each variable thus has an equal weight within the index. An alternative index weights the individual items by their factor scores and it is highly correlated (correlation coefficient = 0.94) with this Index.

20. Training of Rural Youth for Self-Employment (TRYSEM) and Development of Women and Children in Rural Areas (DWACRA).

21. Dreze (1990), Swaminathan (1990), and Yugandhar and Raju (1992) make the general case; Ahuja and Bhargava (1989) make a similar case for Rajasthan.

22. Not surprising, the most favorable assessment is that of a government agency. On the basis of its sample survey, the Rajasthan Government's Department of Rural Development estimates that more than two-thirds of all beneficiaries were able to cross the poverty line permanently, i.e., without any major risk of slipping back into poverty.

23. Land reform is held out by some urban intellectuals as essential for poverty removal (though urban-based assets, such as stock holdings and real estate, are not usually made explicit within this calculus of egalitarian redistribution). In the context of India, however, where average landholdings are usually less than 1 hectare and where the largest holdings are usually no more than 25–30 hectares, i.e., where the middle peasantry is dominant, economically and politically and large landlords are very few in number (Varshney 1995), further land reform is unlikely to be viable politically.

24. Within each village, new leaders rotate employment so that each household has an opportunity for some part of the total time. Rotation of labor is the norm I observed among all 16 case-study villages.

25. Considering three-year figures here (and five-year figures for poverty reduction) helps smooth the random fluctuations that can arise from year to year.

26. This figure would be higher, closer to ten days per capita, if it were averaged, instead, over all poor and adult villagers. Comparative analysis of village performance is not significantly affected, however, no matter which of these two averages one considers for analysis.

27. Each of these scores is standardized to have a range from zero to one, so that each has an equal weight in the index. The four-point aggregate is transformed to have a range from zero to hundred, which makes it easier to interpret regression results, reported later in this chapter.

28. "Practitioners" include those couples where either the male or the female has gone in for sterilization, or where some other birth-control implant or support is regularly used. Health Department records were available for only 48 villages, so this relationship could not be tested for all 60 villages in Rajasthan.

29. The variable STR_PCR is not separately represented here. Patron-client links have scores that are consistently low within all villages, i.e., there is no variation among high-performing and low-performing villages. For nearly all villagers, patron-client linkages are an inheritance from the past that are related in the present time with a small and dwindling set of activities. People contact patrons mostly for obtaining consumption loans. Hardly any villager contacts this type of agent for any other purpose. Reasons for the declining salience of this kind of agency were presented earlier in chapter 3.

30. Interview with Chaturbhuj Gujar, 75 years old and one of the patriarchs of Balesariya village, July 25, 1998.
31. Interview with Mangilal Sharma, Sarpanch, Balesariya Gram Panchayat, July 28, 1998.
32. Interview with Bhanwarlal Garg, Pradhan, Panchayat Samiti, Bhilwara, March 21, 1999. A *panchayat samiti* is composed of a group of village *panchayats*. Funds from most state programs have usually been allocated to village *panchayats* through the medium of *panchayat samitis*.
33. Interview with Jagdish Joshi, 40 years of age, and a young leader of Ghodach village, June 16, 1998.
34. Interview with Sarup Singh, previously Sarpanch of Ghodach village, June 18, 1998.
35. Interview with J. P. Shrimali, Assistant Engineer of the Watershed Development Department, under whose charge watershed development activities were implemented in Losing and Ghodach villages. Interviewed in Losing village, July 17, 1998.
36. Literacy is not, strictly speaking, a "structural" variable. Since it is measured at the level of the village society, however, it has been displayed here alongside other societal variables.
37. Though some independent variables are correlated with each other, for instance, STR_CASTE is correlated with CASTEDOM, and literacy with PERCPOOR, pairwise correlation among the independent variables is not greater than 0.5 in any case. The value of the Condition Index is 24.68 for model 1, indicating moderate multicollinearity, and less than 15 for Models 2 and 3, indicating low collinearity. White's general test does not reveal the presence of any significant heteroskedasticity.
38. 73 percent of villagers in Madhya Pradesh said they would contact the new leaders if they had any business to transact with banks or with the District Rural Development Agency; 69 percent said they would go to these leaders for getting employment on government construction sites; and 68 percent said they would seek the assistance of these leaders for interacting with suppliers, insurance agencies, and other market operators.
39. Interview with Vandana Meena, Zila Pramukh (head of the district-level panchayat organization), Udaipur, March 10, 1999.

Chapter 6

1. Unlike in the United States and in other countries with a federal system, the police in India are not appointed or controlled by mayors or any other form of local government. Instead, they form part of a vertical hierarchy, which is responsible to the Director-General of Police in each state. Police officers form part of a permanent cadre, and they move between positions within the state

at the instructions of the Director-General and the Home Ministry. For a recent overview of the police in India, see Verma (2001).

2.   The term "Village Council" is mine. Villagers refer to these bodies as *mukhiya sabha* (meeting of elders) or *gaon-ki-panchayat* (traditional village assembly). I must distinguish these traditional bodies from the official *Panchayats*, which are modern, introduced institutions, inserted within the institutional landscape by the Indian state. The older and more informal local institutions, which I call Village Councils, are also sometimes referred to by villagers as *panchayats*. Villagers make a critical distinction, however, between *Gaon-ki-panchayat* (the villagers' panchayat) and *Sarkari panchayat* (the government's panchayat). To avoid any terminological confusion, I will refer to the villagers' homegrown and traditional bodies as Village Councils, saving the term *panchayats* to refer only to government-introduced institutions.

Though there is a significant correlation between the level of social capital in a village and the strength of its informal Village Council, the strength of this correlation is not very high (correlation coefficient = 0.45). High social capital in many villages is not accompanied by especially strong Village Councils; and strong Village Councils (VCs) co-exist with medium or low levels of social capital in some villages (see table 4.4).

Different sets of factors influence the levels of social capital and VC strength in villages. Villages located closer to the market tend to have relatively weaker Village Councils, in general. However, social capital in these villages is not always lower.

3.   For an excellent review article that examines the origins and functions of these traditional institutions in different parts of India see Cohn (1965).

4.   Interview with Roshan Lal Jain, Advocate, Udaipur, March 10, 1999. Other practicing lawyers interviewed in Udaipur and in Bhilwara supported this assessment.

5.   Interview with Saubhagya Singh, Police Station-Incharge, Bhilwara Police Station, March 21, 1999.

6.   Interview with Onkar Ba, Dantisar village, Rajsamand district, June 22, 1998.

7.   Interview with Radheysham Sadhu, 35 years of age, a successful businessman and a new leader of Palri village, July 27, 1998.

8.   Cited in *India Today* (March 29, 1999).

9.   "Temple of Justice," a report in the same issue of *India Today* (March 29, 1999) describes a *Jana Adalat* (people's court) that has sprung up over the past five years in the city of Bhubhaneshwar, Orissa. It tells of how this court has helped "settle over 400 cases — mostly civil disputes like disagreements over property and land. But with its fame spreading to even distant [urban] areas like Cuttack, Phulbani, and Nayagarh, the court is now also hearing divorce suits and criminal offences. At the moment, about 100 cases are pending with the court . . .

[which meets] bi-weekly. . . . While the country's civil courts take years and decades to settle disputes, the *Jana Adalat* is a simpler alternative, [even] though it has no legal sanction."

10. The effectiveness of the different Village Councils differs in terms of range of activities, frequency of meetings, and extent of popular participation. The variable Str_VC, defined in chapter 4, scales the strength of Village Councils in these terms.

11. Records of Sub-Divisional Magistrates' courts were consulted for the purpose of compiling the numbers of land-related cases for these villages. In all, 13 different courts have jurisdiction over this group of 60 villages. I was able to get information from 11 of these courts for a total of 51 villages.

12. A group of six villages, all of which lie within the tribal belt of Dungarpur district, have scores of zero, i.e., not a single land dispute case has been filed in the courts by any resident of these villages. These villages did not form part of the sample of 16 villages that I studied intensively as cases. Their records are analyzed, instead, with the help of regression analysis.

13. Since a random sample of villagers was interviewed in each village, the sample mean is an unbiased estimator of the mean for the village population.

14. Factor loadings for the four separate items are 0.779, 0.717, 0.824, and 0.698, respectively. Communality is 2.82, i.e., 71 percent of the combined variance of the four separate items is explained by the single common factor. The Index of Communal Harmony was constructed by adding together village scores for the four separate items after first dividing each item by its range so that each has an equal weight in the index. A further transformation results in giving the index a range from zero to hundred, which is helpful for interpreting the regression results that follow.

15. Both of these correlation coefficients are significant at the 0.01 level. Since official records for criminal cases and land dispute cases were not available for all 60 villages, it was not possible to aggregate these items within the Index of Communal Harmony.

16. None of the other significant variables — i.e., neither social capital nor the capacity of Village Councils — is consistently higher in villages of Dungarpur district. In fact, none of the variables associated with any of the three competing hypotheses being examined here is in any way markedly higher or lower in the 12 Dungarpur villages compared to the other 48 villages (only literacy is considerably lower, but this variable does not achieve significance in the present regression analysis). One is forced to the conclusion, thus, that factors outside the scope of the present inquiry are responsible for the greater observed harmony that is found among Dungarpur villages. The dummy variable, DUNGARPUR, includes the omnibus effect of these unidentified causes.

17. Some of these independent variables are significantly correlated, for instance,

Str_VC has a correlation coefficient of 0.45 with the Social Capital Index. However, the pair-wise correlation among the independent variables is not greater than 0.5 in any case. The value of the Condition Index is 25.72 and 24.62 for Models 1 and 2, indicating moderate multicollinearity, and it is less than 15 for Model 3, indicating low collinearity. White's general test does not reveal the presence of any significant heteroskedasticity.

18. Additionally, R-squared does not change by very much when this variable is dropped from the regression model.

19. This is shown further by Model 3, which includes only the three significant variables of Model 2, Str_VC, the Social Capital Index, and the dummy variable, DUNGARPUR. The F-ratio rises to 15.43 when the nonsignificant variables are removed from the model.

20. Interaction variables, constructed by multiplying together the Social Capital Index with each of these agency variables, were also considered in regression analysis, but none of these variables achieved significance.

21. And not a multiplicative effect, as they did in the case of economic development, reviewed in the previous chapter.

22. Streets in this village are strewn with garbage and dotted by pools of stagnant water. No one feels responsible for cleaning these streets or for fixing streetlights. In spite of having lived and worked in these rural areas for thirteen years before, I had a severe bout of gastroenteritis while living in this village, most likely brought on by its lack of hygiene and polluted drinking water.

23. Interviewed in Palri village, July 24, 1998.

24. Interview with Radheysham Sadhu, Palri village, July 27, 1998.

25. Interview with Laduram Jat, chairman of the watershed Users Committee, Palri, July 28, 1998.

26. Interviewed in Palri village, July 30, 1998.

27. Interview with Fateh Balai, Palri, July 25, 1998.

28. An amusing instance was provided in this regard by Gopichand Kumhar, a leader of the faction aligned with the Congress Party in Palri: "The BJP burst five atomic bombs and as a result there was a heat wave. Many people fell ill. This was very bad decision-making. If only they had burst these bombs during the winter time, then the increase in heat would have benefited people. . . . Our Congress government also burst an atom bomb [in 1971]. But the Congress cares more about the people; they exploded this bomb in winter." Interviewed in Palri, July 27, 1998.

29. Regression analysis reveals that party strength is not generally significant for communal harmony — the variable Str_PARTY did not achieve significance in alternative specifications of the regression model.

30. Dantisar village scores 58 points on the Social Capital Index, which places it in the Medium category, not as high as Balesariya and Nauwa but not as low

as Kundai or Ghodach, indicating that social capital alone does not account sufficiently for higher levels of community harmony.

31. Interview with Badan Singh, Dantisar, June 17, 1998.

32. Interview with Nathulal Bhoi, Dantisar, June 21, 1998.

33. Interviewed in Dantisar village, June 18, 1998.

34. Interviewed in Dantisar village, June 22, 1998.

35. Carstairs (1912: 12–13). The author was, in his own words, "a member of the Indian Civil Service, who, after serving for nearly twenty-nine years with credit, but without distinction, retired in the year 1903" (page 3).

36. "The draft of the Indian Penal Code was prepared by the First Law Commission when Macaulay was the President of that body. Its basis is the law of England. . . . Suggestions were also derived from the French Penal Code and from Living-stone's Code of Louisiana. The draft underwent a very careful revision at the hands of Sir Barnes Peacock, Chief Justice, and puisne Judges of the Calcutta Supreme Court who were members of the Legislative Council, and was passed into law in 1860" (Business Guide to India, *The Economic Times*, Bombay, Web Edition). The people of India were not involved, and certainly no village custom was consulted, while framing these laws that continue to govern society, including the Evidence Act (1872) and the Criminal Procedure Code (1883).

37. Report in *India Today* (March 29, 1999).

38. Reported in a daily newspaper, *Dainik Bhaskar*, Udaipur, March 8, 1999.

39. Interviewed in Bhilwara, March 20, 1999. Dangi went on to quip, "The IPC [Indian Penal Code] applies to ordinary people, then there is the VIP-C. [Ex-Prime Minister] Narasimha Rao's bail application moved very fast from the lowest court to the Supreme Court [of India, and it was heard and decided] in just two days. For the poor guy, this could take more than two years and [his case may] still not be heard. Poor persons do not have the knowledge [or] the funds to get justice [within the system]."

40. "Cases are brought to court to harass one's opponent, as a punishment, as a form of land speculation and profit making, to satisfy insulted pride, and to maintain local political dominance over one's followers. The litigants do not expect a settlement that will end the dispute to eventuate from recourse to state courts" (Cohn 1965: 105).

41. Interview with Kapil Garg, Deputy Inspector General, Rajasthan Police, Jaipur, August 10, 1998.

42. "Believe it or not," says a report in *The Times of India* (January 8, 2000), "Delhi policemen devote just about 40 percent of their time for preventing and detecting crime. The rest is spent guarding VIPs, and tackling rallies and processions." Police in rural areas, while not so hard pressed for VIP duties, still devote a considerable proportion of resources for guarding VIP convoys, escorting visiting dignitaries, etc.

43. Interview with Panna Singh, SHO Raipur police station, March 17, 1999.
44. Interview with Saubhagya Singh, SHO Bhilwara police station, March 21, 1999.
45. While Mukerjee details the working of these Village Councils for southern India and the Punjab, Tod (1971 [1829]: 120) describes the operation of these bodies among villages in Rajasthan. "Of their *punchaets* I will only remark that their import among the vassals is very comprehensive; and when they talk of the *punch*, it means the 'collective wisdom.' "
46. Saxena and Charan (1973, 1993) report the continued salience of the Village Council over twenty years in Dingri village of Udaipur district. Purohit (1974) and Census of India (1961, 1981) speak of the role played by similar councils in Zawar and Janvi villages, respectively. Foster and Simmons (1978) reflect upon the changes in the operation of the traditional council brought about in one village (Bhanapur) of Uttar Pradesh on account of changes in the pattern of land ownership. Srinivas (1987) reviews the literature and indicates the duties performed by such councils in different parts of India.
47. Feeding corn to pigeons is the most common penalty imposed by Village Councils in this region. In Balesariya, for instance, a person who had misbehaved in public after consuming alcohol, was required to scatter four bags of maize in a place designated for this purpose. A similar practice is observed in villages in a wider area, as observed by Fisher (1997: 66ff) for a village in Jodhpur district, about five hundred kilometers distant from Balesariya.
48. Historically, according to Cohn (1965: 91–92), even though dominant castes were more influential in these Councils, "in general, the attempt [was] to settle disputes on the basis of some sort of equity. . . . The power and influence of the dominant caste is not absolute over lower caste people. . . . The dominant caste is subject, as a part of the village, to some of the same norms as others in the village."
49. One panch in Nauwa village who was frequently drunk in public was kicked off the Council by his caste fellows and replaced by a younger and more respected member of the same caste. In Sunderchha, a panch was replaced when it became known that he had conspired to take a bribe from an affected party.
50. No official statistics exist to confirm this 80:20 division of cases between the informal Village Councils and the formal court system. A number of key respondents independently mentioned the same set of numbers, however, including a police station officer-in-charge (Panna Singh, officer-in-charge of Raipur police station, Bhilwara), a leading advocate (Roshan Lal Jain of Udaipur), political party officials (Dharmanarayan Joshi of the BJP's Udaipur unit), and several knowledgeable villagers, including long-time members of Village Councils. This widespread convergence on the rough distribution of adjudication between VCs and the police cannot be entirely coincidental.

Chapter 7

1. Some analysts of Indian politics, including Kohli (1990) and Sabharwal (1997), are fearful that democracy might indeed break down in these circumstances.
2. There is a tendency, common to surveys undertaken in different parts of the world, for respondents to over-report participation in voting. 91 percent of these north Indian villagers said they had voted in the last-held election; however, the average voting percentage recorded in these villages was only 63.3 percent. "As is always the case in surveys," state Verba et al.(1995: 50, fn. 2), "the reports of voting are exaggerated. . . . Because other forms of activity are both less frequent than voting and less firmly attached to notions of civic duty, [however,] . . . the problem [of over-reporting] is less severe for other activities than it is for voting." Bratton (1999: 556) similarly finds that "as is common in other parts of the world for political acts considered to be socially obligatory, respondents in Zambia over-reported their involvement in voting" but not in the other three forms of political participation.
3. The interpretations that respondents give to the same set of questions vary from one context to another. Table 7.1 is useful to the extent that it allows some gross or aggregate comparisons to be made.
4. Bi-variate correlation coefficients among responses to these seven survey items are all positive and they all have high statistical significance (at the 0.0001 level). These seven variables load commonly on a single common factor, and factor loadings are all 0.67 or higher. Communality is 3.4, implying that nearly half of the combined variance of the seven separate variables is accounted for by the single common factor. Similarly, the three survey items related to voting are all highly correlated and load highly on a single common factor.
5. Each item is first re-scored to have a range between zero and one. Consequently, each item has an equal weight in the Index. The summed score is re-scaled to give it a range from zero to one hundred points, which makes it easier for interpreting regression results, reported later. Correlations of the six individual items with the Index are all 0.73 or higher; Cronbach's Coefficient Alpha = 0.845.
6. Mean individual score on the Index is 26.4 points, and standard deviation is 24.1. Skewness = 0.871.
7. Additionally, R-squared was not significantly affected when this variable was removed in alternative specifications of the regression model.
8. Other interactive variables were also constructed by considering the other five agency variables. None of these interactive variables was significant, however, in alternative specifications of the regression model.
9. In addition to landholding, herd size and quality of house construction were also considered as proxies for wealth, but these results did not change appreciably no matter which among these indicators was utilized for this purpose.

10. Each of these three correlation coefficients is significant at the 0.01 level or better.

11. The variable "Gender" is measured for the purpose of this calculation as Women = 1, Men = 0.

12. The variable "Information" was constructed from responses to the following survey question. Which among the following sources do you consult regularly — i.e., at least once a month — for news and information: household members, neighbors, village leaders/prominent persons, radio or TV, newspapers, the village assembly, other (specify)? Scores were assigned depending on the number of sources a respondent had indicated. Information calculated in this manner is only weakly correlated with the Education variable, which corresponds to the number of years a respondent spent at school. Of the seven sources of information, only one, newspapers, is inaccessible to the illiterate. Further, neither Information nor Education are correlated to any great extent with Wealth. The coefficient of correlation between landholding and education, for instance, is only 0.34 — and it is even lower (0.16) among villagers aged 18 years or less. Villagers of all caste groups and income categories are preferring increasingly to send their children to school, as seen in chapter 3, and at least for the primary school level, there is no appreciable difference in enrollment by caste or wealth categories.

13. Only extremely capable women rise to positions of real (as opposed to titular) leadership in villages. Effective women leaders whom I met were all relatively highly educated, energetic, and forceful. Despite being in leadership positions for several years and having filled those positions competently and with distinction, some, such as Rajkumari Goswami (Deputy Pradhan, Mandsaur District, Madhya Pradesh), had yet to acquire the respect they deserved, especially among older males.

14. Though a similar set of influences accounts for the rise of new leadership in all villages, the capacities of these leaders vary significantly from village to village. It is not easy to account fully for differences in agency capacity since a number of random and contingent factors intervene. Among non-random factors, however, two were found to be significantly correlated with agency strength. Distance from high school is significantly negatively correlated with the variable Str_NEW, and inequality of land ownership, as measured by the Gini coefficient, is significantly positively correlated with this variable. All else being the same, easier access to high school education tends to add to agency strength, which is understandable. But why should greater asset inequality be positively correlated with high agency strength? I suspect that inequality affects agency strength through increasing the demand for new leadership among poorer villagers. Higher inequality and greater poverty may be associated with a greater desire to support new leaders who can help villagers obtain employ-

ment and other economic benefits from the state. More research will be required to establish these relationships conclusively.

15. Except for the states of Kerala and West Bengal, where the Communist parties have organized at the village level, forcing other parties to compete by providing similar contact points for villagers, there is little by way of village- or even district-level party organization in most of the rest of rural India. See Kohli (1987) for West Bengal, and Heller (1999) and Herring (1983) for Kerala.

16. Reports of the last twenty years from other parts of India also provide indication of increasing political efficacy among ordinary villagers. "The rural elites are losing some of their powers," concludes Robinson (1988: 10), writing of rural Andhra Pradesh in the early 1980s, "the vote banks are collapsing. . . . The critical factor is that some members of the central, state, and district bureaucracies, and increasing numbers of the poor have both begun to realize that their 'interpreters' have been carefully and systematically distorting their messages in both directions."

17. More than 270 households reside in this village, and about 70 are Muslim. The rest are Hindu, including 90 of the Jat caste, 80 of the Gujar caste, and 20 of the Regar caste.

18. Interviewed in Gangapur City, Bhilwara district, July 14, 1998.

19. For an excellent discussion of how caste associations have been reconstructed into political parties geared toward delivering particularistic economic benefits to members of particular caste groups, see Chandra (2000). For a more general discussion of strategies of "embedded particularism," see Herring (1999). Bates (1999) demonstrates how urban based political entrepreneurs in Zambia have built political action groups based on ethnic ties with kin in rural areas, suggesting that a similar logic of reconstructing ethnicity is attractive as well in other parts of the developing world.

20. Summarizing the results of the 1999 national elections, the *Economist* (October 9, 1999) states that "no party, bar those on the left, offered voters a clear-cut ideology or philosophy of government. Instead, voters judged parties mainly on their performance at state level, and often found them wanting." Ideological appeals (of a special kind) were held out by the BJP in 1985 (and to a lesser extent also in 1990) when it drummed up religious fervor among Hindus by promising to rebuild a mythical temple in Ayodhya. But the party has adopted a less strident stance on these divisive issues after coming to power in New Delhi, and villagers have also ceased to be moved by these appeals. As one district-level BJP organizer told me: "People say 'When the temple in our own village is not even cleaned regularly, what will we gain by building a new temple there [in Ayodhya]?' The *mandir-masjid* [temple-mosque] thing has lost its charm. Local issues prevail in elections" (Interview with L.N. Daad, Member of the Executive Committee of the BJP for Rajasthan. Bhilwara, March 23, 1999).

21. "Despite the apparent centralization of decision-making power in New Delhi, it is the national leadership that is more dependent on effective local leadership than vice versa" says Brass (1997a: 321), speaking of an essential continuity in Indian politics. The nature of local leadership and the relative effectiveness of different types of leaders have changed substantially, however, in the last twenty years.

22. Interview with Chunnilal Garasiya, Congress Party leader in the Udaipur region, and cabinet minister in the Rajasthan Government during the 1980s (Udaipur, March 13, 1999). Similar electoral strategies are reported by leaders of the other major party, the BJP (see chapter 3).

23. Hardly any new leaders among those I met were keen to tie themselves down to a permanent relationship with any political party. Their status in the village depends on getting greater economic benefits for villagers, and much higher benefits can be obtained by those who are successful in playing off parties against one another. Even in terms of their own personal ambitions, there is not much that these village leaders hope to gain through allying themselves loyally with any one party. "Most of these political formations, which serve as instruments of democratization of society . . . are themselves completely undemocratic in their organizational set-up as well as style of functioning (Yadav 1996: 100). New leaders are aware that party nominations are not usually awarded in any democratic or transparent manner, and ability ranks alongside, and often below, a host of other characteristics, such as family connections.

24. Interview with Logar Lal Dangi, Nauwa village, Udaipur district, June 26, 1998.

Chapter 8

1. *Panchayats* have very limited utility for this purpose partly because they function as no more than "mere implementing agencies of a centralized state" (Mayaram 1998). They enable the state to reach down to villagers, but communication in the reverse direction — upward, from village to state — is much more constrained.

2. Scores for these three activities are closely correlated with each other, and they were combined together with the help of factor analysis to construct the Index of Political Activity.

3. "Informal (grassroots) and formal (state) institutions often contradict each other. . . . Russia today continues to suffer from a *missing middle* of organizations linking informal grassroots networks and modern organizations. . . . this gap is sometimes filled by anti-modern enterprises run by ex-nomenklatura officials or by Mafia organizations" (Rose 1999).

4. "Village residents in Uganda find it hard to connect with agencies of the state. What they know and what is available to them — their traditional laws and

deliberative bodies — are not valuable for these purposes; and what is valuable — state programs and state assistance — is usually hard to access. . . . Decentralization has not helped. . .to reduce this distance" (Opio-Odongo and Lwanda-Ntale 2000).

5.   "Bolivia's agrarian reform of the 1950s created an institutional vacuum in the rural areas. . . . it annulled the old feudal patterns . . . but little was done by the state or its agencies to build linkages with peasant organizations" (Demeure and Guardia 1997: 91).

6.   There are few "local and accessible links between townspeople and government." Locally evolved "community development organizations act as local-level town governments and see themselves as responsible for making national and local governments more responsive to the townspeople" (Seligson 1999).

7.   Connections are important. Grassroots groups and NGOs that are unable to make effective connections with their national governments are increasingly going around governments to make contact with international advocacy networks. National NGOs use transnational networks to communicate with and put pressure upon their national governments, thereby connecting with them through a tedious and long drawn-out route. Advances in communication technology have made such transnational routes feasible, though it is likely that these avenues are more readily available to richer citizens and better endowed NGOs (Keck and Sikkink 1998).

8.   Even in the case of Italy, however, some analysts have stressed the role that middle-level institutions, in this case, political parties, have played for organizing citizens and articulating their demands. "Sports clubs, choral societies, cooperatives and cultural associations have been organized by and for two major political parties, the Communists and the Christian Democrats," claim Foley and Edwards (1996: 42) for the Emilia-Romagna region. Tarrow (1996) enlarges this claim to include other Italian regions as well. Agency capacity — in the form of well-organized political parties — is strong in the very regions where social capital is also high, and both of these factors count equally for institutional performance.

9.   The two southern districts, Udaipur and Rajsamand, experienced nearly unbroken rule for more than ten centuries by a single dynastic ruling house (Mewar). Villagers of these districts experienced relatively stable rule and continuity in local traditions (Pinhey 1996 [1909]). Villagers of the two northern districts, Ajmer and Bhilwara, had a more turbulent history and long periods of unstable rule. Because of its strategic position in the Aravalli range of mountains, Ajmer was almost continuously fought over by various contenders. It was ruled by the Mughals for sporadic intervals in its history, and it was finally annexed by the British and ruled directly by the imperial power (Lupton 1908). Bhilwara, situated directly south of Ajmer and directly north of Rajsamand, was put together

as an administrative district after independence. Some parts of its territories were taken from Ajmer, and other parts from the northern and more turbulent part of Mewar.

10. Krishna et al. (1997) present the experience of 18 such programs.

11. "The liberty it brings," claims Yadav (1999b: 34), speaking of Indian democracy at the current time, "is distributed in extremely unequal measure. The power it brings to the people as an abstraction is rarely, if ever, exercised by real people. And there are still many people — full citizens of the republic of India — who feel as powerless under this democracy as they did under British rule."

12. Their utility to parties for electoral purposes allowed large landowners to successfully avoid or evade the most stringent provisions of the land reform laws that were implemented in the fifties and sixties. Parties and state governments connived with landlords to water down the implementation of these laws (see, for example, Ladejinsky 1972).

13. Interviewed in Kundai village, Udaipur district, June 15, 1998.

14. Interviewed in Kundai village, June 14, 1998.

15. The Tahsil is sub-district-level office — a critical feature of the colonial and post-colonial administration — that is responsible for maintaining land records, collecting land revenue, performing magisterial duties at the local level — and, increasingly, with multifarious other duties, including disbursing old-age and disability pensions, supervising famine relief, preparing voters' lists and conducting elections, etc.

16. Interviewed in Ghodach village, Udaipur district, June 16, 1998.

17. Girdhari Singh draws his clout over the local administration through his connections with another politically revitalized Rajput satrap, Mandhata Singh, brother-in-law of ex-Prime Minister, V. P. Singh, and an adherent of the BJP. Caste and party affiliation are only very poorly related to one another even within this small part of southern Rajasthan. While the Rajput Thakur of Kundai is closely aligned with the Congress Party, Girdhari Singh and some other Rajput leaders are affiliated with the BJP.

18. *Apna Gaon Apna Kaam* (Our Village, Our Construction) was a program of the state government intended to finance community infrastructure. Communities contributed 25 percent of the estimated cost and the government supplied the remaining 75 percent.

19. Interviewed in Sangawas village, Rajsamand district, August 1, 1998.

20. Interviewed in Gangapur city, Bhilwara district, July 14, 1998.

21. Interview with Sheshmal Pagariya, President of the Congress Party for Udaipur district, July 12, 1998.

22. Interview with Narayan Upadhyaya, Congress Party activist, son of the sitting Member of Parliament (at that time, but since unseated and lately deceased), and leader of a local labor union; Bhilwara, March 20, 1999.

23. Chapter 5 reports these figures in greater detail.

24. The manifesto of the ruling BJP-led National Democratic Alliance promised, for instance that "the main thrust of the new government will be 'Berozgaari Hatao' [Eradicate Unemployment]. As against the present trend of jobless growth, our government will measure growth by generation of gainful employment . . . [there will be] massive employment creation at all levels" (page 4). "The Government has decided that ten crore [one hundred million] people should get employment opportunities over the next ten years" (page 18). The Congress Party's manifesto (translated by me from Hindi) states that "The Congress will give the highest priority in all its economic plans and programs to creating opportunities for employment generation. We do not want the type of development that does not lead to increases in employment. . . . We need to generate one crore new jobs each year (page 18)" — or one hundred million jobs over ten years, which is exactly the number held out by the BJP.

25. Interview with Mangilal Joshi, President of the BJP for Udaipur district, July 9, 1998.

26. Interview with Sheshmal Pagariya, President of the Congress Party for Udaipur district, July 12, 1998.

27. Interview with Bhanwarlal Garg, district Congress Party official and party worker for the last 25 years, Bhilwara, July 25, 1998.

Appendix A

1. Communal harmony could be compared among villages by relying on data related to criminal cases and land disputes, which could be obtained from police stations and district courts. Figures related to political participation were also relatively easy to access. Voting percentages could be compared among villages by using figures pertaining to panchayat elections, and the other indicators of participation — campaigning, canvassing and contacting — could be scaled using information obtained from household surveys and following the method of Verba, et al. (1995); and Rosenstone and Hansen (1993).

2. The results of this earlier investigation are reported in Krishna and Uphoff (1999).

3. There is a common apprehension among politicians that large numbers of fictitious names are recorded in the voters lists by government officials, particularly at the instance of the ruling party. The present investigation helped additionally to assess the magnitude of this type of misdemeanor in this region.

References

Agrawal, Arun. 1999. *Greener Pastures: Politics, Markets and Community Among a Migrant Pastoral People.* Durham: Duke University Press.

Ahuja, Kanta and Pradeep Bhargava. 1989. "Long-Term Impact of Integrated Rural Development Programme." Jaipur: Institute of Development Studies, mimeo.

Almond, Gabriel and Sidney Verba. 1965. The Civic Culture: Political Attitudes and Democracy in Five Nations. Boston: Little, Brown.

Anderson, Leslie. 1994. *The Political Ecology of the Modern Peasant: Calculation and Community.* Baltimore: Johns Hopkins University Press.

Apter, David E. 1965. *The Politics of Modernization.* Chicago University of Chicago Press.

Attwood, Donald W. 1992. *Raising Cane: The Political Economy of Sugar in Western India.* Boulder, CO: Westview Press.

Baden-Powell, B. H. 1899 [1970]. *The Origin and Growth of Village Communities in India.* London and New York: Scribner's.

Bagchi, Amaresh. 1991. "India," 97–128. In *Fiscal Decentralization and the Mobilization and Use of National Resources for Development: Issues, Experiences and Policies in the ESCAP Region.* Bangkok: Economic and Social Commission for Asia and the Pacific.

Bailey, Frederick G. 1960. *Tribe, Caste and Nation: A Study of Political Activity and Political Change in Highland Orissa.* Manchester, UK: Manchester University Press.

———. 1963. *Politics and Social Change: Orissa in 1959.* Berkeley: University of California Press.

Balagopal, K. 1995. "Democracy and the Fight Against Communalism." *Economic and Political Weekly*, Bombay, 30 (1).

Banfield, Edward C. 1958. *The Moral Basis of a Backward Society.* Chicago: Free Press.

Barber, Benjamin. 1995. *Jihad versus McWorld.* New York: Free Press.

Bardhan, Pranab. 1984. *The Political Economy of Development in India.* Delhi: Oxford University Press.

———. 1992. "A Political-Economy Perspective on Development," 321–37. In Bimal Jalan (ed.), *The Indian Economy: Problems and Perspectives.* New Delhi: Penguin Books.

Baron, J. and Hannan, M. 1994. "The Impact of Economics on Contemporary Sociology." *Journal of Economic Literature*, 32 (September): 1111–46.

Bates, Robert H. 1990. "Macropolitical Economy in the Field of Development," 31–54. In James E. Alt and Kenneth E. Shepsley (eds.), *Perspectives on Positive Political Economy.* Ithaca, NY: Cornell University Press.

———. 1999. "Ethnicity, Capital Formation, and Conflict." *Social Capital Initiative Working Paper No. 12.* Washington, DC: The World Bank.

Baviskar, B. S. and D. W. Attwood. 1995. *Finding the Middle Path: The Political Economy of Cooperation in Rural India.* New Delhi: Vistaar Publications.

Bayly, C. A. 1988. *Indian Society and the Making of the British Empire.* Cambridge, UK: Cambridge University Press.

Berger, Peter L. and Thomas Luckmann. 1966. *The Social Construction of Reality: A Treatise in the Sociology of Knowledge.* Garden City, NY: Doubleday.

Berman, Sheri. 1997a. "Civil Society and the Collapse of the Weimar Republic." *World Politics*, 49 (April): 401–29.

Berman, Sheri. 1997b. "Civil Society and Political Institutionalization," *American Behavioral Scientist*, 40 (5): 562–74.

Béteille, Andre. 1996. *Caste, Class and Power: Changing Patterns of Stratification in a Tanjore Village.* Delhi: Oxford University Press.

Bhargava, Pradeep. 1997. "Concurrent Evaluation of IRDP: Rajasthan Vth Round." Jaipur: Institute of Development Studies, mimeo.

Boix, Carles and Daniel N. Posner. 1998. "Social Capital: Explaining its Origins and Effects on Government Performance." *British Journal of Political Science*, 29 (4): 686–93.

Bokil, Milind. 2000. "Drought in Rajasthan: In Search of a Perspective." *Economic and Political Weekly*, Bombay, 35 (47): 4171–75.

Bollen, K. and R. Jackman. 1985. "Political Democracy and the Size Distribution of Income." *American Sociological Review*, 50 (4): 438–57.

Brara, Rita. 1992. "Are Grazing Lands 'Wastelands'? Some Evidence from Rajasthan." *Economic and Political Weekly*, Bombay, 27 (8).

Brass, Paul. 1974. *Language, Religion and Politics in North India.* Cambridge, UK: Cambridge University Press.

————. 1994. *The Politics of India Since Independence*. Cambridge, UK: Cambridge University Press.

————. 1997a. "National Power and Local Politics in India: A Twenty-year Perspective," 303–335. In Chatterjee (ed.), 1997.

————. 1997b. *Theft of an Idol: Text and Context in the Representation of Political Violence*. Princeton, NJ: Princeton University Press.

Bratton, Michael. 1999. "Political Participation in a New Democracy: Institutional Considerations from Zambia." *Comparative Political Studies*, 32 (5): 549–88.

Brehm, John and Wendy Rahn. 1997. "Individual-Level Evidence for the Causes and Consequences of Social Capital." *American Journal of Political Science*, 41 (3): 999–1023.

Bunce, Valerie. J. 1996. "The Return of the Left and the Future of Democracy in Central and Eastern Europe." Ithaca: Cornell University, unpublished ms.

Carstairs, R. 1912. *The Little World of an Indian District Officer*. London: Macmillan.

Census of India. 1961. *Janvi: A Village Survey, Rajasthan*. New Delhi: Census of India.

————. 1981. *Janvi: A Village Re-Study*. New Delhi: Census of India.

Chakravarty, Anand. 1975. *Contradiction and Change: Emerging Patterns of Authority in a Rajasthani Village*. Delhi: Oxford University Press.

Chambers, Robert, N. C. Saxena, and Tushaar Shah. 1990. *To the Hands of the Poor: Water and Trees*. Boulder: Westview.

Chandhoke, Neera. 1995. *State and Civil Society: Explorations in Political Theory*. New Delhi; Thousand Oaks, CA: Sage Publications.

Chandra, Kanchan. 2000. "The Transformation of Ethnic Politics in India: The Decline of the Congress and the Rise of the Bahujan Samaj Party in Hoshiarpur." *Journal of Asian Studies*, 59 (1) (February): 26–61.

Chatterjee, Partha (ed.). 1997. *State and Politics in India*. New Delhi: Oxford University Press.

Chaubisa, M. L. 1988. *Caste, Tribe and Exploitation: Exploration of Inequality at Village Level*. Udaipur: Himanshu Publications.

Chaudhury, S. N. 1987. *Dynamics of Rural Power Structure: A Case Study of An Indian Village*. Delhi: Ajanta Prakashan.

Chhibber, Pradeep. 1999. *Democracy without Associations: Transformation of the Party System and Social Cleavage in India*. New Delhi: Vistaar Publications.

Cohen, Jean L. and Andrew Arato. 1992. *Civil Society and Political Theory*. Cambridge, MA: MIT Press.

Cohn, Bernard S. 1965. "Anthropological Notes on Disputes and Law in India." *American Anthropologist*, 67 (6): 82–122.

————. 1969. "Structural Change in Indian Rural Society," 53–122. In Robert. E. Frykenberg (ed.), *Land Control and Social Structure in Indian History*. Madison: University of Wisconsin Press.

Coleman, James S. 1988. "Social Capital in the Creation of Human Capital." *American Journal of Sociology*, 94: S95–S120.

———. 1990. *Foundations of Social Theory*. Cambridge, MA: Harvard University Press.

Crook, Richard and James Manor. 1998. *Democracy and Decentralization in South Asia and West Africa: Participation, Accountability and Performance*. Cambridge, UK: Cambridge University Press.

CSE. 1990. *The State of India's Environment: A Citizens' Report*. New Delhi: Centre for Science and the Environment.

CTAE 1999. "Integrated Watershed Development Project. Impact Evaluation Report 1991–1997." College of Technology and Agricultural Engineering, Rajasthan Agricultural University, Udaipur.

Davidson, Basil. 1992. *The Black Man's Burden: Africa and the Curse of the Nation State*. New York: Times Books.

Demeure, Juan and Edgar Guardia. 1997. "DESEC: Thirty Years of Community Organization in Bolivia," 91–101. In Anirudh Krishna, Norman T. Uphoff and Milton J. Esman (eds.), *Reasons for Hope: Instructive Experiences in Rural Development*. West Hartford, Connecticut: Kumarian Press.

De Soto, Hernando. 2000. *The Mystery of Capital: Why Capitalism Triumphs in the West and Fails Everywhere Else*. New York: Basic Books.

Diamond, Larry, Juan J. Linz and Seymour M. Lipset. 1995. *Politics in Developing Countries: Comparing Experiences with Democracy*. Boulder, CO: Lynne Rienner.

Downs, Anthony. 1957. *An Economic Theory of Democracy*. New York: Harper.

Dreze, Jean. 1990. "Poverty in India and the IRDP Delusion." *Economic and Political Weekly*, Bombay, 25 (39).

Dreze, Jean and Amartya Sen. 1995. *India: Economic Development and Social Opportunity*. New Delhi: Oxford University Press.

———. 1997. *Indian Development: Selected Regional Perspectives*. New Delhi: Oxford University Press.

Dumont, Louis. 1970. *Homo Hierarchicus: An Essay on the Caste System*. Chicago: University of Chicago Press.

Eastis, Carla M. 1998. "Organizational Diversity and the Production of Social Capital." *American Behavioral Scientist*, 42 (1): 66–77.

Echeverri-Gent, John. 1993. *The State and the Poor: Public Policy and Political Development in India and the United States*. Berkeley and Los Angeles: University of California Press.

Edwards, Bob and Michael W. Foley. 1997a. "Escape From Politics? Social Theory and the Social Capital Debate." *American Behavioral Scientist*, 40 (5): 550–61.

Edwards, Bob and Michael W. Foley. 1997b. "Social Capital and the Political Economy of Our Discontent." *American Behavioral Scientist*, 40 (5): 669–78.

Edwards, Bob and Michael W. Foley. 1998a. "Beyond Tocqueville: Civil Society and Social Capital in Comparative Perspective." *American Behavioral Scientist*, 42 (1): 5–20.

Edwards, Bob and Michael W. Foley. 1998b. "Civil Society and Social Capital Beyond Putnam" *American Behavioral Scientist*, 42 (1): 124–39.

Engineer, Asghar Ali. 1989. *Communalism and Communal Violence in India*. Delhi: Ajanta Publishers.

Esman, Milton J. and Norman T, Uphoff. 1984. *Local Organizations: Intermediaries in Rural Development*. Ithaca, NY: Cornell University Press.

Etienne, Gilbert. 1988. *Food and Poverty: India's Half Won Battle*. New Delhi and London: Sage Publications.

Evans, Peter. 1996. "Government Action, Social Capital and Development: Reviewing the Evidence on Synergy." *World Development*, 24 (6): 1119–32.

Fanon, Frantz. 1968. *Black Skins, White Mask*. New York: Grove Press.

Farah, Nuruddin. 1992. *Close Sesame*. Saint Paul, Minn.: Graywolf Press.

Fiorina, Morris P. 1977. *Congress, Keystone of the Washington Establishment*. New Haven: Yale University Press.

Fisher, Robert J. 1997. *If Rain Doesn't Come: An Anthropological Study of Drought and Human Ecology in Western Rajasthan*. Delhi: Manohar Publishers.

Foley, Michael W. and Bob Edwards. 1996. "The Paradox of Civil Society." *Journal of Democracy*, 7 (3): 38–52.

Foley, Michael W. and Bob Edwards. 1998. "Is it Time to Disinvest in Social Capital?" Paper presented at the American Political Science Association Meeting, Boston, September 3–6, 1998.

Foster, Phillips and Beverly Simmons. 1978. *Change in a Hindu Village: Bhanapur in 1955, 1968 and 1973*. Department of Agriculture and Resource Economics, University of Maryland, College Park.

Frankel, Francine N. 1978. *India's Political Economy, 1947–1977: The Gradual Revolution*. Princeton: Princeton University Press.

———. 1989. "Introduction." In Frankel and M. S. A. Rao (eds.), *Dominance and State Power in India*. Delhi: Oxford University Press.

Frykenberg, Robert E. 1969. "Village Strength in South India," 227–48. In Robert. E. Frykenberg (ed.), *Land Control and Social Structure in Indian History*. Madison: University of Wisconsin Press.

Fukuyama, Francis. 1995. *Trust: The Social Virtues and the Creation of Prosperity*. New York: The Free Press.

Gadgil, Madhav and Ramachandra Guha. 1992. *This Fissured Land: An Ecological History of India*. Delhi: Oxford University Press.

GOI. 1998. *Indian Economic Survey 1997-98*. New Delhi: Ministry of Finance, Government of India.

————. 1999. *India 1999*. New Delhi: Publications Division, Ministry of Information and Broadcasting, Government of India (CD-ROM).

GOR. 1991. *Districtwise Trends of Agricultural Production*. Jaipur: Agriculture Department, Government of Rajasthan.

————. 1997. *Some Facts About Rajasthan*. Jaipur: Directorate of Economics and Statistics, Government of Rajasthan.

————. 1999. *Progress Report: Eight Five-Year Plan: 1992–1997*. Jaipur: Planning Department, Government of Rajasthan.

Granovetter, Marc. 1973. "The Strength of Weak Ties." *American Journal of Sociology*, 78, 1360–80.

————. 1985. "Social Structures and Economic Action: The Problem of Embeddedness." *American Journal of Sociology*, 91(3): 481–510.

Grootaert, Christian. 1998. "Social Capital, Household Welfare and Poverty in Indonesia." Washington, DC: World Bank, photocopy.

Grootaert, Christian and Deepa Narayan. 1999. "Local Institutions, Poverty and Household Welfare in Bolivia." World Bank, photocopy.

Grootaert, Christian and Thierry van Bastelaer. forthcoming. The Role of Social Capital in Development: An Empirical Assessment. New York: Cambridge University Press.

Hall, Peter. 1997. "Social Capital in Britain." Paper prepared for Bertelsmann Stiflung Workshop on Social Capital, Berlin, June 1997.

Hardin, Garrett. 1968. "The Tragedy of the Commons." *Science*, 168 (124).

Hasan, Zoya. 1989. *Dominance and Mobilization: Rural Politics in Western Uttar Pradesh, 1930–1980*. New Delhi and London: Sage Publications.

Hechter, Michael. 1987. *Principles of Group Solidarity*. Berkeley: University of California Press.

Heller, Patrick 1999. *The Labor of Development: Workers and the Transformation of Capitalism in Kerala, India*. Ithaca, NY: Cornell University Press.

————. 2000. "Degrees of Democracy: Some Comparative Lessons from India." *World Politics*, 52 (4): 484–519.

Herring, Ronald J. 1983. *Land to the Tiller: The Political Economy of Agrarian Reform in South Asia*. New Haven: Yale University Press.

————. 1989. "Dilemmas of Agrarian Communism: Peasant Differentiation, Sectoral and Village Politics." *Third World Quarterly*, 11 (1): 89–115.

————. 1999. "Embedded Particularism: India's Failed Developmental State." In Meredith Woo-Cumings, ed., *The Developmental State*. Ithaca, NY: Cornell University Press.

Hipscher, Patricia. 1996. "Democracy and the Decline of Urban Social Movements in Chile and Spain." *Comparative Politics*, April.

Huntington, Samuel P. 1968. *Political Order in Changing Societies*. New Haven: Yale University Press.

Inkeles, Alex and David E. Smith. 1974. *Becoming Modern: Industrial Change in Six Developing Countries*. Cambridge, MA: Harvard University Press.

Inkeles, Alex. 1981. "Convergence and Divergence in Industrial Societies," 3–38. In Mustafa O. Attir, Burkart Holzner and Zdenek Suda (eds.), *Directions of Change: Modernization Theory, Research and Realities*. Boulder, CO: Westview Press.

Jackman, Robert W. and Ross A. Miller. 1998. "Social Capital and Politics." *Annual Review of Political Science*, 1, 47–73.

Jain, S. P. 1993. "Reorganizing Grassroots Institutions for Sustainable Development." *Indian Journal of Public Administration*, 39 (3): 396–405.

Jalal, Ayesha. 1995. *Democracy and Authoritarianism in South Asia: A Comparative and Historical Perspective*. Cambridge, UK: Cambridge University Press.

Jayal, Niraja Gopal. 1999. *Democracy and the State: Welfare, Secularism and Development in Contemporary India*. New Delhi: Oxford University Press.

Jodha, Narpat S. 1990. "Rural Common Property Resources: Contributions and Crisis." *Economic and Political Weekly*, Bombay, 25 (24).

Kaviraj, Sudipta (ed.). 1997. *Politics in India*. Delhi: Oxford University Press.

Keck, Margaret and Kathryn Sikkink. 1998. *Activists Beyond Borders: Advocacy Networks in International Politics*. Ithaca, NY: Cornell University Press.

Kenworthy, Lane. 1997. "Civic Engagement, Social Capital, and Economic Cooperation." *American Behavioral Scientist*, 40 (5): 645–56.

Kerr, John M., N. K. Sanghi and G. Sriramappa. 1999. "Subsidies in Watershed Development Projects in India: Distortions and Opportunities," 178–93. In Fiona Hinchcliffe, et al. (eds.), *Fertile Ground: The Impacts of Participatory Watershed Management*. London: Intermediate Technology Publications.

Khilnani, Sunil. 1997. *The Idea of India*. New Delhi: Penguin Books.

Knack, Stephen and Philip Keefer. 1997. "Does Social Capital Have an Economic Payoff? A Cross-Country Investigation." *Quarterly Journal of Economics*, 52 (4): 1251–87.

Kohli, Atul. 1987. *The State and Poverty in India: The Politics of Reform*. Cambridge, UK: Cambridge University Press.

———. 1990. *Democracy and Discontent: India's Growing Crisis of Governability*. Cambridge, UK: Cambridge University Press.

———. 1997. "From Breakdown to Order: West Bengal," 336–66. In Chatterjee (ed.).

Kothari, Rajni. 1988. *State Against Democracy: In Search of Humane Governance*. Delhi: Ajanta Publishers.

Krishna, Anirudh. 1997. "Participatory Watershed Development and Soil Conservation in Rajasthan, India," 255–72. In Anirudh Krishna, Norman T. Uphoff and Milton J. Esman (eds.), *Reasons for Hope: Instructive Experiences in Rural Development*. West Hartford, Connecticut: Kumarian Press.

————. 2000. "Creating and Harnessing Social Capital," 71–93. In Partha Dasgupta and Ismail Serageldin, eds., *Social Capital: A Multifaceted Perspective*. Washington, DC: The World Bank.

Krishna, Anirudh and Elizabeth Shrader. 2000. "Cross-Cultural Measures of Social Capital: A Tool and Results from India and Panama.". Social Capital Initiative Working Paper Series. Washington, DC: The World Bank.

Krishna, Anirudh and Norman Uphoff. 1999. "Mapping and Measuring Social Capital: A Conceptual and Empirical Study of Collective Action for Conserving and Developing Watersheds in Rajasthan, India." Social Capital Initiative Working Paper #13. Washington, D. C.: The World Bank.

Kuhn, Berthold. 1998. *Participatory Development in Rural India*. New Delhi: Radiant Publishers.

Kurien, George. 1999. "Empowering Conditions in the Decentralization Process: An Analysis of Dynamics, Factors and Actors in Panchayati Raj Institutions From West Bengal and Karnataka, India." *Working Paper Series No. 228*. The Hague, Netherlands: Institute of Social Studies.

Ladejinsky, Wolf. 1972. "Land Ceilings and Land Reforms." *Economic and Political Weekly*, Bombay, 7 (7).

Laitin, David D. 1995. "The Civic Culture at 30." *American Political Science Review*, 89 (1): 168–73.

Lecomte, Bernard and Anirudh Krishna. 1997. "Six-S: Building upon Traditional Social Organizations in Francophone West Africa," 75–90. In Anirudh Krishna, Norman T. Uphoff and Milton J. Esman (eds.), *Reasons for Hope: Instructive Experiences in Rural Development*. West Hartford, CT: Kumarian Press.

Lehmann, N. 1996. "Kicking in Groups." *Atlantic Monthly*, 277: 22–26.

Lerner, Daniel. 1958. *The Passing of Traditional Society: Modernizing the Middle East*. New York: Free Press.

Levi, Margaret. 1996. "Social and Unsocial Capital." *Politics and Society*, 24: 45–55.

Lin, Nan. 2001. *Social Capital: A Theory of Social Structure and Action*. Cambridge, UK: Cambridge University Press.

Linz, Juan and Alfred Stepan. 1996. *Problems of Democratic Transition and Consolidation*. Baltimore: Johns Hopkins University Press.

Lipset, Seymour M. 1960. *Political Man: The Social Bases of Politics*. New York: Doubleday.

————. 1994. "The Social Requisites of Democracy Revisited: 1993 Presidential Address." *American Sociological Review*, 59: 1–22.

Lodha, Sanjay. 1999. "Caste and Two-Party System." *Economic and Political Weekly*, Bombay, 34 (48): 3344–48.

Lowi, Theodore J. 1985. "The State in Politics: The Relation Between Policy and Administration." In Roger G. Noll (ed.), *Regulatory Policy and the Social Sciences*. Berkeley and Los Angeles: University of California Press.

Lowndes, Vivien and David Wilson. 2001. "Social Capital and Local Governance: Exploring the Institutional Design Variable." *Political Studies*, 49, 629–647.

Lupton, W. J. E. 1908. *Report on the Question of the Assessment of Land and Water Revenue in Ajmer-Merwara with Proposed Revenue Rates for District Ajmer.* Ajmer: Scottish Mission Industries Co. Ltd.

Lyon, Fergus. 2000. "Trust, Networks and Norms: The Creation of Social Capital in Agricultural Economies in Ghana." *World Development*, 28 (4), 663–681.

Magagna, Victor V. 1991. *Communities of Grain: Rural Rebellion in Comparative Perspective.* Ithaca, NY: Cornell University Press.

Mamdani, Mahmood. 1996. *Citizen and Subject: Contemporary Africa and the Legacy of Late Colonialism.* Princeton: Princeton University Press.

Manor, James. 1990. "How and Why Liberal and Representative Politics Emerged in India." *Political Studies*, 38: 20–38.

———. 1997. "Karnataka: Caste, Class, Dominance and Politics in a Cohesive Society," 262–73. In Kaviraj (ed.).

Mathew, George. 1994. *Panchayati Raj: From Legislation to Movement.* New Delhi: Concept Publishers.

Mayaram, Shail. 1993. "Communal Violence in Jaipur." *Economic and Political Weekly*, Bombay, 28 (46).

———. 1998. "Panchayats and Women: A study of the processes initiated before and after the 73rd Amendment in Rajasthan." Jaipur: Institute of Development Studies, mimeo.

Migdal, Joel S. 1988. *Strong Societies and Weak States.* Princeton: Princeton University Press.

Minkoff, Debra. 1997. "Producing Social Capital: National Social Movements and Civil Society." *American Behavioral Scientist*, 40 (5): 606–619.

Mishra, S. N. 1997. "Agricultural Liberalization and Development Strategy in the Ninth Plan." *Economic and Political Weekly*, 32 (13): A1–19.

Mitchie, Aruna N. 1979. "Agricultural Policy and Political Viability in Rural India." *Comparative Political Studies*, 12 (3): 362–84.

Mitra, Subrata K. 1991. "Room to Maneuver in The Middle: Local Elites, Political Action, and the State in India." *World Politics*, 43 (April): 390–413.

———. 1992. *Power, Protest and Participation: Local Elites and the Politics of Development in India.* London and New York: Routledge.

Moog, Robert S. 1997. *Whose Interests Are Supreme? Organizational Politics in the Civil Courts in India.* Ann Arbor, MI: Association for Asian Studies.

Moore, Barrington. 1966. *Social Origins of Dictatorship and Democracy: Lord and Peasant in the Making of the Modern World.* Boston: Beacon Press.

Morlino, Leonardo. 1995. "Italy's Civic Divide." *Journal of Democracy*, January, 173–77.

Morris, Matthew. 1998. "Social Capital and Poverty in India." Working Paper, Institute of Development Studies, Sussex.

Mukherjee, Radhakamal. 1923. *Democracies of the East.* London: P. S. King.

Nandy, Ashish. 1990. "The Politics of Securalism." In Veena Das (ed.), *Mirrors of Violence: Communities, Riots and Survivors in South Asia.* Delhi and New York: Oxford University Press.

Narain, Iqbal and P. C. Mathur. 1990. "The Thousand Year Raj: Regional Isolation and Rajput Hinduism in Rajasthan Before and After 1947," 1–58. In Francine N. Frankel and M. S. A. Rao (eds.), *Dominance and State Power in Modern India: Decline of a Social Order, Volume II.* Delhi: Oxford University Press.

Narain, Iqbal, K. C. Pande and M. L. Sharma. 1976. *The Rural Elite in an Indian State: A Case Study of Rajasthan.* Columbia, MO: South Asia Books.

Narayan, Deepa and Lant Pritchett. 1997. "Cents and Sociability: Household Income and Social Capital in Rural Tanzania." World Bank, photocopy.

Nehru, Jawaharlal. 1946. *The Discovery of India.* Calcutta: Signet Press.

Newton, Kenneth. 1997. "Social Capital and Democracy." *American Behavioral Scientist,* 40 (5): 575–86.

North, Douglass C. 1981. *Structure and Change in Economic History.* New York: Norton.

North, Douglass C. 1990. *Institutions, Institutional Change and Economic Performance.* Cambridge, UK: Cambridge University Press.

North, Douglass C. and Robert P. Thomas. 1973. *The Rise of the Western World: A New Economic History.* Cambridge, UK: Cambridge University Press.

O'Donnell, Guillermo and Philippe C. Schmitter. 1987. *Tentative Conclusions About Uncertain Democracies.* Baltimore: Johns Hopkins University Press.

O'Donnell, Guillermo. 1973. *Modernization and Bureaucratic-Authoritarianism.* Berkeley: Institute of International Studies, University of California.

Offe, Claus. 1996. *Modernity and the State.* Cambridge, MA: MIT Press.

Oldenburg, Philip. 1976. *Big City Government in India: Councilor, Administrator, and Citizen in India.* Tucson, AZ: University of Arizona Press.

———. 1999. "The Thirteenth Election of India's Lok Sabha (House of the People)." Available at http://www.asiasoc.org/publications/indian_elections.13.a.html.

Oliver, Pamela E. 1984. "If You Don't Do It, Nobody Else Will: Active and Token Contributions to Local Collective Action." *American Sociological Review,* 49 (5): 601–10.

Oliver, Pamela E. and Gerard Marwell. 1965. *The Logic of Collective Action.* Cambridge, MA: Cambridge University Press.

———. 1982. *The Rise and Decline of Nations.* London and New Haven: Yale University Press.

————. 1988. "The Paradox of Group Size in Collective Action: A Theory of the Critical Mass, II." *American Sociological Review,* 53 (1): 1–8.

Omvedt, Gail. 1993. *Reinventing Revolution: New Social Movements and the Socialist Tradition in India.* New York: M. E. Sharpe.

O'Neill, Claire M. 1996. "Making Democracy Work: Putnam and His Critics." *South European Society and Politics,* Autumn 1996.

Opio-Odongo, Joseph and Charles Lwanga-Ntale. 2000. "Participation and Empowerment Through Participation: Some Lessons From Uganda." In Anirudh Krishna (ed.), *Changing Policy and Practice From Below: Community Experiences in Poverty Reduction.* New York: United Nations Development Programme. (web edition: http://www.undp.org/csopp/CSO/NewFiles/toolboxcase.htm)

————. 1990. *Governing the Commons: The Evolution Of Institutions For Collective Action.* Cambridge, UK: Cambridge University Press.

————. 1996. "Crossing the Great Divide: Co-production, Synergy and Development." *World Development,* 24 (6).

Paige, Jeffery M. 1975. *Agrarian Revolution: Social Movements and Export Agriculture in the Underdeveloped World.* New York: Free Press.

Pal, Mahi. 2000. "Uttar Pradesh Panchayat Elections: From Politics to Tactics." *Economic and Political Weekly,* Bombay, 35 (37): 3289–91.

Patel, Tulsi. 1994. *Fertility Behavior: Population and Society in a Rajasthan Village.* New Delhi: Oxford University Press.

Piattoni, Simona. 1998. "Can Politics Create Community? Evidence from the Italian South." Paper presented at the 1998 meeting of the American Political Science Association, Boston, September 3–6.

Pinhey, A. F., Lt. Col. 1996 [1909]. *History of Mewar.* Jodhpur: Books Treasure.

Polanyi, Karl. 1944. *The Great Transformation: The Political and Economic Origins of Our Time.* Boston: Beacon Press.

Popkin, Samuel. 1979. *The Rational Peasant.* Berkeley: University of California Press.

Portes, Alejandro. 1998. "Social Capital: Its Origins and Applications in Modern Sociology." *Annual Review of Sociology,* 24: 1–24.

Portes, Alejandro and Patricia Landolt. 1996. "The Downside of Social Capital." *The American Prospect* (May–June, 18–21): 94.

Portney, Kent E. and Jeffrey M. Berry. 1997. "Mobilizing Minority Communities: Social Capital and Participation in Urban Neighborhoods." *American Behavioral Scientist,* 40 (5): 632–44.

Pretty, Jules. 1995. *Regenerating Agriculture: Policies and Practices for Sustainability and Self-Reliance.* Washington, DC: Joseph Henry Press.

Przeworski, Adam. 1991. *Democracy and the Market.* Cambridge, UK: Cambridge University Press.

Purohit, S. D. . 1974. *Zawar (Udaipur District, Rajasthan): A Tribal Village in the Vicinity of Zawar Mines.* Village Study No. 19, Agro_Economic Research Centre. Vallabh Vidyanagar, Gujarat: Sarder Patel University.

Putnam, Robert D. 1995. "Bowling Alone: America's Declining Social Capital." *Journal of Democracy,* January, 65–78.

———. 1996. "The Strange Disappearance of Civic America." *The American Prospect* (Winter): 34–48.

———. 2000. *Bowling Alone: The Collapse and Revival of American Community.* New York: Simon and Schuster.

Putnam, Robert D., Robert Leonardi, and Raffaella Y. Nanetti. 1993. *Making Democracy Work: Civic Traditions in Modern Italy.* Princeton: Princeton University Press.

Reddy, G. Ram and G. Haragopal. 1985. "The Pyraveerkar: The "Fixer" in Rural India." *Asian Survey,* 25 (11): 1147–62.

Robinson, Eva Cheung. 1998. *Greening at the Grassroots: Alternative Forest Strategies in India. .* New Delhi: Sage Publications.

Robinson, Marguerite S. 1988. *Local Politics: The Law of Fishes. Development through Political Change in Medak District, Andhra Pradesh (South India).* New Delhi: Oxford University Press.

Rogers, Everett M. 1969. *Modernization Among Peasants.* New York: Holt.

Rose, Richard. 1999. "Getting Things Done in an Anti-Modern Society: Social Capital and Networks in Russia." *Social Capital Initiative Working Paper No. 6.* Washington, DC: The World Bank.

Rosenau, James N. 1992. "The Relocation of Authority in a Shrinking World." *Comparative Politics,* 24 (3): 253–272.

Rosenstone, Steven J. and John M. Hansen. 1993. *Mobilization, Participation and Democracy in America.* New York: Macmillan.

Rosin, R. Thomas. 1994. "Locality and Frontier: Securing Livelihood in the Aravalli Zone of Central Rajasthan," 30–63. In Karine Schomer, Joan L. Erdman, Deryck O. Lodrick, and Lloyd I. Rudolph (eds.), *The Idea of Rajasthan: Explorations in Regional Identity, Vol. II: Institutions.* New Delhi: Manohar.

Rothstein, Bo. 1998. *Just Institutions Matter: The Moral and Political Logic of the Universal Welfare State.* Princeton: Princeton University Press.

———. "Social Capital in the Social Democratic Welfare State." *Politics and Society,* 29 (2), 207–241.

Rudolph, L. I. and S. H. Rudolph. 1987. *In Search of Lakshmi: The Political Economy of the Indian State.* Chicago: University of Chicago Press.

Sabharwal, Satish. 1997. "On the Diversity of Ruling Traditions," 124–40. In Kaviraj (ed.).

Sampson, Robert J., S. W. Raudenbush and F. Earls. 1997. "Neighborhoods and Violent Crime: A Multilevel Study of Collective Efficacy." *Science,* 277 (August 15): 918–24.

Sartori, Giovanni. 1970. "Concept Misformation in Comparative Politics." *American Political Science Review*, 64 (4): 1033–53.

Saxena, N. C. 1994. *India's Eucalyptus Craze: The God That Failed*. New Delhi: Sage Publications.

Saxena, S. B. and A. S. Charan. 1973. *Dingri (Udaipur District, Rajasthan): A Village in the Vicinity of a New Rail Link*. Indian Village Studies No. 18, Agro-Economic Research Centre. Vallabh Vidyanagar, Gujarat: Sardar Patel University.

———. 1993. *Dingri: A Re-Survey*. Indian Village Studies, Agro-Economic Research Centre. Vallabh Vidyanagar, Gujarat: Sardar Patel University.

Schneider, Mark, Paul Teske, Melissa Marschall, Michael Mintrom and Christine Roch. 1997. "Institutional Arrangements and the Creation of Social Capital: The Effects of Public School Choice." *American Political Science Review* 91 (1): 82–93.

Schomer, Karine, J. L. Erdman, D. O. Lodrick and L. I. Rudolph. 1994. *The Idea of Rajasthan: Explorations in Regional Identity, Vol. II. Institutions*. Delhi: Manohar Publishers.

Scott, James C. 1976. *The Moral Economy of the Peasant: Rebellion and Subsistence in Southeast Asia*. New Haven: Yale University Press.

———. 1985. *Weapons of the Weak: Everyday Forms of Peasant Resistance*. New Haven: Yale University Press.

Seligson, Amber L. 1999. "Civic Association and Democratic Participation in Central America: A Test of the Putnam Thesis." *Comparative Political Studies*, 32 (3): 342–362.

Sen, Amartya K. 1999. *Development as Freedom*. New York: Knopf.

Shefter, Martin. 1994. *Political Parties and the State: The American Historical Experience*. Princeton: Princeton University Press.

Sheremeta, Pavlo, David Koenig, Olexiy Vynogradov, and Oleksander Sydorenko. 2000. "CEREBRAL: A Grassroots Initiative for Assisting Children with Cerebral Palsy in Ukraine." In Anirudh Krishna (ed.), *Changing Policy and Practice From Below: Community Experiences in Poverty Reduction*. New York: United Nations Development Programme. (web edition: www.undp.org/csopp/CSO/ NewFiles/toolboxcase.htm).

Sheth, D. L. 1999. "Secularization of Caste and Making of New Middle Class." *Economic and Political Weekly*, Bombay, August 21, 2502–10.

Singh, Rajendra. 1988. *Land, Power and People: Rural Elite in Transition, 1801– 1970*. New Delhi and London: Sage Publications.

Singh, Sukhpal. 1995. "Structural Adjustment Programme and Indian Agriculture: Towards an Assessment of Implications." *Economic and Political Weekly*, Bombay, 30 (51).

Sisson, Richard. 1972. *The Congress Party in Rajasthan: Political Integration and Institution-Building in an Indian State*. Berkeley: University of California Press.

Skocpol, Theda. 1979. *States and Social Revolution*. Cambridge, U.K.: Cambridge University Press.

Spear, T. G. P. 1973. *Twilight of the Mughals: Studies in Late Mughal Delhi*. Karachi: Oxford University Press.

Srinivas, M. N. 1987. "The Indian Village: Myth and Reality," 20–59. In M. N. Srinivas, *The Dominant Caste and Other Essays*. Delhi: Oxford University Press.

Stolle, Dietlind. 1998. "Making Associations Work: Group Characteristics, Membership and Generalized Trust." Paper presented at the 1998 meeting of the American Political Science Association, Boston, September 3–6.

Stolle, Dietlind and T. Rochon. 1998. "Are All Associations Alike?" In Edwards and Foley (eds.), *Beyond Tocqueville: Civil Society and Social Capital in Comparative Perspective*. Thematic Issue of the *American Behavioral Scientist*.

Swaminathan, Madhura. 1990. "Village-Level Implementation of IRDP: Comparison of West Bengal and Tamil Nadu." *Economic and Political Weekly*, Bombay, 25 (13).

Swidler, Ann. 1986. "Culture in Action: Symbols and Strategies." *American Sociological Review* 51: 273–286.

Tarrow, Sidney. 1977. *Between Center and Periphery: Grassroots Politicians in Italy and France*. New Haven: Yale University Press.

———. 1996. "Making Social Science Work Across Space and Time." *American Political Science Review*, 90, 389–397.

Tendler, Judith. 1997. *Good Government in the Tropics*. Baltimore and London: Johns Hopkins University Press.

Tocqueville, Alexis de. 1945 [1980]. *Democracy in America*, Volumes I and II. New York: Vintage Books.

Tod, James. 1971 [1829]. *Annals and Antiquities of Rajasthan*.

UNDP. 1998. *Human Development Report 1998*. New York: United Nations Development Programme.

Uphoff, Norman. 1992. *Learning From Gal Oya: Possibilities for Participatory Development and Post-Newtonian Social Science*. Ithaca, NY: Cornell University Press.

———. 2000. "Understanding Social Capital: Learning from the Analysis and Experience of Participation," 215–52. In Partha Dasgupta and Ismail Serageldin, eds., *Social Capital: A Multifaceted Perspective*. Washington, DC: The World Bank.

Vanaik, Achin. 1990. *The Painful Transition: Bourgeois Democracy in India*. London and New York: Verso.

Varshney, Ashutosh. 1995. *Democracy, Development and the Countryside: Urban-Rural Struggles in India*. Cambridge, UK: Cambridge University Press.

———. 2001. "Ethnic Conflict and Civil Society: India and Beyond." *World Politics*, 53 (April), 362–398.

Verba, S., Norman H. Nie and Jae-on Kim. 1971. *The Modes of Democratic Participation: A Cross-National Comparison.* Beverly Hills, CA: Sage Publications.
————. 1978. *Participation and Political Equality: A Seven-Nation Comparison.* Cambridge, U.K.: Cambridge University Press.
Verba, S., Schlozman, K. and H. Brady. 1995. *Voice and Equality: Civic Voluntarism in American Politics.* Cambridge, MA: Harvard University Press.
Verma, Arvind. 2001. "Design, Performance and Adaptability of the Police in India." Paper presented at the conference on Public Institutions in India: Performance and Design, Harvard University, February 9–10.
Vithal , B. P. R. 1997. Evolving Trends in the Bureaucracy, 208–31. In Chatterji (ed.), 1997.
Wade, Robert. 1994. *Village Republics: Economic Conditions for Collective Action in South India.* San Francisco: Institute for Contemporary Studies.
Walzer, Michael. 1995. "The Concept of Civil Society," 7–28. In Walzer (ed.), *Toward a Global Civil Society.* Oxford, U. K.: Berghahn Books.
Weiner, Myron. 1963. *Political Change in South Asia.* Calcutta: K. L. Mukhopadhyaya.
————. 1967. *Party-Building in a New Nation: The Indian National Congress.* Chicago: Chicago University Press.
————. 1989. *The Indian Paradox: Essays in Indian Politics.* New Delhi and London: Sage Publications.
Wolf, Eric R. 1969. *Peasant Wars of the Twentieth Century.* New York: Harper and Row.
Woolcock, Michael. 1998. "Social Capital and Economic Development: Toward a Theoretical Synthesis and Policy Framework." *Theory and Society,* 27 (2): 151–208.
Woolcock, Michael and Deepa Narayan. 2000. "Social Capital: Implications for Development Theory, Research and Policy." *World Bank Research Observer,* 15 (2), 225–249.
World Bank. 1993 *The East Asian Miracle: Economic Growth and Public Policy.* New York: Oxford University Press.
————. 1997. *World Development Report: The State in a Changing World.* New York: Oxford University Press.
————. 1999. *World Development Report 1999/2000: Entering the 21st Century.* Oxford University Press.
————. 2000. *Voices of the Poor: Can Anyone Hear Us?* Deepa Narayan (ed.). New York: Oxford University Press.
Yadav, Yogendra. 1996. "Reconfiguration in Indian Politics: State Assembly Elections, 1993–95." *Economic and Political Weekly,* Bombay, January 13, 95–104.
————. 1999a. "Electoral Politics in the Time of Change: India's Third Electoral System, 1989–99." *Economic and Political Weekly,* Bombay, August 21, 2393–99.

————. 1999b. "Politics," 3–38. In Marshall Bouton and Philip Oldenburg (eds.), *India Briefing: A Transformative Fifty Years*. New York: Asia Society.

Yugandhar, B. N. and B. Y. Raju. 1992. "Government Delivery Systems for Rural Development: Malady-Remedy Analysis." *Economic and Political Weekly*, Bombay, 27 (35).

Zoetelief, Jochem. 1999. "Finance From Below: Savings Arrangements and Credit Mechanisms in Dodoma Rural District, Tanzania." M.Sc. thesis, Department of Social Science, Wageningen Agricultural University, The Netherlands.

Index